African American Women Playwrights

A Study in Race, Gender and Class

African American Women Playwrights

A Study in Race, Gender and Class

T. Sarada

Prestige

an international publishing house

Published by

Prestige Books

New Delhi 110 058

Ph. 9818755529

email: prestigebooks@gmail.com

website: asiabookclub.com

ISBN: 81-7851-072-3

Printed at Chaman Offset Press, New Delhi 110 002

Contents

Foreword

To the best of my knowledge, very few Indian academics have attempted to work on African American women playwrights. Sarada must be commended on bringing out this book on three significant women playwrights, Sonia Sanchez, Adrienne Kennedy and Ntozake Shange. Sarada places these playwrights in the context of other African American women playwrights and goes on to examine the three playwrights in terms of three significant issues—race, gender and class. While the themes of individual plays are significantly dealt with, Sarada is acutely aware of the fact that plays cannot be treated as mere words on the page but must also be looked at as performances. The strength of her work lies is her ability to examine and analyse language, including the use of metaphors and images, so as to bring out the triple oppression the African American women are subjected to. Sarada does not wish to see only that side of African American life which is ridden with violence. So in her conclusion she posits the overcoming of differences and violence through spirituality.

With growing interest in marginalised literatures, particularly in African American literature, women's writing and theatre studies, this book is bound to be useful to students, research scholars and teachers.

Hyderabad

Alladi Uma
Professor and Head
Department of English
University of Hyderabad
Hyderabad 500 046

Preface

When I started my research in the area of African American Women's theatre nearly a decade ago, I remember the belittling expressions on the faces of many on account of the "unfashionableness" involved in the process, since the literary arena is currently flooded with research in the areas of postcolonial and Indian writers. But serious literary research to me, is no fashion shop and therefore the term "trend" is absolutely irrelevant.

As one interested in theatre, performance and gender studies, the area of African American women's theatre only seemed apt for its power, dramaturgy, vibrancy and its strength to shake all complacency. My chance reading of Kennedy's play *Sun* and visualizing of a performance of Shange's *for colored girls*, further heightened my interest in this area. Having decided upon the three dramatists: Adrienne Kennedy, Sonia Sanchez and Ntozake Shange, the task of collecting their works was a challenging one, since not all their works were available within the country. Researching on Sanchez in particular was problematic since her works remain unanthologised even to this day. After an assiduous search at the then ASRC, Hyderabad, I could procure only a single play of her. It was my mentor Prof. Krishna Sarma, my all-time well-wisher, who procured her plays during his personal trip to the U.S., which he had painstakingly collected from different journals.

To work in the area of "class" was the most challenging since the notion of "class" lacks proper conceptualization and research to this day. The paucity of supportive material in this area was yet another impediment. However, I have attempted at analyzing the plays from this perspective to the best of my ability. Further suggestions would be welcome.

Words can hardly express my gratitude to the Department of English, University of Hyderabad, from where this research was pursued, Dr. Alladi Uma, my guide, for also having written the foreword, Prof. Mohan Ramanan, for his critical insights, Dr. M. Sridhar, for his meticulousness in perfecting the mechanics of my research, Dr. V. Rangan, who was then my continuous source of inspiration and the former ASRC for its research grant. Above all I thank my family members and the Lord of Seven Hills for making this happen.

Tirupati **THALLAM SARADA**

Chapter 1

Introduction

> Black women are a prism through which the searing rays of race, class and sex are first focused, then refracted. The creative among us transfer these rays into a spectrum of brilliant colours, a rainbow which illuminates the experience of all human kind. (Wilkerson xii)

These words of Margaret Wilkerson in her introduction to *9 Plays by Black Women* (1986), while vindicating the glory of African American women's writing, also encapsulates the theme of their works, their anxieties and their creative tensions in the early part of the twentieth century All women are twice-born, since their elevative metamorphosis demands their transcendence of issues like gender and class, each of which is a re-birth for them. But African American women, like the Indian women, are thrice born since their sustenance in this world demands their surmounting of the triple mountains of race, gender and class issues while the Indian women need to traverse the gender, caste and class issues.

Race and class are the issues which form the nucleus of all African American writing since its inception. But women are also additionally burdened with the trauma of gender. Physically exploited and psychologically mutilated, the African American women, as social pariahs, often reach the nadir of degradation and humiliation in a society which denies and deprives them of any human value. The three issues are a culmination of complex socio-cultural-economic-psychological values and perceptions that the White race, or rather the human community has been cherishing since times immemorial.

Racism, colour complex and the superior attributes given to the White colour have been driven into the human consciousness since the earliest times. Cultural critics like Todorov, Bosnak and Sloane speculate colour as "a supplement to the symbolism of light" (Adams 34). Although the symbolism of light and dark cannot be called absolutely universal, it is at least "international," appearing in many cultures. Sloane cites the moral imperatives of colour in the Bible, where White is a symbol of "purity" and Black that of "death," "mourning," "sexual provocativeness" and "sex." It is not just the Judaeo-Christian tradition, but also the Islamic tradition that associates Black with "sin" in a symbolic manner since the sacred Black stone of Mecca was originally White when it fell down from heaven and eventually became Black from the sins of human beings who touched it.[1] Therefore, the symbolic "purity" of White influences the racial designation wherein there is established a hierarchy based on colour, and therefore even as per certain linguistic conventions, the "white intentions are pure; black motives are evil" (Sloane 191).

Apart from the religious symbolism, W.D. Jordan in his *White over Black: American Attitudes toward the Negro* (1968) provides a culturalist account of the encounter between the Whites and Blacks, between the English and the Africans in the sixteenth century. Jordan mentions how the most significant characteristic of the newly discovered African was his complexion: "Travellers rarely failed to comment upon it; indeed when describing Negroes they frequently began with complexion" (Jordan 4). The dark complexion of the negroes therefore had a powerful impact on the Whites since suddenly the fairest people had encountered one of the darkest people. The emotional impact that the White race had on the Black race must have also been great since their fair complexion must have inculcated a feeling of awe in them which later paved the way for notions of conquest. But much before the encounter between the Whites and the Blacks, the English had assigned numerous negative aesthetic and moral values to the term "black" as being "dirty," "ugly," "evil," "deadly" and "devilish" whereas to be "white" was to be pure, clean, beautiful, godly and everything positive. Jordan rightly remarks, "No other colors so clearly implied opposition" (Jordan 7). It is actually a culmination of numerous cultural, religious and psychological factors.

As a contrast to Jordan, Todorov considers the supremacy of the White colour as almost universal, by referring to universal symbolism like "white-black," "light-dark" and "day-night," he arrives at the fact that "[t]he history of humanity being what it is, the exemplary racism [. . .] is thus of Whites toward Blacks" (Todorov 95). Psychology and Jung's theories on "race" and the unconscious have further compounded the issues of race, and skin colour. Jung does not undermine the influence of "colour" since he believes that all the implications of colour do get under one's skin, the effect being both "unconscious, subcutaneous, subliminal, subconscious" (Jung 46-47). Jung feels that the other gets under the skin of the self, because although human beings are different on the surface, they still remain the same inwardly.[2] Therefore, he also contends that the colour of the skin matters not as a "natural" or "racial" phenomenon, but on "cultural and historical grounds" (Jung 49-50). The differences do exist, although their grounds may vary.

But racism is not merely a product of the growth of psychological research. It is also the consequence of the growth of the colonial powers wherein the process of constructing one's power destroys the civilisation and the power-structures already existing there. It involves a number of practices including trade, plunder, negotiation, warfare, enslavement, rebellion and suppression. It is "the conquest and control of other people's land and goods" (Loomba 2). Although this has been a recurrent feature of history, Marxist thinking distinguishes between precapitalist colonialism and modern colonialism. The latter has subtly been involved in the process of re-structuring the economies and created a more complex network so as to facilitate the passage of human and natural resources between the colonised and the colonising nations which has altered their economics and their human relationships. In this context, slaves were moved from Africa to America and the West Indies in order to work in the large plantations. The movement of slaves under forced conditions has led to the evolution of the Black predicament in America.

While abolition and emancipation technically ushered freedom to the entire African American race, the women still continued to remain under the multiple bondages of race, gender and class since the political freedom in the larger sense failed to cater to the particular needs of the African American women. One of the sanctions with which the African American women were subjugated was the Bible, on the basis of God's curse in the book of Genesis on account of Eve having tasted the forbidden fruit.[3] Although the White American women were treated as inferior to the White male folk, the position of the African American women was the most peculiar since they were at the rock-bottom position of both the White and the Black cultural norms. Slave women had always been treated as property to be owned by their masters. The Biblical god incites his followers to treat "bondmen" and "bondmaids" as permanent possessions and property to be inherited by future children.[4] Therefore the African American women were groaning under the multiple burdens of race and gender both of which had biblical sanction, so much so that an intellectual like Robert Ingersoll, the famous nineteenth century orator and statesman of America candidly opined: "The real oppression, enslaver and corrupter of the people is the Bible"[5] (Ingersoll 32).

Apart from the Biblical sanction, the rise of patriarchal values and the "advancement" made in terms of "civilization" had contributed towards the suppression of women. The African American women were suppressed in multiple ways for several reasons other than the general above-mentioned values. From the beginning, African American women were of intrinsic value to the capitalist patriarchal modes of production in America. Their bodies were not only cheap sources of labour but also free labour production machines to the White patriarchal capitalistic forces of America. Many European travellers and colonialists felt that the promise of sexual pleasure rested on the assumption that "the darker races [. . .] were immoral, promiscuous [and] libidinous" (Loomba 158). As a result, the African American women are often labelled as "Jezebels" referring to their enormous sexual potential, which is often missing in the White women who are synonymous with angelic qualities and virtuousness. Therefore, the rise of colonial powers have only positioned the African American women in an absolute state of degradation, since, according to Helen Carr, women and non-Europeans occupy the same "symbolic space." Both of them are often perceived as being unsuited for governments on account of their "passive, child-like, unsophisticated, needing leadership, guidance [. . .] [with] no initiative, no intellectual powers, [and] no perseverance" (Loomba 159-60).

The situation is more complicated in the case of African American women as they were always perceived as being inferior on account of their race, gender and weak economic positioning. Moreover, they were merely perceived as objects of sexual pleasure. The complicity between race and gender was therefore one of the fundamental ways of exploiting the African American women who were brought to the land by force, to be only exploited through multiple means. Stepan and Gilmea mention how the analogy between race and gender was common in the nineteenth century. Low brain weights and deficient brain structures were linked to the "lower" races especially the Negroes.[6] Therefore, the pseudo-scientific theories of the nineteenth century had abandoned the empirical modes of study for a metaphorical system that created the difference. The African American women were further relegated to the lowest positions since they were considered even inferior to African American men.

Another scientific theory used to undermine the position of African Americans is Darwinism. Darwin's *Descent of Man* (1871) had a great impact on western thought. In his introduction to *Social Darwinism in American Thought* (1944), Richard Hoftstadter also mentions that although England gave Darwin to the world, the United States readily absorbed his philosophies since it suited their materialist progression, and Darwin's ideas also acted as a challenge to the prevailing "conservative political mood." Moreover, Hofstadter points out how Darwinian catch phrases like "struggle for existence" and "survival of the fittest," when applied to the American society would suggest that the best competitors would win, leading to a continuous improvement of a few privileged classes, while relegating many as underprivileged. The use of natural selection as a vindication of militarism or imperialism was also not new in European or American thought. The subtitle of Darwin's book *The Preservation of Favoured Races in the Struggle for Life* appealed to the power-hungry minds. Although Darwin was talking about pigeons in his book, imperialists applied the ideologies to human life. But racism was not a strictly post-Darwinian phenomenon, since the doctrine of *Macht politik* (power politics) already existed there. Gobineau's *Essai sur Negalite des Races Humaines* (*Essay on the Neglect of the Human Races*) (1853-55), an important milestone in the history of Aryanism, was highly influential during the pre-war times, since the southern politicians were thoroughly grounded in notions of racial superiority. Therefore, the Anglo-Saxon dogma became the chief element in American racism. Although Darwinism was not the only source of the American belligerent racism, it did become a novel weapon for the power-hungry Anglo-Saxon race for conquering the weak.

These dominant scientific ideologies of race have dovetailed into gender bias wherein the Black women have been pushed to the lowest rung of the American racial ladder. Vaughan, when analysing the African situation mentions that the African men alone were treated for schizophrenia and confined to lunatic asylums since their women were not considered to have reached the "level of self-awareness" so as to go mad. The women therefore represented the "primitive" state of Africa prior to colonization. (Vaughan 22). Therefore, even "madness" which is perceived here as a trait in advanced minds, is an aspect of progress in which the Black women lag behind their men who themselves slowly follow the Europeans.

Psychology also further enhanced the poor status of women, especially the African American women in particular. When Freud labelled the incomprehensibility of women's sexual life as a "dark continent"[7] (that the woman places herself in an "inferior" status on account of "penis envy"), he was unconsciously further debasing the position of African American women. Freud's contention that both sexuality and Africa are beyond comprehension, indirectly implies that a dark woman is totally beyond any apprehension on account of her sub-human status. Freud had unconsciously equated "darkness" with femininity and the unknown, thereby complicating the position of African American women who were both.

The position of the African American women is further worsened by the lowest "class" which she occupies. It is not unfamiliar for us to watch Hollywood films projecting African American women as maids, sweepers, toilet cleaners and as being engaged in sundry labour.[8] Their advent to the new continent as field labourers has stratified them permanently into the lowest class. The African American women groan under these heavy burdens since they are already being continually tormented on account of their being Black and women. In an era of rapid industrialisation, the African American women are commodified as objects meant to serve various purposes. The intervention of Marxist ideology made women believe that their work and its material culture shaped their thoughts and therefore capitalism is seen as a system of power relations as well as exchange relations. According to this, every kind of transactional relation is fundamentally exploitative. Rosmarie Tong feels that although women do not constitute a single "class" in the strict Marxist sense (since they have relationships with both the bourgeois and proletarian men), most of the domestic experiences of women give room for their coming together for housework campaign.

But the plight of the African American women is worsened in this system since she labours often in the fields/factories, her home and that of her master/mistress. The politics and culture of the American women's movement have mainly catered to the experiences and priorities of White middle-class women, whereas Black women have been excluded from the group, thereby categorising them under the lowest of classes. While the African American discrimination has been frequently located in racial ethnic strifes, the broader dimensions of political, economic and social discrimination have been largely ignored. Although class and race overlap in the lives of African American women, one category does not wholly encompass the other. This is because, although Marxism speaks of the general oppression of women, it fails to theorise the specificity of gender oppression.[9] Feminists feel that Marxism does not precisely point out how women have been marginalised.

The most important issue of how the oppression of women is connected with economic systems like capitalism remains unexplored till feminists undertook it. This is a crucial area for the African American feminists since they have been exploited at manifold levels at the altar of capitalist forces. Marx and Engels strongly believe that our ideas originate from our immediate milieu: "It is not consciousness that determines life, but life that determines consciousness" (Marx and Engels 36). Therefore all ideas, self-conceptions and even illusions spring from the world in which we live. Money has the power to distort even reality.

Thus with the advancement of capitalism, money and commodities are mistaken for human values leading to the establishment of a false consciousness. The economic power of America has further debased the already humiliated status of African American women by pushing them to the periphery of existence. Their struggle for their daily bread most often all alone, has further compounded the agony of their women, since, they have had to work their way towards social mobility. Survival is therefore a difficult process since their existence remains fissured by race, gender and class divides.

The African American women are therefore forced to combat the ideologies of the dominant classes which Gramsci has labelled as "hegemony."[10] In his *Prison Notebooks* (1929-34), Gramsci discusses the failure of the proletarian revolution, owing to the failure of the Italian workers to come to power after the First World War. To Gramsci, the revolution had failed, in spite of the fact that "the objective material conditions for its success had been in place" (Hawkes 116). He believes that revolutions not only facilitate shifts in economic structure, but also on the levels of ideologies. At this point, Gramsci examines the different schools of ideas and their conflicting existence. Gramsci agrees with Marx and Engels who in their Communist Manifesto (1848), contend that "the ruling ideas of each age have ever been the ideas of its ruling class" (38). This is the "dominant ideology thesis," suggesting that the economically powerful class will impose its way of seeing the world leading to a class conflict. By hegemony, he means the connection between material and ideological instruments, through which the dominant class maintains its power, leading to the formation of a "praxis," since, power is achieved through both coercion and consent. Modifying the Machiavellian suggestion that power can be achieved through both fair means and guile, Gramsci opines that the ruling classes attain power through direct and indirect mechanisms. The African American women who are deprived of all power, and virtually rendered sterile, are often forced to accept their dehumanising predicament. This is because the Gramscian idea of hegemony emphasises the forced imposition of ideas rather than a simple consent. The French Communist theorist Louis Althusser also in his "Ideological State Apparatuses" (1971) mentions how in modern capitalist societies, the ideological hegemony is achieved through the school, the church, the family, media and political systems. This machinery assists in the reproduction of the ideologies of the dominant system, by creating subjects who remain conditioned to accept the values of the system.

Despite the multiple oppressions confronting them, the African American women continue to make pioneering efforts in the field of creativity. It is significant to note that the African American literary tradition was born of a woman—Phillis Wheatley. Her *Poems on Various Subjects: Religious and Moral* (1773) lays the foundation of all African American writing. Henry Louis Gates Jr. mentions: "Wheatley launched two traditions at once—the Black American literary tradition and the Black women's literary tradition" (Andrews x). Ann Plato was the first African American woman to publish a book of *Essays* (1841) and Harriet E. Wilson was the first African American to publish a novel *Our Nig* (1859) in the United States.

Although the African American women have continued to act as forerunners in the world of writing, they still remain unknown and unrecognised. Hence, their experiences differ from that of their male counterparts. Many works have been lost, unclassified, uncatalogued and therefore remain unread. The "Black Experience" has been therefore a male experience, which has remained insensitive to the needs of their women. Anna Julia Cooper in *A Voice from the South* (1892) points out that just as the "Caucasian barristers" can never fully assimilate the consciousness of Black men, the latter can never completely apprehend the sensibilities of Black women. (Cooper 7) Any writing which does not give its due to Black women is myopic indeed, since it ignores the inner lives of one half of humanity, thereby negating its universal value. Until the Black woman's works are also brought to the limelight, to use Cooper's significant lines, "[t]he world has had to limp along with the [. . .] one-sided hesitancy of a man with one eye" (Cooper 3). Therefore, the discovery, the publication and the greater awareness of African American women's writing has added a greater vibrancy to it, thereby rendering it holistic.

Among the various genres of creativity, drama is an area where the African American women have faced greater hurdles. Although the women mothered other genres like poetry, fiction and prose, in theatre, it was William Wells Brown who preceded his women folk. Brown's *Escape: or a Leap to Freedom* (1858) was the first African American play to be produced. It was only twenty-two years later that Pauline Hopkins, an African American woman dramatist first performed her musical play on July 5, 1880, at Oakland Garden, Boston, *Slave's Escape: Or Underground Rail Road.*[11] It was performed by the members of her family and friends. But the play is not considered by many drama critics the first play by an African American woman as it lacked proper production. Moreover, the gap of twenty-two years between the first African American male and female playwrights may be attributed to the multiple hurdles that women faced in this genre. Drama being more public and requiring a greater participation from the others in terms of action, production and the like, also necessitated a greater economic investment which remained a serious handicap to African American women. Pauline Hopkins also wrote a second play *Drama of Early Days* (1882) which dramatised the Biblical story of Daniel in the lion's den. The economic infeasibility of production forced her to forego her dramatic career for a more "stable" occupation. In order to curb the intellectual stiflement of the African American women dramatists, W.E.B. Du Bois, Montgomery Gregory and Alaine Locke encouraged them to write "native dramas" which evolved directly from their own experience. Du Bois proposed that the plays must be "[a]bout us [. . .] by us [. . .] [and] near us" (446).

A number of women writers responded to this call. Kathy Perkins points out that when Crisis and Opportunity sponsored play-writing contests, "most of the winners were women" (Perkins 9). Nellie McKay remarks that between 1918 and 1930, "eleven black women published twenty-one plays [. . .] in comparison to no more than half a dozen [black] men who saw their works in print" (625). Perkins suggests that the sudden blossoming of the hitherto suppressed talent is because "black women were not in any leadership position compared to black men [and therefore], these plays provided a unique opportunity for their voices to be heard" (7).

Margaret Wilkerson catalogues a number of other factors which have activated the process of play-writing by African American women. Because most of the women dramatists lived in Washington DC rather than Harlem, their work reflected a different aspect of Black life when compared to the writers who wrote from the Harlem experience. But the fact remains that much of Black women's writings of these times is shrouded in oblivion. Christine Gray mentions how in 1987, Richard Bernstein, theatre columnist for *New York Times* wrote that the "tradition of a Black American Theatre is not a long one, going back only a generation or so to the work of play-writings like Amiri Baraka" (Murphy 243). The fact remains that there were 100 African American playwrights who wrote 350 plays before 1930. Of these, 47 were women. In 1916, Black women became actively engaged in writing plays for the non-musical stage. African American women's theatre is undoubtedly a legislative theatre, since it simultaneously authenticates their space, bodies and creativity.

When Du Bois organised the NAACP's drama committee in 1915, it sponsored Angelina Weld Grimke's *Rachel* which became the first properly produced African American woman's play in the year 1916. She has been labelled by James V. Hatch as "the mother of African American women's theatre" (Murphy 245). The playbill of *Rachel* considers it as "the first attempt to use the stage for race propaganda in order to enlighten the American people [. . .] to the lamentable condition of ten millions of coloured citizens in [. . .] the free Republic" (Perkins 8). Grimke is the first Black woman playwright to counter the negative stereotypes of the Black race in general and the Black women in particular. Harris mentions the cluster of themes included in the play like "social inequality, hiring discrimination, the Black frustration and familial erosion which have resulted from economic strictures and the [. . .] blighting effects of racism" (Harris 206).

Rachel is significant from manifold points of view. Apart from its condemnation of lynching, it is a powerful depiction of colour psychology. It also reveals the sexist determination of Rachel when she forcefully renounces motherhood. The play throws insights into the prejudices faced by Blacks in the realm of employment, since, even with a college degree, Rachel's fiancé finds employment only as a waiter. It counters the negative depictions of the Blacks as lazy, ignorant and superstitious. The Blacks in the play are middle-class, educated and soft spoken. Christine Gray points out how the play challenges the stereotypes of African Americans in the racist movie *Birth of a Nation* (Murphy 242).

By 1930, 46 African American women had written plays, Georgia Douglas Johnson (22 plays), May Miller (14 plays), Zora Neale Hurston (13 plays), Eulalie Spence (13 plays) and Thelma Duncan (9 plays). As Elizabeth Brown-Guillory mentions, these women "were able to turn theatres into nurseries where the Black race [was] given roots, tested, healed and provided with the spirit to survive" (Guillory 5). They lived at Washington DC and were influenced by the Howard dramatic community. They frequently interacted with Du Bois and Locke. The common themes were lynching, sexist oppression, life in the south, poverty, miscegenation and the aftermaths of oppression.

Although these women wrote during the times of the Harlem Renaissance, recent critics like Gloria T. Hull in *Color, Sex and Poetry: Three Women Writers of the Harlem Renaissance* (1984), and Cheryl Wall in *Women of the Harlem Renaissance* (1995), have pointed out that these women's writing communicated a very different sense of the experience as they were being continuously oppressed. Christene Gray points out how "although Harlem was seen as a Mecca for [. . .] Black writers and artists, it was not a hub of plays by African American women" (Murphy 247). Indeed, there was a silent revolution which was going on in the meeting rooms of Black churches, in the basements of public libraries and in the school and college auditoriums. Their revolution was indigenous and a rather silent one since they have been always excluded from the mainstream

White experience and the writers of the Harlem Renaissance. In fact, many of the plays produced by the Black women attempted to present the folk traditions of their race (for instance those of Hurston) and through it they re-enacted the problems and the situations that they currently encountered. Christene Gray aptly mentions that "it was in the plays produced in church basements that many African Americans learned Black history, not in the flash and adventure of the Harlem writers" (Murphy 247). These writers met frequently at Georgia Douglas Johnson's house where they discussed their works and their common oppressions. Johnson, for instance, highlights the challenge of being both a housewife and a writer and pleads for greater creative spaces on Wolfian lines:

> If I might ask some fairy Godmother special favours, one would sure be for a clearing space, elbow room in which to think and write and love beyond the reach of Wolfe's fingers. (Hull 165)

Shirley Graham also faced multiple problems in producing her plays. Her second marriage to Du Bois rather late in her life ironically ended her career as a dramatist. Her *Tom Tom* (1932) aptly delineates her artistic frustration. Both May Miller and Mary Burrill lost their audience when they retired from teaching. Marita Bonner could get three of her plays published, but not performed (Brown-Guillory 1-2). Gloria Hull contrasts Locke's misogynistic treatment of Hurston with the encouragement meted out to male dramatists like Langston Hughes. Only Eulalie Spence was lucky enough to see six of her plays published and seven performed. The control of the theatre economy by the Whites was a major hurdle which was confronted by all these artists. Harris cites the statistical details of Theophilus Lewis to show how "Whites controlled 50 percent of the theatres and 75 of the patronage of blacks in New York" (208). The feeble economic position of Black women dramatists was a major device of silencing the creativity of Black women. The struggle that these women faced in the course of begetting their creativity has been unearthed by recent critics. Cheryl Wall has found out that while Alain Locke's essay "The New Negro" (1925) conveyed "a revigorated consciousness of race, Marita Bonner's "On Being Young—A Woman and Colored" (1924) evoked "images of silence, entrapment and a sense of stasis" (10).[12]

Only in the recent years, have the plays by African American women won serious acclaim. One of the reasons for this delayed recognition is the non-availability of these works as these women have been systematically marginalised in American history. Freda Scott Gills, a theatre professor at the university of Georgia points out that the lack of reviews, commentary and press coverage makes it difficult to piece production histories (Brenda 250). James V. Hatch, an authoritative scholar on African American drama mentions that in order to locate reviews, commentaries and production notes, one needs to "go through piles of microfilm of Black newspapers of the twenties, but the women are in there" (Brenda 250). The recovery work which precedes publication describes the process of locating and editing materials that have been lost, neglected or forgotten. It requires reading archival materials, contacting families, reading newspapers for theatre reviews, journals, poring through biographies and autobiographies. Although 350 African American plays have been written before 1930, their location is not always known. Despite such practical problems, a certain amount of recovery has been arduously made. But Judith Stephens remarks that "many times African American female playwrights are still ignored even after their importance to theatre in this country has been documented" (Gray 250).

Put cumulatively, the triple issues of race, gender and class are constructs which act as identificatory signifiers often creating hierarchal relationships, tension zones and power structures. Its very act of suppression circulates novel cultural and political values which need to be re-defined and re-configured in their cumulative positioning. The knowledges thus produced are invested with endless chains of social, political and cultural signification wherein the individual consciousness of the characters in these plays is often seen as representing the collective consciousness of all the women of the entire race. Heuristically positing, these triple burdens are not "natural" borders but socio, cultural and political constructs which circulate convoluted notions of the oppressed. What then formed as identificatory signifiers, are often transformed into ideological constructs. The aim of this study is to prove how these trifurcated divisions are often (mis)represented as being ontogenic that is (mis)constructed as being natural.

The fact remains that these African American women playwrights have continued to assert their creative selves and have provided alternate and positive images of Black women. They have borne the multiple burdens of race, gender and class and still remain valiant enough to strike back at the dominant culture with the power of their pens.

Notes

1. The Islamic influence in the lives of African Americans cannot be undermined. Back home in their native Africá, Islam was one of the first cultural invasions which threatened their native faiths. In America, on the other hand, a large number of African Americans converted themselves to Islam. Malcolm X's call to Islam was one of the profound influences on African Americans. In fact, Sonia Sanchez was temporarily converted to Islam before she came back to Christianity.
2. Jung writes: "You cannot live in Africa or any such country without having that country get under the skin. You cannot prevent it [. . .] in the collective unconscious. You are the same as the man of another race; you have the same archetypes [. . .] [so] [. . .] it does not matter that his skin is Black." (Vol. ii 321).
3. Genesis (3:16) states: "Unto the woman he said, I will greatly multiply thy sorrow and thy conception; in sorrow thou shalt bring forth children; and thy desire shall be thy husband, and he shall rule over them."
4. See Leviticus (25:46): "And ye shall take them as an inheritance for your children after you, to inherit them for a possession; they shall be your bondmen for ever."

5. Ingersoll's statement is of immense importance to the African American women writers since many of them questioned the validity of the Bible since it led to oppression of their gender.
6. Their essay is significant since it deals with the undue appropriation of pseudo-science with little validity as one of the tools of reinforcing racist values within the dominant White culture.
7. In *The Question of Lay Analysis* (1926e), Freud wrote, "We know less about the sexual life of little girls than of boys. But we need not feel ashamed of this distinction; after all, the sexual life of adult women is a 'dark continent' for psychology" (212). The term "dark continent" connotes a geographic space that is deep and one that defies understanding. Freud has borrowed the expression from the African explorer John Rowlands Stanley's description of the exploration of a dark forest—virgin, hostile, impenetrable. By using this phrase and comparing the adult woman's sexual life to an unknown continent, Freud indicates the obscure and incomplete nature of the clinical material on the sexual life of girls and women for the psychoanalyst. African American women feel doubly marginalized at such a term, since they are doubly excluded from their subjective positions as women and for being "dark," thereby compounding their problems of exclusionist identity politics.
8. The recent worldwide television ads of Saint Gobain projects African American women as being mere charwomen and stewards.
9. For feminists, the issues of culture and ideology have been vital for several reasons. Although women's oppression has been considered to be a matter of culture and taking place within the family, the actual exploitation of their labour power has been obscured by a gender-blind and colour-blind economic analysis.
10. The notion of hegemony is of relevance to the African American women since they remain criss-crossed by various forms of power which oppress them simultaneously.
11. Although Pauline Hopkins had written and produced a play nearly thirty five years before Angelina Grimke, Pauline is never considered the mother of African American women's theatre since she lacked proper modes of production. She wrote in worse circumstances than Grimke since she had no literary mentors like Du Bois and Locke as had Grimke. Still her effort requires to be mentioned

since she had the courage to write and enact the play as it is a reflection of her conviction.

12. Marxist criticism contends that the "absences and silences in a text are places where the real history is embedded. That is, the absences link a text to the history from which it is produced, it effaces instances of class struggle, exploitation and the true dynamics of history" (Nayar 111).

Chapter 2

Bein' Colored and Bein' Loved

This chapter begins with the origins of racism in the human psyche, including numerous social, psychological, anthropological, political and religious theories which directly or indirectly propound racism. After probing into the genesis of the African American women's theatre with regard to racism, the main dramatists taken up for the present study are dealt with in detail. Racist issues like marginalisation on the basis of their skin, the resultant psychological trauma, its effects on the family, religion, and the racist policies in education are discussed. The chapter ends with a detailed analysis of the techniques used by these women dramatists in highlighting their racist predicament

Racism is a great blot on the American nation though the constitution was based upon lofty principles. One of the greatest paradoxes of American history is the fact that the sword and the Bible have worked simultaneously ever since the land was founded by the puritan fathers. The marginalisation of the pre-Columbian civilisation by the White colonial masters is the beginning of the "white man's burden" to both alienate and suppress the native from his own land. Triggered by a reformist zeal, the ideas of "conquest" and "alienation" operated in the psyche of the American Whites ever since the land was founded by the puritan fathers. Manning emphasizes that the alienation was at multiple levels: "from God, from nature and *from other men*." (Manning 39; my italics) This signifies the beginning of the systematic process of exclusion which the Americans have adopted with other ethnic minorities, especially the Blacks, since they were the only race in the "el dorado" who had been brought by force.

To Sowell, "The peopling of America is one of the greatest dramas in human history" (Sowell 3). The term "ethnicity" derived from the Greek word "ethnos" originally meant "a number of people living together, and subsequently came to be used in the sense of a tribe, group, nation or people" (Henderson 7). Although "ethnicity" and "race" are closely allied, they are never wholly synonymous. The difference lies in the fact that while "ethnicity" denotes the carrying of a specific culture, race refers to one's phenotype of physical appearance (Henderson 7). It is the Black phenotype that is primarily responsible for the unwarranted agony that the race faces in all parts of the globe. The polarisation of "black" and "white" has ushered in a sense of colour-consciousness. It promoted a basic knowledge of racial differences which was needed to understand the differences in the bewildering varieties of human beings in a larger schema. This is "Racial Difference" which is different from "Racism" and in all probability, the former idea must have first emerged in human consciousness. Racial "awareness" emerged out of human beings' need to classify themselves to establish a sense of group identity. But it is the deeper gregarious instinct in man that has contributed towards the oppression and alienation of certain ethnic groups. Thus, racism is ultimately transformed into an ideological instrument that separates human beings from their own species while also blocking the possibilities of common identification and mutual co-operation.

Racism is camouflaged with a number of convoluted, ethnopolitical and cultural theories. Although cruel exploitation and naked forms of oppression have characterised human behaviour since times immemorial,[1] the distinctive quality of the modern times is "the emergence of a racial order dominated by Whites in which much of this [. . .] brutality has been channelized along the dimension of color" (Blauner 20). Thus, systematic inequality and injustice have been built into stratified societies, and African Americans are victims of such well-established methods of discrimination. The entire gamut of African American writing is an attempt at establishing their racial identity.

The Black Power Movement and the Black Arts Movement empowered their intellectuals to project an authentic African American vision that both articulates and caters to the innate needs of the American Blacks. As a protest against the ideological tyranny of the Whites, a large corpus of African American writing emerged in the form of narratives, songs, poetry, speeches and fiction. Dramatists like Amiri Baraka, Ron Karenga and Ed Bullins staged their works. Its vibrancy offered "[a] radical alternative to the sterility of the American theatre." It is basically "a theatre of the spirit" (Neal 33) wherein the Black Man is seen interacting with the entire spiritual continuum, thereby elevating the theatre to higher realms. In his early play *Dutchman* (1964), the protagonist Clay is murdered by the White bitch-goddess Lula. The murder is committed the moment Clay realises himself. The relationship between Clay (Black American) and Lula (White American) represents the historical mutilation of Black manhood in a racist land. Within the larger issue of racism, the gender distinction within African American race has also attained a significance because this is discrimination within discrimination. bell hooks construes the "male turf," as "hard politics," and a "playing field where women do not really belong." Since they are "male locker rooms, spaces no real women would want to enter" (hooks, *Killing Rage* 1-2). Not only racism, but even the connection between the Black woman and the theatre had initially been an uneasy one. Theatre had posed the greatest number of hurdles to African American women. The plays of early dramatists like Angelina Grimke, Marita Bonner, Georgia Douglas Johnson, Alice Dunbar Nelson, Zora Neale Hurston and others, voiced a definite protest against racism, along with gender and class issues.

Angelina Grimke's *Rachel* (1916) is the first play on record to be staged by a twentieth century African American woman. The play not only forms a stern protest against racist discrimination, but also gives an insight into the lynchings of innocent African Americans. These harrowing experiences transform an innocent girl Rachel into a confused and horror-struck adult. Initially, in an almost Blakean state of innocence, she asks her friends: "Is life so terrible? I had found it beautiful! How can life be terrible when the world is full of little children?" (Wilkerson, 9 Plays 9). From innocence, she moves on to experience which transforms her world-view. God now appears to her as a "terrible-being" (Wilkerson, *9 Plays* 11). She renounces motherhood by symbolically snatching rosebuds from the flower vase and stamping them under her feet. She vows never to beget children so as to lose them to the evil clutches of racism.

Margaret Wilkerson, an African American theatre critic feels that although Rachel protests against racism, it is rather passive since she contends that "Rachel is neither a super woman, nor a loose character; she is a tender, vulnerable person whom the evils of society overwhelm" (Wilkerson, *9 Plays* 9). The resolution cannot be labelled as "passive" since renunciation of fertility and motherhood is not an easy task for any woman. The protest is rather radical, given the historical subjugation of the African American women at the turn of the century. Lynching was the predominant theme in the early plays by African American women.[2] It was a device through which the White masters ruthlessly exercised their power over the Black folks. Lynching did not remain a male issue, since Grimke had successfully appropriated it to both breach the "male discourse" and to prove its physical and metaphorical aftermaths on Black women.

From its genesis as anti-lynching plays, African American women's theatre has matured to explore the deeper psychological causes of racism. This brings us to the fundamental question: Are all human beings alike or different? Is racism a primary attribute of difference? Colonial and racist writings have been continuously pondering over these issues. Consequently, a systematic "othering" of certain specific racial groups and a deliberate projection of the "othered" as being inferior have taken place. The connection between the coloniser and the colonised is rather a complex one. It is based on a premise that all human beings are not one and that there are inherent differences between them. Racism thus becomes a primary attribute of the differences. Therefore, the coloniser systematically marginalises certain specific cultural groups. Abdul Jan Mohammed labels this as "Manichean allegory" (Jan Mohammed 18), which produces a binary and implacable opposition between races. In such a situation, a certain form of ambivalence between the coloniser and the colonised is itself a product of "imperial duplicity" (Jan Mohammed, *The Post Colonial Studies Reader* 19), since a tug of power is always inevitable in the relationship between the coloniser and the colonised.

Basically, racial stereotyping is not a consequence of modern colonial powers. It could be detected in the Greek and Roman civilisations wherein certain sections of humanity were branded as slaves and barbarians. These ideological references were reworked in medieval and modern Europe wherein Christianity became the major ideological filter through which all forms of knowledge was refracted. Slavery and racist discrimination was deeply instigated in modern times on the basis of the biblical story of Ham, Noah's "bad" son, who was cursed with blackness. While the male African American theatre was dabbling with the ideas of protest and revolution,[3] it was the African American women's theatre which fathomed into the foundation of the White Christian view of racism. Zora Neale Hurston through her play *The First One* (1927)[4] mocks at the Biblical sanction supposedly bestowed on the Whites by God, as a justification of their racist attitude. The play is based on the biblical story of Noah and his son Ham in the Book of Genesis in the Bible. In the hands of Hurston, the inclusion of a strong female character determines the outcome of the play. The play is set in the valley of Arafat, three years after the flood. Noah curses his youngest son Ham for showing disrespect towards him. In an intoxicated state, Noah curses Ham to be turned "Black" along with his "seed" for ever (Perkins 85) thereby equating black with sin. Noah refuses to lift the curse and remains steadfast. When Noah orders Ham to quit the place, it is Eve, Ham's wife, who offers her wisdom and ability to face the future with optimism. She beckons him to the place where "the sun shines forever, to the end of the earth," where he may "never behold those faces again nor would he weep" (Perkins 85). The conversation is also significant given the fact that it is Eve who spurs Ham to action and also acts as an anchor in his distress.

The racist issue has since then, been the major theme for many women dramatists, the most notable among them, being Lorraine Hansberry. Hansberry's *A Raisin in the Sun* (1959) is a significant play focusing on the race's assertion of space in America. Despite the hostility of the White neighbours when Mama declares that "it makes a difference in a man when he can walk on floors that belong to him." (Hansberry 16). It is a symbolic affirmation of her inner space, since by defining and forging external territories, the dramatist is actually reinforcing her psychological terrain, both of which are needed for one's complete living. After Hansberry, although a number of dramatists have emerged on the African American feminist theatrical scenario, Sonia Sanchez, Adrienne Kennedy and Ntozake Shange are among the most prominent in projecting deep perceptions about the triple issues of race, gender and class which torment the African Americans in general, more particularly their women.

Race talk to them is not a product of a militant "*Killing Rage*," but a positive "narcissistic rage" (hooks, *Killing Rage* 34). This is because their subaltern experiences make them view themselves as someone more deserving. Maria Berghahn, a social-psychiatrist contends that the foundations of racism lie in its "colour shock" which the Elizabethans experienced when they encountered the Africans. Elizabethans were very different from the Spaniards and Portuguese (who also travelled a great deal), who were more familiar with other skin colours. It therefore made a much more lasting impression on them. (Berghan 14) The "colour shock" of the Europeans was easily transmitted to

Americans. While the African dark skin shocked the White race, their White skin created a sense of astonishment among the Blacks. This sense of "wonder" is labelled as "ethnographic gaze," by bell hooks (hooks, *Killing Rage* 35). To her, the term itself is an expression of racism. She speculates that the very act of thinking not only perpetuates subjugation, but also denounces them as "subhuman," thereby negating their very status as human beings. It promotes the hegemonisation of power and aids to internalise certain "well accepted" systems of repression and reproduce them in multifarious means Kennedy, Sanchez and Shange wage relentless wars against such stifling power systems. Many of their characters are rudely shocked at the recognition of their colour. The polarisation of colours is deeply ingrained in their minds. "Black" and "White" remain irreconcilable opposites of them. Kennedy's female protagonist Sarah in her play *Funny House of a Negro* (1964) is unable to accept the relationship between her father and her mother. As the Duchess (one of her selves) mentions:

> Duchess: How dare he enter the castle, he who is the *darkest* of them all, the *darkest* one, my mother looked like a White woman . . . but he is *black*, the *blackest* one of them all. (Kennedy, *In One Act* 3; my italics)

The repetitive emphasis on "dark" reveals how to even a "mulatto" like Sarah, the mixture of White with Black is tantamount to contamination, and subsequently death. As she adds, "the beast put his hands on her, she died" (3).

Like Sarah, Kennedy's Clara in her *The Owl Answers* (1965) initially appears a doomed figure who cannot overcome the condition of her colour. Her mixed blood paves the way for frustrations, thereby leading her to a state of psychological limbo. Both Sarah and Clara find it difficult to coalesce their diverse colours and cultures as illustrated through symbolic means. In Kennedy's *Funny House of a Negro* (1964), Sarah is split into multiple selves. She is both Black and White, male and female, she is simultaneously a mulatto, Queen Victoria Regina, and Patrice Lumumba. The stage symbols constitute a number of masks, European antiques, photographs of Roman ruins, a piano, oriental carpets and a white table. Clara in *The Owl Answers* is simultaneously a mulatto, Virgin Mary, a bastard and an owl. Both Sarah and Clara are conceived through violent rapes. *The Owl Answers* marks a further progress in the technique of Kennedy, for she incorporates an animal self into the human self of Clara. The scathing racist experiences in America splinters holistic personalities into fragmented individuals with multiple selves. James M. Glass, a postmodern psychiatrist in his *Postmodernism and Multiplicity: Shattered Selves* (1993) deems such a condition as both "bizarre" because it is extremely complex to comprehend the difficulty of having to live with multiple and often warring personalities in a single body; and it is also "real" because of the horrendousness involved in the "switching of personalities" (Glass 53).

While modernist psychiatry is an attack on the rational self of human beings, postmodernist psychiatry is an attack on their unitary selves. This is because no single self defines his/her being. That Kennedy has been influenced by these and numerous other playwrights is evident throughout her autobiography *People Who Led to My Plays*. Strindberg in his *Miss Julie* (1885) refers to the multiplicity of human existence which has made him "deliberately" discard the traditional mode of characterization. As his characters are contemporary, their existence is in a transitory world where everything is in a state of "turmoil." He further states that the characters are "shifting, changing, vacillating, a blend of old and new." They are "drawn from a mixture of past and present ideas, snippets from books and newspapers, scraps of real people, rags and tags of Sunday papers, all sewn together like every, human soul" (xxviii-xxix). Pirandello's *Six Characters in Search of an Autho*r (1921) may be seen as one of the further manifestations of this concept to herald the multiple selves of a creator's conscience. The difference lies in the fact that Kennedy's characters are fragmented because of the suffocating racist experiences.

Lack of place, inner space, identity and the continued oppression for centuries has had a heavy toll on their psyche so much so that their holistic selves remain splintered. The host selves are a bundle of contradictions. As Glass continues to mention, "It is as if the self were made up of disconnected, non-communicating images whose existence [is] in the world derived directly from terror and pain." (53) This statement holds partially true in the case of Sarah and Clara. Sarah's host self has undergone terror and pain. But the different selves are not entirely disconnected. The Duchess of Hapsburg and Queen Victoria represent the aristocratic White female selves of Sarah, with whom she longs to identify. She continues to do so although she is rejected by them. Jesus is the White male saviour of both the Blacks and Whites. Lumumba, the Ghanian leader is the saviour of the Black race to which Sarah partly belongs. All the characters are emanations of a single personality. The connection between the different selves also lies in the fact that they have in some way or the other touched upon a poor Black woman's consciousness. The Duchess and Queen Victoria represent the class of White women to which Sarah can never rise. Jesus representing Christianity has both blessed the race and has also acted as a curse since he represents the erosion of their ethnic faiths. The different selves thus enhance our understanding of Sarah's inscape, which struggles for identification with the White of Black worlds though she ultimately does not belong to both the places. The presence of icons that belong to the White world are vital for Sarah's inner sustenance and existence since she considers them as "embankments" which are vital for maintaining "a stark fortress" against recognition of her much detested blackness (Kennedy, *In One Act* 5). The icons therefore serve the dual purpose of both recognition and non-recognition. By acting as a shield against excessive recognition of her self, she is only more painfully aware of her acute Blackness.

Clara Passmore in Kennedy's *The Owl Answers* is yet another character with multiple personalities lodged within her.

She is also Anne Boleyn, the Virgin Mary, the bastard and the owl. Her love for the English land, literature and culture is highlighted through her longing to walk on the streets of London. She is denied passage into the White world by the self-same masters of English (whom she loves) like Chaucer, Shakespeare and Dickens. Instead, she is imprisoned in the Tower of London. Clara's holistic self suffers from the hegemonic superimposition of race and power. When her human selves offer little solace, she is transformed into a bird[5]. She is an owl.[6] Bird imagery dominates the play. Throughout the play, there are haunting ravens, and also a god's White dove, which keep fluttering. Along with these two birds, Kennedy introduces aptly, the owl's self of SHE. This is the most poignant of Kennedy's bird imagery: "In contrast to the play's haunting raven and god's White dove, the owl can see through the darkness that empowers it. But for Clara, the silence of the darkness and of the owl's world, undermines its power" (Meigs 174). As an owl, Clara is able to see through the darkness that covers her physically and shrouds her metaphorically. Therefore, an obsession with darkness continues to haunt her till the end. It consolidates the "self" and marginalises the "other." A number of reasons, social, cultural and psychological have contributed to the formation of a biased attitude towards the coloured race. Lind uses the term "blood complex" (104) (a term borrowed from social psychiatry) which believes in the superiority of the White race. Adler labels it as "inferiority complex" (Lind 104). Both these complexes have sunk into the human psyche, contributing towards the evolution of a prejudiced socio-cultural network.

The discourse on race is also the product of science in the eighteenth century. Debates over the colour of the skin were centuries old in Europe. Science, instead of dismantling the notions of inferiority attached to races, only strengthened them. The race which detested the view that man was a mere biological product of the evolutionary process (and not created by god) accepted Darwin's notion of racial supremacy as presented in his *Descent of Man* (1871). Thus, racial concepts slowly evolved. Gradually, it connoted not only the skin colour, but also its cultural, genetic and civilisational imputations. Nearly all the characters in the plays of Kennedy, Sanchez and Shange suffer from the negative attributes made to their colour.

Kennedy's Sarah in *Funnyhouse of a Negro* suffers from colour complex. Her complexion is sometimes called "yellow" or "whitish yellow" and the expression on her face is an "alabaster" one. A "mulatto" herself, she detests the mixture of Black and White. To her, it is equivalent to contamination. She shudders at the thought: "It was because of him that my mother died because she let a black man put his hands on her." (Kennedy, *In One Act* 20-21)

To Sarah, the mixture of Black with White not only amounts to contamination but death itself. This brings us to the crucial issue of hybridisation. In recent times, hybridity is understood as stressing the interdependence of the coloniser and the colonised. Homi Bhabha cites Fanon and concludes that both liminality and hybridity are essential features of the colonial condition. Throughout his *Black Skin, White Masks*, Fanon asserts that the trauma of a Black person arises from the realisation that one can never attain the Whiteness that one is conditioned to desire. Therefore, a certain amount of mimicry cannot be ruled out. Bhabha does not consider Fanon's image of Black Skin/White Masks as a "neat division." Rather it is "A doubling, dissembling image of being in at least two places at once." The process defies the "devalued" individual "to accept the coloniser's invitation to identity" because though the offer may superficially equate him with the whites, implied differences continue to prevail. It is precisely in that ambivalent use of "different" that the liminal problem of colonial identity and its vicissitudes emerge (Bhabha "Of Mimicry and Man" 117). Therefore, skin becomes an important signifier, marking the difference between the "self" and "other." For Bhabha, it does not merely signify the agony of the colonial subject, but also the workings of the colonial authority. Hybridity therefore becomes an important consequence of contact zones, everywhere.

Like Sarah, Clara in *The Owl Answers* is also a "hybrid" product. The play explores the psychological terrain of Clara who is ravaged between the conflicting desires of the two worlds. Her love for England is a product of her English education. The play being partly autobiographical, it would be relevant to quote from Kennedy's *People Who Led to My Plays* with regard to her own mixed heritage. Kennedy mentions how most of her ancestors came from England and therefore she becomes "very interested in England." (72) "Heritage" becomes a troublesome issue for Clara, since she is not allowed to embrace it. While the White patriarchy considers her inferior on account of her "contaminated" blood, the Black race also fails to take her into its fold. The father figure is one colour Clara longs to love. She longs for understanding from her father. He is a "dead white father." Clara J. McDonnough mentions in her "God and the Owls: The Sacred and the Profane in Adrienne Kennedy's *The Owl Answers* that the term "Dead White father" is a fascinating one for today's audiences (not in 1965 when the play was originally written) since currently the term invokes the "multi-cultural literary attitudes" that focus excessively on the works of "dead white males," and recognising the importance of other non-white, non-male writings. McDonnough is right in pointing out how Clara seems to be "unaware that there might be a culture worth embracing besides that being defined by white males" (McDonnough 393), which is a strong proof of the internalised racist values that almost bamboozles them into believing that there exists nothing beyond.

Sonia Sanchez's characters are also initially enmeshed in the web of colour complex. The difference between the characters of Kennedy and Sanchez lies in the fact that while the characters in Kennedy are inextricably caught in the lattice of colour-complex, totally devoid of any positive affirmation, the characters in Sanchez present a positive change. Although the characters are initially overwhelmed by their dark complexion, slowly they grow to assert their stigmatised colours. In her play *The Bronx is Next* (1970), Sanchez depicts the appalling conditions of the Blacks living in ghettoes. Charles, a Black man, voices the human racial memory when he alludes to the connotations associated with Black and White colours as a "colour thing" which places them in a position inferior to the poor Irish whites (Sanchez, "The Bronx"; 80).Therefore, the inferior status of the Black race in America according to Charles is because of his "colour."

Patricia Sloane in her work *The Visual Nature of Colour* (1989) gives a path breaking insight into the colours "Black" and "White" as achromatic or non-colours. Sloane rejects the notion that they are opposite colours. To her, the Black-White logic is not a visual but a strictly psychical/symbolic one. The interpretation of the world "as a collection of opposites" leads to positioning of a positive against a negative. "Black for this reason is said to symbolize [. . .] night, darkness, the void, Satan, evil." She further adds how black colour is devoid of all positive connotations which remain the prerogative of "white" on account of its connotative value with "day, light, salvation, God, goodness, or other concepts." Such forms of polarisation leave little space for ambiguities, thereby reinforcing the divisions with an element of fixity. (Sloane 88-89)

Despite such probing psychological studies on the black-white colour complex, it is a hard fact that inequalities do exist. In the play *The Bronx is Next* by Sanchez, Charles creates the idea of role-reversal. While the White cop acts as a Black man, the Black man acts as a White cop. Initially, the White cop denigrates the idea as being "ridiculous" and "silly." Charles questions if he thought it was "silly" to be Black. (Sanchez, *The Bronx* 80). Sanchez is actually asking the White man for the ultimate, which is imagining himself as being "Black." While it is easy for a Black man to assume a White role (since he often craves to be so on account of internalised racism), the same is difficult for the White man. The White cop's sympathy alone would be inadequate because it requires an empathetic perception of the Black race's colour complex, and an inordinate ability to transcend the psycho-cultural perceptions of colour which would place him in the shoes of the Black race. Thus, the initial reluctance on the part of the White cop to don the role of a Black man is only natural. The moment he accepts that role, he is immediately branded a "robber" and hit since "Black" is traditionally associated with negative qualities. This is a unique case of reverse-lynching since it is a White man being lynched by a Black. Historically, it was a weapon used by the Whites to keep the Blacks in a perpetual state of terror. Ida B. Wells in her autobiographical work mentions that lynching was an "excuse to get rid of Negroes [. . .] and thus keep the race terrorised" (Duster 64). Anti-lynch plays were therefore seen as a diatribe against dominant racial and gender ideologies of late U.S.

In her play *Uh! Uh! But How Do It Free Us?* (1974) Sanchez explains the internalised colour-complex within the Blacks. The play is ironically set in the mid 1960s (at the time of the Black Arts Movement and the Black Power Movement) during which there was a vindication of everything Black including the colour of the skin. The play is divided into three sections. The myth of narcissism runs through all the sections in the play. Freud believes in two types of narcissism. "In its healthy state, it leads men to accomplish things and develop self-esteem. In its unhealthy manifestation it becomes a dominating factor in a person's life, since a narcissistic individual sees himself superior to others" (Berger 116). The men in the three sections of the play are obsessed with the latter form of narcissism. Out of extreme self-love, they rate their mediocre potentials very high. In the second section, the Brother Man rates his average performances on the stage as "perfect." He also thanks the efforts of their leaders like Malcolm X and Eldridge Cleaver who had upheld their racist stances. Sanchez is actually focusing on the negative aspects of narcissism, which hampers their progress. The prime motto of the Black Arts movement and the Black Power movement was to make the African Americans work hard to realize their true worth. On the other hand, a false self-esteem and unwarranted pride in their mediocrity would actually pave way only towards their downfall. Speaking about the Sixties to Zala Chandler, Sonia Sanchez mentions how it was the time for contradictions among the Blacks: “It was a period when we felt the necessity to write about our internal contradictions, and we often juxtaposed the public image and the private image” (Braxton and Mc Laughlin 358). The play lays bare these confusions, since sensitive artists like Sanchez were pained to see the empty pride of many African Americans who wanted to catapult to fame with little work of substantial merit. As a woman she is also hurt by the African American male insensitivity to the oppression of their women. Therefore the narcissism of the Brother man in *Uh! Uh! But How Do It Free Us?* is a negative one since he lives in an illusory world which actually impedes his progress. Sanchez visualises these movements as moments of self-discovery when they could be their “natural self[ves]” when they were no longer concerned about their hair, nose or ears. It was a moment of “relief from a peculiar kind of bondage,” a positive narcissism which actually enhances their creative potential. For the first time, they had time to do something with their “brains” instead of their hair. (Braxton and McLaughlin 357).

The plays of Sanchez, Kennedy and Shange can therefore be perceived as protest theatre which attempt to gain respite from restrictions on creativity. While Kennedy and Sanchez present characters who are struggling within the webs of colour complex, it is Ntozake Shange who raises a direct protest against the racist colour issue in America. Although her first play *for colored girls who have considered suicide when the rainbow is enuf* (1981) is clearly a voice for the Black American woman, her racist protest is more vocal in her second play *spell #7* (1981). Parodying the traditional American minstrel shows popular in the nineteenth century, the play introduces the magician/narrator Lou who claims to cure many problems. He remedies issues in romance, banishes nightmares, solves sexual problems, but is immobilized by the request of a Black child who asks to be made

"White." This is a clear case of colour complex, which is entrenched in the psyche of children. A child's first awareness of its blackness arises the moment it realises the contrast between "self" and the "other." The "othering" is a systematic and deliberate act of the hegemonic racist attitudes. Lou's hostility towards racist colour complex is a consequence of Shange's own childhood encounters with southern racism. She recollects the trauma of that experience when she narrates her experiences in a school where there were only white children. Not only did the kids refuse to play with her, but they would also take away her cookies and ask her to prove that she was not "colored" to get them back. (Ribowsky 46)

Every coloured child in a racially bigoted nation like America undergoes a schizophrenic shock of recognition. Having been nurtured in a bias-free domestic atmosphere, which treats it like any other normal child, it faces a shock of recognition, when exposed to the outer world. The conflict between the two worlds scathes its psyche. The moment it realises that its natural/biological complexion is smirched, it longs to transform itself into a White person. Fanon mentions in his *Black Skin, White Masks* that "for the Black man there is only one destiny. And it is White" (8). The internalisation of inferiority begins in childhood. Rightly does Fanon quote Nietzsche who said that "man's tragedy [. . .] is that he was once a child" (8). In order to raise the positive self-esteem of the child, Lou uses not voodoo, but the "magic of changing their mental perceptions" (Lester 89). This is one of the most potent ways for the race to overcome the crippling effects of racist colour complex and to perceive its true worth.

The theme of blackness and colour complex is further intensified in her fourth published play, *boogie woogie landscapes* (1979). Like the plays of Kennedy which are always located in the mind of the protagonist, Shange's play is set in the subconscious layer of the protagonist's psychic existence. The play exposes the inner fears, fantasies and dreams of a coloured girl, nay, every coloured girl. Dreams are also an integral part of it.

When the realities of life are rather too harsh for the characters to bear, they transport themselves into a world of dreams. Dreams have a special significance for the African Americans as they have always cherished dreams of equality in a racially bigoted nation like America. Martin Luther King's famous speech, "I have a dream" signifies dreams as a harbinger of hope for the African Americans. To probe into the dream world, expressionistic and impressionistic techniques are intermingled with dance, music and poetry. Basically, African drama is by itself a mixture of several art forms, amalgamating magic, music, dance and a melange of colours which add to the vibrancy and vitality of primitive life forces as reflected in their theatre. It was one of the ways through which the primitive tribes combated with the hostile nature around them. As in Rugyendo's *The Contest* (1977), song and dance form the dynamics and mechanics of magic which is crucial for the inner sustenance of the Africans.

While primitive African theatre was a struggle against eternal cosmic forces, the African American feminist theatre was a complex struggle against the added socio-political cultural environment in which they were enmeshed. The union of several aesthetic forms renders a cumulative effect in the minds of the spectators. Theatre becomes closer to Artaudian idea of "expression in space" (Artaud 51). Through such an amalgamated medium, Shange probes into the inscape of Layla's acceptance and discovery of blackness. Her colour reveals itself slowly before her. Each movement shreds and reveals Layla's complex identity. Her "self" is always at war against the oppressive White cultural forces which are continuously undermining and "othering" her. Shange attributes Layla's racial awareness to her adolescent times, where she existed as a confused individual, trapped between "Black and White." Both these worlds do not accept her. Home too, offers little solace, as it is "a cave." Using the womb/oven imagery, Layla probes into the emptiness of her life, which has been haunting her since her birth. At still another level, the oven imagery recalls a myth that explained to Black children that their skin is darker than that of White children because they were baked longer (Lester 183).

Layla's angst makes her frantically resume efforts to wipe away the darkness of her skin. It is a "charcoal life" for her. Whatever she touches becomes darker.[8] The self-alienation[9] caused in Layla makes her seek solace in outer media. When the print media offers little comfort for her, she turns to the radio for help. The radio evangelist helps her discover Jesus. This is religion in Christian terms. Spiritual healing makes her discover new meanings for the word "colour." Her "charcoal life" which was filled with "overwhelming darkness," and "grime" is now transformed into a state of brightness, as illustrated through her colour symbols like "sun" and "yellow." The life which was earlier "Black and crusty," is now jubilant with the "great light steering in her soul." Layla's spirit undergoes a new birth. Words like "bathed" and "washed" suggest not only purgation but also the Christian ideas of baptism. It is through her renewed birth that she is able to overcome her colour complex.

Along with colour, another major African feature, which stands out prominently is their "hair." It is an essential part of the African American anti-racist agenda.[10] In Kennedy's *Funny House* the protagonist Sarah is extremely conscious of her hair because that is the only "glaring negroid" feature in her appearance: "My one defect is that I have a head of frizzy hair, unmistakably Negro kinky hair, and it is indistinguishable." (Kennedy, *In One Act* 6). The hair is the only vestige of Sarah's racial identity from which she deliberately wants to alienate herself. All the various selves of Sarah are also obsessed with their hair. After an insomniac night, the Duchess agonises over the loss of hair on her temples and crown which is indeed shocking. (Kennedy, *In One Act* 10). Throughout the play, the hair keeps falling out whenever the characters pass through tempestuous times. For Patricie Lumumba, his hair falls whenever his mind becomes turbulent. To Lumumba, the falling of hair was directly linked to a state of self-hatred. The presence of violent negative feelings has an impact on his hair. It falls because his mind has become tempestuous. Even Jesus screams "My hair. [. . .] My hair" (Kennedy, *In One Act* 16).[11] Sarah thinks in terms of baldness as a solution to the conflict in her mind. It is a sort of "compromise formation" through which "she attempts to nullify the opposition kinky-straight, Black-White." But the state of baldness is only a temporary solution to the problem of racism. Symbolically, baldness signifies the state of "fallenness." It is an "unfortunate fall from a state of grace into a state of "race." In the "racial" funny house, the fall out is not just of hair, but of love. "Sarah's mother falls out of love with her father, falls out of love with blackness [. . .]. Falling out of love is falling into hate." (Adams 94). The theme of baldness has continued to find a place in other plays too. In George Woolfe's play *The Colored Museum* (1992) a bald head is used to satirize the kinky-straight opposition. Michael Vannoy Adams feels that the bald head in both Kennedy and Woolfe can be interpreted in Barthesian terms of the "zero degree." He quotes Barthes saying that the absence of something is itself a signifier: "The zero degree testifies to the power held by any system of signs, of creating meaning out of nothing" (Adams 77). Therefore, having no hair is also meaningful. Baldness is an absolute zero degree. It is a "nothing" that has produced a continuum of signifiers with racist connotations.

When the characters are not born with straight hair, they at times wear wigs to conceal their springy hair. In Kennedy's play *The Owl Answers*, Rev. Passmore conceals his dark, kinky hair with a straightened blonde wig. Kennedy describes his act thus: "the DEAD FATHER remembers his hair [. . .] beneath his White hair is dark negro hair" (Kennedy, *In One Act* 28-29). A similar act of concealing the dark wild hair is also adopted by the Black woman in Sanchez's play *The Bronx is Next* (1970). Pushed to flesh trade on account of poverty, she does not despise her race although she hates her men. The appalling ghetto conditions and the harsh treatment meted out to her race have only made her racially assertive instead of weakening her. Paradoxically, although she loves her race, she also wears "a powdered wig" to frantically conceal her racial identity. Charles calls it "her passport to the White world" (Sanchez, "The Bronx" 83). The wig becomes a mask with which she conceals her racial roots and also with the help of which she lures her White male customers. The wig then becomes a sort of "fetish," because she believes that it grants her the passage into the dominant White culture.

Attempts to conceal one's real hair are an initial stage of the African American racial struggle. In *The Autobiography of Malcolm X* (1965), the leader says how he purchased lye, potatoes and eggs to get his hair "processed" or "conked." Little did he realise that the false consciousness was really the fist step towards degrading his own self.[12] But later, Malcolm X moves on to vindicate his real self and no longer feels ashamed of it. In the later part of his racist struggle, the protest is transformed into love and a positive highlighting of his racist features.

The issue of kinky-straightened hair is analysed by Shange in *spell #7*. In this play, Lily, an African American woman fantasises about being the Black counterpart of Rapunzel, a fairy tale heroine. When trapped in a tower, Rapunzel is ultimately united with her lover by allowing him to climb her long, straight, golden hair. Lily is excluded from playing this popular role in the theatre, as she is not gifted with such a mane. But still, she nurtures a secret hope that her hair may be straightened some day with rigorous brushing at the rate of 200 times/day. (*three pieces* 26). Lily believes that such an act of frenzied brushing would radically transform her social and professional life paving way to greater acceptance. Throughout the speech, Lily knows that she's not Rapunzel. But she deliberately dreams to sustain her psychic existence. The obsessional complex with skin and hair is an integral part of African American literature, which John E. Lind calls skin complex. He calls this as "extremely common say, almost universal in the Negro" (Adams 120). It is the result of the social subordination of the African Americans. To Lind, colour complex (which in the large sense may include both the skin and hair) is also found in African Americans who are not psychotic. The African American writers try to overcome these dermato-psychological states through their writings. They may fly into a world of fantasy, later they may realise the innate beauty lodged within them and move towards a greater acceptance, or as Layla does in *boogie woogie landscapes* they may attempt to find salvation in the White Christian religion.

This brings us to the crucial issue of the role played by Christianity in "conquering" the natives and the relevance of the White religion to the African Americans. Africa is a land of diverse sub-cultures and multiple forms of faith. A belief in God did exist there, though not in the Christian sense of the term. While Christianity may use the destructive word "heathen" to describe their original faith, Jan Abdul Mohammed considers it a part of the colonial mission that distorts it as a world which has not been "domesticated" (a euphemism for colonisation and cultural devastation). Therefore it is represented as being "uncontrollable, unattainable, and ultimately evil." Thirst for conquest and domination often trigger the imperialist to devalue the colonised on the basis of "differences in race, language, social customs, cultural values and modes of production" (Jan Mohammed 18). The world is perceived by the polarised mind of the coloniser as being in a state of flux where he has come to impose order. The coloniser thus starts his process of "reformation." Religion is used as a major weapon of "transformation."

The diasporic experience of the African Americans has uprooted them from their native religions. In the new land, they were confronted with hostile socio-cultural circumstances, which did not permit the retention of their original faith. Gradually, they were converted into the White man's religion which slowly permeated their beings. The initial process of indoctrination may have been easy since the coloniser had the power to do so. But, the process of acceptance may not have been uniformly simple. While some may have accepted the faith as a source of comfort, others viewed Christianity as a White man's religion, hence its troubled acceptance. Both these facts have to be borne in mind.

By refracting the race through the prism of Christianity, the coloniser impressed upon the colonised that the Bible was the ultimate revelation unto the "savage" race. Homi Bhabha contends that it is an "Enstellung," involving "a process of displacement, distortion, dislocation" [since] "the discovery of the English book established both a measure of mimesis and a mode of civil authority and order. (Bhabha, "Signs Taken For Wonders" 31-32). The mimetic nature of the Bible can never be undermined since we see its impact in all the dramatists taken up for the current study. But to accept it as the only source of order into what is otherwise distorted as a chaotic universe is to deliberately undermine the innate value of their native beliefs. African Americans zealously adopted the faith as it gave them the hope of freedom. Like the Biblical Moses who freed the Israelites, they nurtured secret hopes of freedom from White bondage. Christianity also acted as a unifying factor, for, the diverse tribal groups in the pluralistic American landscape, imbuing them with what Milton L. Sernett labels as "an elemental bond of group identity" and "a set of religious beliefs, symbols and rituals" (Sernett 6).

One of the earliest responses to Christianity was by a woman. Phillis Wheatley, an American poet who is generally claimed as the forerunner of African American literature, welcomes Christianity as a delivering factor since it has enlightened her "benighted soul" to "understand" since she once redemption neither sought nor knew. (Reinfro 12) W.E.B. DuBois in his *The Souls of Black Folk* calls the church a "social centre of Negro life" (DuBois 142). Booker T. Washington in *The Story of the Negro* considers the church as the pioneer offshoot of African American life that still holds its sway upon them. The prevailing social conditions had placed special burden on the Black churches. They had to be political forums, educational centres, places of worship and above all, asylums from racism and its associated violence. Both Catholicism and Protestantism were enforced on the African Americans. To uphold Christian values was not an easy task for the African Americans since it was the religion of the colonisers. It tried their souls especially during slavery:

> To hold Christianity while receiving blows from its professed practitioners, to avoid wishing evil upon those who prayed with them on Sunday but beat them on Monday, tried the souls of Black Christians. (Sernett 6)

Clearly, the African American attitude towards Christianity remains shrouded in ambiguity since its inception. Such an attitude is quite visible in Kennedy, Sanchez and Shange.

Adrienne Kennedy's faith in Catholicism is clear from *People Who Led to My Plays*. She was influenced by Christianity since her childhood days when the miniature photographs of Jesus "hypnotised" her (Kennedy, *People* 11). At the same time, she also mentions a certain amount of fear that frequently accompanied her in the process of being Christianised. In her *People Who Led to My Plays* she mentions the fear that she often experienced in the congregations when she met a particular minister who was always "angry." She was afraid of his "black eyes" and "evil robes" (20). The passage is also an apt illustration of the internalised notions of the colour black with evil. Although her elementary school life had made her experience the faith in its pristine form, her later racist experience makes her adopt a rather ambivalent attitude towards Christianity.

In her play *A Rat's Mass* (1966), she uses the Catholic ritual like mass to depict the grime and filth that surrounds the African American life. The brother rat and sister rat are named Blake and Kay respectively. The name "Blake" is significantly suggestive of the lost state of innocence of the Blacks in the American diaspora. Sister rat is named 'Kay' after the character K in Kafka's existential novel *The Trial* (1925). The moral dilemma of Kay almost borders on nihilism, which is a metaphor for their grime-filled existence. The very appearance of the brother and the sister fills the spectators' minds with a sense of the gruesomeness. While brother rat has a rat's head and a human body, sister rat has a rat's belly and a human head. The imagery of "rat" had been introduced to Kennedy through her acquaintance with fairy tales. Commenting on the Pied Piper of Hamelin (along with other fairy tale characters), she mentions that it "was a world that existed where unusual terror reigned, a world my parents and friends couldn't reach" (Kennedy, *People* 4). Kennedy's apprehension of terror in the seemingly simple fairytale world is reflected in her play *A Rat's Mass*. Like the rats who are snared to death by the Pied-piper, the African Americans live a terror-filled life. While cats are usually pet animals (signifying Whites) who are a privileged race, rats are associated with slime, dirt and disease (signifying the American Blacks). They are the guinea-pigs of the racist American culture. They lead a trapped existence from which there is no salvation. Elinor Fuchs in "Kennedy and the First Avant-Garde" compares the plays of Kennedy with Strindberg's *To Damascus* and focuses on the complexity of Kennedy's religious vision. While the religion "waits patiently for Strindberg's stranger," "Kennedy's view of the religious sign is more complex. It can turn punishing and vengeful, or its affirmative power may be exactly balanced by a sign from another culture [. . .] leading to spiritual doubt and paralysis." (Fuchs 82) The complexity stems from the fact that there is a balancing of religious symbols. The symbol of the "Virgin Mary" and the "dove" is juxtaposed with that of the "owl," and Jesus with Lumumba, signifying the uneasy compromise that is reached in the Black racial memory. Religion offers Kay and Blake little consolation as the cathedral in which they live is bombarded by violence. They scream:

> The Nazis! The Nazis have invaded our house [. . .] the rats. The rats have invaded our cathedral [. . .] yet we weren't safe long. (Kennedy, *In One Act* 57)

A paranoiac feeling grips them in the cathedral which is actually a haven for the oppressed. In her *People*, Kennedy relates her memories of Hitler who had created terror in her psychological space. Having lived through the Second World War, she was gripped with a paranoid fear of persecution: "If Hitler came to Cleveland and we resisted, would we be beaten and sent to the concentration camp? [. . .] I didn't want Hitler to come [. . .] or go to a camp." (28) The persecution-complex is amplified in *A Rat's Mass*. The mass is not attended by human beings, but by rats. They are present in "the church books"; and also "behind every face in the congregation" (Kennedy, *In One Act* 58). Religion, instead of acting as a liberating force, has become an engulfing one. Jesus in *Funny House* is a "hunch-backed yellow skinned dwarf" (Kennedy, *In One Act* 7), dressed in White rags and sandals. Jesus is both a God and her rapist father who had haunted her mother's conception. Jesus is the saviour of the Black race. Sarah mentions how her paternal grandmother cherished a dream of her son becoming a Christ-like figure in Genesis in order to save her race: "You must walk with a white dove and heal the race, heal the misery, take us off the cross. (Kennedy, *In One Act* 14)

Contrary to the expectations of the mother who dreamt that her son would save the race, he turns into a "wild beast." Sarah turns aghast at the thought of her mother's rape by her father since she believes that "Christ would not rape any one." (Kennedy, *In One Act* 21). The yawning gap that exists between expectation and fulfillment in their newly adopted religion, gives the African Americans a dubious feeling. Their depiction of Christ is unconventional. In one of his interviews, Lind mentions how the African American theological conception is a contrast to the traditional representation of God as White as proved by African American art pieces which project Black celestial figures and Black paradise (Lind 407). Lind further feels that such an attempt is probably "a protest against the orthodox colour scheme of salvation" (Lind 408). This leads us to the debatable issue if Jesus was "Black" or "White." While traditional Judaeo-Christian ideologies conventionally perpetuate the fact that Christ was blue-eyed, other researches seem to give different opinions. A study conducted at the University of Manchester leads to the conclusion that Christ could have had kinky hair, dark eyes and a broad nose.[13]

An iconoclastic perspective of Christianity was advocated by African American leaders like Malcolm X. In an anti-integration speech delivered at the University of Michigan in the year 1963, he beckoned the men of his race to counter the "Uncle Tom" stereotype who has only a blind faith in Christianity. With faith in a "White Jesus, White Mary" etc. He considers this a consequence of "400 years of brain washing . . . in America" wherein the Black man's heart and brain have been thoroughly whitewashed. (*Malcolm X* 131). Kennedy (who has dedicated a poetic play called *Sun* in 1968 to Malcolm X) has responded to this call. Although we do not find any hint of her response to the Islamic faith of Malcolm X, she had deliberately gone against the "Uncle Tom" image. Though Jesus is not black-skinned in her play, he is one of the many selves of a Black woman. In *A Lesson in Dead Language* he becomes more conspicuous by his mute presence because he stands powerless to ameliorate the plight of African American adolescent girls. Religious characters are often transformed into religious symbols. Mary is an important figure in *The Owl Answers*. She is one of the selves of Clara Passmore, an African American woman. In her autobiographical work *People Who Led to My Plays*, Kennedy mentions how she played the role of mother Mary in one of the school's Christmas parties (10-11). In the play, Clara's mother wants her daughter to always remain "Mary" since it would assure her virginity. But unfortunately, Clara is unable to protect her virginity and thus, she moves from the kingdom of God to "owldom," from which she longs for her ultimate resurrection.[14] The dead White father Rev. Passmore, has significantly embraced the "White" Bible, a symbol of the White man's religion. Christianity is questioned in this play (as in *Funny House*) since it indicates the religion of the coloniser. Robert Tener mentions how Clara "has been brought up in the White man's Christian religion, where none of whose symbols have the mythic power of uniting man with the sacred for the Black person" (2). Towards the end of the play, Clara is transformed into an owl with the "oww" expression signifying rape and Clara's painful initiation into sexual knowledge, where sex, in Christian terms, equals a fall from grace (Curb 142).

Sanchez is closer to Kennedy in depicting an inevitably uneasy attitude towards Christianity. In her play *Uh! Uh! But How Do It Free Us?* (1974), the Black woman in the third section of the play is deserted by her man. She realises that Christianity offers little comfort since she was expecting succour from someone who had never helped her race to achieve anything except making them "stay on their knees." (Sanchez, *"Uh! Uh!"* 213) But the feeling is merely a passing phase, for she immediately moves towards a greater sense of hope. As a mother, she does not want her child to live in a spiritual wasteland. She wants it to enter into a world of "light" in the place of darkness and madness. (Sanchez, *Uh! Uh!* 213) Longing for a spiritually enlightened world for her progeny, she moves towards a higher plane of realisation that religion alone would act as an antidote for all modern maladies which may otherwise make them neurotic.

In Shange's *boogie woogie landscapes*, the dramatist speaks of religion in Christian terms for the first time. In *colored girls*, her seven women love God "fiercely" with an inner strength, paving the way for a greater amount of self-awareness. Their spiritual experience kindles in them a state of sisterhood, as they join their hands chanting. In *spell #7*, there is an atmosphere of religious conversion that characterises a spiritual revival. Ultimately, the characters emerge with renewed racial self-awareness. But in *boogie woogie landscapes*, religion plays a traditional role of providing peace and haven from a hostile secular, materialistic and antagonistic White world. African American Christian churches are "louder" than the White Christian churches. In his "Black religion in the Post-Reconstruction South" (1880), William Wells Brown mentions how "shouting" was a part of the African American church conventions. Initially, it was difficult to erase from the mind of the Negro the loud outward demonstrations of faith, such as the loud "Amen" were not the necessary "adjuncts to piety"

(Lester 187), since they had viewed Christianity through the filter of their native faiths. Whether loud or calm, the influence of Christianity in the lives of African Americans cannot be ruled out. Layla's transformation takes place through a radio-voice, rather than a direct conversion: she discovers that there were new "dimensions" and new modes of evaluation. Since good and bad are ultimately not external, but internal, lodged within her own darkness (Shange, *three pieces* 117).

But that such a discovery has been made possible through a radio evangelist's voice and not through the voice of Jesus is paradoxical. Perhaps Shange is here simultaneously praising and attacking religious conversions as it has been traditionally associated with Black people's psychological and emotional survival in racist America. While it has helped them to survive all tribulations in a racially bigoted nation, it still remains an unresolved paradox to the Black race, especially their women since they wage a war against White men while they are forced to accept a White male god as their protector. The New Jerusalem, while promising to accept them, simultaneously becomes an oppressive factor by itself. But still the African American women do not give up faith. There may linger elements of doubt but they never renounce it. They need it because it is necessary for their individual spiritual existence and the well-being of the entire family.

The family is the centre of African life. But in the new soil, it was one of the much thwarted institutions. During the Sixties and Seventies of the last century, much debate was generated over the African American familial patterns. Franklin Frazier's *Social History of the African American Family* (1952) believed that although exceptional slave men and women made attempts to triumph over the system, the most ordinary of them were transformed into "lumpenproletariats"—a powerless aggregate of displaced African American men, women and children. Frazier holds the view that "environmental determinism" interprets slave behaviour as an imperfect imitation of the dominant culture. He also opines that the African American family survived because it "reacted" to the multiple oppressive systems. Ralph

Ellison significantly questions if the African American familial system could "live and develop over these hundred years by "simply reacting" (Berlin 10). Ellison's question did not arise in a vacuum. It was a call made to probe deeper into the domestic unit—the family. True, like the Indians, the Africans also had their own familial systems. In White America the Black families were torn asunder to cater to the needs of the White, patriarchal norms. Members of a single family were often sold to different slave owners. While the slave man was forced to till the ruler's land the slave woman was often pushed into the domestic service of the plantation owner's household.

Therefore, family and domestic harmony have become the central points of discussion for many of the African American women dramatists. Such themes dominated African American women playwrights even at the turn of the century as Georgia Douglas Johnson's *The Plumes* (1927), *A Sunday Morning in the South* (1927) and Shirley Graham's *It's Morning* (1942).

Adrienne Kennedy's female protagonists are deeply concerned with family life.[15] The mulatto Sarah's identity crisis in her *Funny House* is not merely a domestic one. Margaret B. Wilkerson sees the deeper historical implications when she perceives Sarah to be the progeny of two mighty continents Europe and Africa. Her "personal identity crisis is at once a crisis with political and social resonance—a legacy of the historical confrontation between White Europeans and Black Africans" (Wilkerson, "Diverse Angles" 73). The Duchess frequently complains that it was her Black father who caused the death of her fair-skinned mother: "It is because of him that my mother died" (Kennedy, *In One Act* 3). It is a symbolic representation of the native rebellion against the colonial process of raping. Colonised countries usually figured themselves as naked women and their colonisers as rapists (see Loomba 13). In *The Tempest*, Miranda might be constantly threatened of rape by Caliban, but Sarah's mother is actually raped by her husband. The family is thus used as a metaphor for a nation. No longer is it merely a "private realm," but also a "public space," thereby investing it with a dual claim. The private worlds are symbolic representations of the public worlds wherein the particular becomes the metaphor of a larger struggle. In projecting the private world, the creative writer is actually trying to present a wider reality which may otherwise escape our attention.

In Kennedy's play *The Owl Answers*, the "mulatto" Clara is the daughter of the Dead White Father/Reverend Passmore. Sarah makes frantic efforts to identify herself with England/father. She revels in "Hyde Park," "Buckingham Palace," "The Tower," "Big Ben," "The Thames" etc. Through education, the colonisers construct a cultural authority for the colonised. To summarise Mary Lousie Pratt's idea, literature serves as an important "contact zone" where "transculturation" assumes complex proportion (Loomba 70). In this process, two or more cultures may be fused, modified or at times, the culture of the subaltern may acquire a marginal place, with that of the dominant one ironically influencing the oppressed. But the White patriarchal culture refuses to accept Clara and instead prefers to imprison her, a symbolic representation of her intellectual and social imprisonment. The intellectual elite of the White patriarchal culture like Chaucer, William the Conqueror and Shakespeare undermine her on account of her colour. They merely label her a "bastard." Kennedy's stage direction clearly indicates their "othering" of her: "Their lines are spoken coldly. SHE WHO IS only a prisoner to them" (Kennedy, *In One Act* 27). This line establishes the fact that their attitude towards them is only that of a White/Black or a coloniser/colonised. This is further reinforced by the fact that THEY represent not merely the icons of the White cult of creativity, but also remain Clara's co-passengers in the subway car. Most importantly, they are "guards in the Tower of London" (27). The Tower of London being an important historical landmark for royal imprisonment (Edward II, Richard II, Anne Boleyn, Bacon etc. are all examples of all those who were either executed of killed), Clara is also metaphorically/physically stifled for the "blasphemy" of identifying herself with the Anglo-

Saxon race. English imperialism is a powerful factor in American racism since England remained the intellectual and cultural capital of America for years after the latter's political freedom. Their common Anglo-Saxon heritage and Caucasian blood is an added factor.[16] While the education of the colonised necessitated their love for England/Anglo-Saxon White race, the practical socio-political norms suppressed them on the pretext of race creating a conflict. When the tormenting realities of racial existence are too harsh for the characters, they are often transformed into birds/animals. Clara is metamorphosed into a multi-dimensional character i.e., an owl, a nocturnal bird, from which she demands resurrection.

The multi-faceted characters of *The Owl Answers* are reduced to stark monolithic figures in *A Beast Story* (1969). While the former play deals with the identity quest of a Black woman with her ancestral culture, the four characters of a Black family are here enmeshed in a web of desires, wills and hatred. While Clara in *The Owl Answers* is transformed into an owl, the four members of a family resemble beasts in this play. The lines of distinction between the human and animal world are blurred. This is an integral part of what Paul Carter Harrison labels as the African "Kuntu Drama" (Harrison 1). Beasts and animals form an integral part of the African spiritual perception. According to this, a common life-force pervades all living things. All forms of life are on a single plane. The roles between the humans/beasts become interchangeable. This is because the Africans perceive "power" as "the basis of all their endeavour." It is a "life-force" with the help of which they establish nexus with other human beings as also "nature and to the cosmos itself." (Harrison 3)

The earthly "cosmic" power is translated in terms of temporal power. Gross imbalances of power create disharmony and conflict. Conflict is the soul of great drama. The ability to go through the conflict also endows the protagonists with a sense of universality. This particular African American family in *A Beast Story* is used as a trope to analyse the anguish of the race in the diaspora. The four characters of an African American family "resemble beasts." They do not resemble any particular beast, but still look like "beasts." Settings of this sort often create complex problems for the performance since the director is left with little clues of establishing the bestial resemblance. The play abounds in bestial imagery, like jackals, mice, toads, wolves and bears. Kennedy's poetic theatre emphasises not merely the physical semblance of the beasts with the human world but a deeper nexus between the human and the animal world which is highlighted through characters who resemble beasts. Kennedy mentions in her interview with Ogunbiyi that "the whole inner relationship between humans and beasts fascinates me" (Ogunbiyi 36). Shredding the layers of human consciousness, she lays bare the two instincts which are predominantly found in animals (human beings inclusive)—the carnal instinct and the murder instinct.

The Beast Man and Beast Woman have a daughter, the Beast Girl. The Dead Human is the murdered son-in-law of the family. He sings lullabies to their murdered child. The four members of this family hardly communicate to each other. Their relationship with each other is both intriguing and destructive. The Dead Human frequently alludes to his ungratified fleshly desire in his married life. He mentions: "The beasts that came to the windows each night knew" (Kennedy, *A Beast Story* 195). When his wife falsely evades him night after night on the pretext of bleeding, his bestial desires continue to torment him. He gratifies his rapacious instinct by molesting his wife in the fields.[17] The beasts silently "watch from the trees" (Kennedy, *A Beast Story* 142). The elemental sexual struggle, which lay between her mother and father, is repeated in her life. Her girl child is killed with whisky and quinine. Ultimately, she also kills her husband. After killing the child, the mother and daughter feel: "The jackals are glad. The toad and the jackals knew" (Kennedy, *A Beast Story* 143).

The latent bestiality in the lives of the characters is highlighted through multiple ways. Throughout the play, an axe hangs on the wall of the room. It emerges as a dual symbol in the play. It is basically used as a weapon to protect her virginity. At another level it becomes a symbol of violence in the characters. The axe also represents the precarious condition of the Blacks, since their lives remain always uncertain. When the Beast Girl commits the murders, they are not mere thoughtless acts. Kimberly Benston sees them in two terms: "the religious outrage of life's denial and the chaotic sensuality of passion in which death too plays its part" (Benston 243). The deliberate denial of the latent primal force in human beings leads to a chaotic conception and the gruesome act of infanticide. The play is a powerful expression of a deeply felt experience. It is a clash between expectation and reality. As the Beast Man says: "I expected to find love in our married life" (Kennedy, *A Beast Story* 195). But "love" remains elusive to the couple from the day of their marriage. The wedding itself starts on a note of disharmony. The music is a discordant one. The sky is filled with "darkness," a "dead blue crow" floats; there are also "floating corpses." Thus the wedding is vitiated with evil portents. These are merely external signs of horror that await the young couple. The first word spoken by the Beast Girl to the Dead Human on the day of the wedding is "death." The discordant wedding note makes the characters move towards a greater degree of self-realisation. The latent destructive instincts are revealed to themselves. As the Beast Girl says: "At last I knew who I was [. . .] no shadow of myself, I was revealed [. . .] to myself." (Kennedy, *A Beast Story* 177)

The self-revelation turns destructive, for she commits the act of infanticide. Robert L. Tener calls this a recognition of "the destructive cycle of suppressed desire, bestiality and death which her ancestors, southern Negroes who came to the city have traversed" (Benston 243). The play is a powerful psychological drama, with simultaneity of action. It takes linear progression. The surrealistic mode of the play allows for the "rooms" to be interpreted as layers of human consciousness, for only there do multiple actions take place at the same time. The psychological conflict within each character allows little room for communication. The only sustainable efforts at communication are made between the father and daughter. The Beast Man tries to establish a communication with the Beast Girl although the latter thwarts all attempts at it. But she understands that the father had cherished a dream for his daughter. She recollects her infant stages when her father had built for her a crib which was circled by a golden aureole, a positive sign of hope despite her mother's "endless wakeful fits." But now there is no moon, and instead of the golden aureole it is only a toad, a symbol of the nadir of human debasement which agonises her to the extent of performing the heinous crime on infanticide, since she kills her child with quinine and whisky. (Kennedy, *A Beast Story* 177)

In the absence of maternal love, she is given paternal love which is refused by her. Like her father who cajoled her as a child, her dead husband sings lullabies for the dead child in the attic. Lullabies, a form of emotional bonding and communication, which usually exist between a mother and child, are here established between the father and daughter. But Kennedy is attempting at a deliberate role reversal.

A number of reasons could be cited for this. All the attempts of the Beast Man to establish even a minimum connection with the Beast Woman having failed, the need for some kind of companionship in the family remains unsatisfied and unfulfilled to him. So, he takes his daughter as a potential companion to compensate for this loss. The attempts of the living father to connect with the living daughter could be seen as a replication of a similar effort by the dead father towards the dead child. In the primitive world view, all life is one—single and continuous. There are two interacting orders of reality: the living and the after-life. As she mentions in the preface to the play, the important thing is ""the materialisation of the ancestral spirit so that one is able to identify a precise source of a particular piece of wisdom. (Kennedy, *A Beast Story* 12). But the primitive mind does not distinguish between these two because the dead can always be involved and a contact can be established. Therefore, the singing of a lullaby by the dead father to the dead child offers only another dimension of the neglected parent seeking companionship with the child, which is what all the attempts of the Beast Man vis-à-vis his daughter are about.[18]

The atmosphere of the play is one of unredeemed gloom. The members of this Black family are unable to transcend their doomed circumstances. They are reduced to a menagerie, each afraid and suspicious of the other. It marks a transition from a well-ordered, regulated society to a forest. An impression is given that the action moves from a family which is supposed to be well-ordered and regulated with normal relations existing between the members, to an absurd situation like in a zoo where the animals seem to be looking at each other with suspicion and fear. In short the family is reduced to a zoo. Kennedy's early plays do share many traits with the theatre of the absurd. Bryant-Jackson mentions how Kennedy makes an effective use of the burlesque and grotesque as in Ionesco, who considers these as the "essence" of an effective theatre which adopts magnification to the maximum. Such devices, contends Bryant-Jackson, should not be concealed, but on the other hand be made "still more evident deliberately obvious, go all out for caricature and the grotesque, way beyond the pale irony of witty exaggeration of parody" (Bryant-Jackson 51). Such techniques are an essential part of twentieth century theatre in laying bare the complexities of life in spatial terms. The experiences being unique, the medium also needs to be so. There is little solace to be drawn from life. The characters experience what John Killinger mentions as "metaphysical emptiness," which leads to chaos and anarchy since "God is the lynchpin suddenly discovered missing from the machinery of the living," (Killinger 25).

The family receives no comfort from traditional religion. The religious symbols present in the room offer them little consolation. The "hymnals" present in the Beast Man's room, "the doleful picture of the virgin," and "a picture of downcast Christ" are all symbolic representations of traditional Christianity which means little to the family. At times, these religious symbols as well as the mundane are juxtaposed for effect. Kennedy makes use of collage to attain this effect. For instance, the play presents a series of images which are juxtaposed to focus on the numerous jeopardies that surround the lives of this family. The picture of the Virgin, that of the downcast Christ, the empty wine bottles in the Beast Woman's room, the dead toad, the dead blue crow together insist on highlighting the predicament of a typical African American family. One important point of contrast is between the Beast Man and Christ. Being a minister, he fails to appear as a Christ-like figure. The living room has a picture of "downcast Christ." While Christ looks "downcast" on account of his humility, the Beast Man stands "downcast" on account of his moral shallowness which has instigated him to rape his wife. He looks down because he suffers from a guilt-complex. While the Beast Man's room has "a book of hymnals," the Beast Woman's room is full of "empty wine bottles." He shows traces of interest in spirituality, but the woman is engrossed in a worldly existence. The Beast Man finds solace in "a golden light," which gives him a mysterious peace despite the howling environment. Towards the end of the play there is a "strange bright sunlight, then darkness" (Kennedy, *A Beast Story* 16). The hope therefore is only a passing phase.[19]

On the whole, the play is a powerful expression of a deeply felt experience. The four members of this Black family fail to attain a psycho-racial identity. Their mummified existence is connoted through surrealistic images of death like "floating corpses," "dead blue crow," "dead infant" and "dead human," all of whom are set in a dark atmosphere. Kennedy uses these symbols to penetrate into the inner psychological states of the characters. This particular image connotes the African Americans who are suspended in a limbo without a sense of identity. The lack of socio-cultural-political space renders them "floating" in a White racist land. Like in Ellison's *Invisible Man*, the members of their family are haunted by a racial paranoia. The injustice meted out to the race for centuries, has not only transformed the

African Americans into "beasts," but it has also led them to a nullified existence.

In inquiring into the consequences of racism and its impact on the African American family, the three dramatists—Kennedy, Sanchez and Shange—understand that racism is not merely an adult experience. Children also go through it. In a bigoted society, its fangs are felt the moment the child is exposed to the devastating values of the dominant culture. Prejudice is first formed at home when the child adapts ready-made ethnic attitudes from its parents. Parental beliefs and antagonisms are transferred to the child. Psychologists D.B. Harris and others in *Child Development* (1957) believe that the development of prejudice is more predominant among children with prejudiced parents, especially mothers. Such a training has an innocuous bearing on the child's psyche whether they are boys or girls, making them understand their powerlessness and conditioning them.

When the sordid racial experiences of the world become unbearable, writers like Kennedy look forward to an ideal state where they remain untouched by racial prejudices. In *A Rat's Mass* the adult "experience" of racism is sharply contrasted with the childhood experience of "innocence." It is a spontaneous and unalloyed state of existence which is free from the faintest touch of self-consciousness. Sister Rat Kay personifies spiritual vacuum that exists in their lives. Their "experience" makes them long for a state of innocence. The "slide" in the play is symbolic of the great fall that the siblings have from their state of innocence "to experience." After the "fall" they find no escape from the Sisyphean plane of survival.

The "past" of the children is depicted through a number of positive symbols like "sunflower," "white birch trees," "spring" and "Holy Songs." Their racist experience is best depicted through a series of horrendous imagery like "worms," "grey cats," "dying babies," "bombs," "nazis," "blood," "ambulance," "winter," bullet," "dead rat babies," "gnawed petals," "battlefield," and "rat voices in the beams." These ghastly images continue to haunt their innocent minds. Rose Mary forms an important link between both the states of the children's existence. Symbolising Catholicism, her hair is Medusa-like, for, it is filled with worms. She is synonymous with the ambivalent attitude of the African Americans towards Christianity since the White Christians failed to live up to the Christian ideals of compassion and mercy in their relationship with the African-Americans.

Shange in *spell #7* introduces the song of the pickaninnies to highlight the causes of racial prejudice in children. Very few children are actually allowed to form their own uninhibited views of people and their colour. Not only do the White children grow up in an atmosphere that nurtures their superior attributes to their colour, but Black children are also sometimes taught to hate their own colour, leading to a low self-esteem. When racial awareness dawns in them, it is not uncommon for children to exhibit a nebulous sense of inferiority with dark skin. To counter such psychologically negative attitudes, Shange beckons the children to bask in the positive glory of blackness. The play itself opens with Lou's rendition of a song about pickaninnies. In the beginning of the play, a third grade Black child resents his blackness and asks the magician to transform him into a White person. Lou brands such a request as "outlandish," and the song exhibits the playful mockery of coloured children towards each other. Not only does the song exhibit the mutual Black-White hatred, but it also questions the true validity of emancipation. Pained by the external forces that undermine the Black children's self-image, Lou asserts the beauty of blackness and makes the child achieve a positive self-esteem. This is a difficult task indeed, in a society that is continually bombarded with racist ideas of beauty, intelligence, success etc. Education also actually does little to exonerate their race. Even the so-called "integrated schools" fail to achieve this purpose, since as Shange mentions, it was one of the "worst" periods of her life.[20] But such childhood adversities have not actually crippled Shange. These have in turn helped her to teach the African American kids a sense of self-respect. The multiple oppressions of the African Americans have made them accentuate the positive aspects of their culture and colour. Lou thus creates a "segregated territory" through his magical powers. This is no mere technical embellishment to the play. It is actually an alternative to the psychological displacement of their race in the American diaspora. It creates an ideal with which they emotionally identify. This kingdom harnesses creative fantasy to overcome all inhibitions. Lou summons all the actors to shed their masks and fully experience their inner lives as Blacks. Thus, it changes their mental perceptions and makes them attain a positive self-hood.[21]

A major cause for the low self-esteem of the African Americans is the lop-sided education they receive. Schools and colleges are breeding grounds of racism in its multiple forms. Carter A. Woodson in *The Miseducation of the Negro* (1933) mentions how several concepts have been absorbed into the consciousness of the African Americans unknowingly. Education is a double-edged weapon, constructive and inspiring for some, destructive and oppressive for others like the Blacks who are systematically inculcalted of their inferiority (Woodson xiii). In the process of being "mis-educated," African Americans fail to see themselves in the proper perspective. Not only is their self-image grossly distorted but they also fail to have authentic first-hand experience of their native cultural values. The experience is closely akin to Edward Said's idea of "Orientalism" which is both distorted and also an essential aspect of European historico-cultural approach (Ashcroft et al, *Post Colonial Studies Reader* 87). Not only does the west distort the orient's image of the world, but the power-play within the countries distorts the subalterns within themselves.

The systematic attempt to incapacitate young African American girls' minds has been of immense concern to many African American writers, including Kennedy in *A Lesson in a Dead Language* (1962) and *The Ohio State Murders* (1972). The former play is a protest against the outmoded and irrelevant American educational system, which is of little value to the African

Americans. When Jesus, Joseph, Mary and the Wisemen stand a mute witness to the drudgery of indoctrination in the name of education, Kennedy is actually lashing out at the misdirected missionary education, which was a regular feature in all colonial countries.[22] The process of translating the terror on the stage in terms of performance was indeed complex. Gadby Rodgers, one of the leading actresses of Kennedy's plays mentions in an interview with Howard Stein how the play's central issue was the "terror" of being Black in a White world. In the performance, the nun was depicted as a big White dog who spoke through an amplification system in order to drill the catechism classes into them. "A lot of their education is a terror trip. The little girls spoke in union like a corps de ballet or chorus. Their individuality was practically obliterated." (Bryant-Jackson and Overbeck 200 my italics) Not only is the medium an extinct one (Latin) but the syllabus is also obsolete. The instructive method only inculcates a sense of horror into the African American girls, as regards the White world. Their teacher/big White dog/nun is a symbolic representation of formal convent education. The statues of Jesus, Joseph, Mary and a shepherd are merely conspicuous by their presence, since the ideals of mercy and compassion are absent in the White Christian world. Ultimately, the Gradgrindian educational system means little to the African American girls who are oblivious of their own histories and ethnic values.

As women, the lesson "I bleed," is of immense relevance to them, since, like Jesus who bled on the cross, the Black women in America bear the triple burdens of race, gender and class. In this short play (seven pages) she refers to "blood" and "bleed" together thirty seven times. Her symbolic use of blood is probably derived from Lorca's *Blood Wedding*. In her autobiography she mentions Lorca as the most profound influence in her dramatic career.[23] "Blood" is a recurrently multiply loaded metaphor in Lorca's plays. While it signifies revenge in his *Blood Wedding*, it symbolises life and birth in his *Yerma*. In *Funny House*, the blood oozing from the bludgeoned head is used as a symbol of violence that mars the lives of the African American women.

It is a symbol of revenge, by extension, hatred and violence. In Kennedy's *Funny House*, there is a "bludgeoned head"; in *A Beast Story*, the Beast girl pretends bleeding; her *Electra* and *Orestes* (1980) are all about violence, bloodshed and the cycle of hatred. In *Lesson*, "blood" has many connotations. Basically it symbolises the violence that mars the lives of the African Americans in the White land. At times it symbolises guilt too. In *Lesson* also, the red marks signify the increasing sense of violence in African American women. The marks slowly enlarge in proportion to the guilt which torments the psyche of the African American adolescent girls on attaining puberty. Blood also may connote sacrifice, since the race has been crucified in New Jerusalem, for its development. Basically, blood symbolises life itself. Here, it connotes the vitality of the race which has been sapped by the dominant culture. Similarly the education of the White race in America is only meant to convert every ethnic minority to English tastes and opinions while simultaneously distancing them from their indigenous racial heritage

While Kennedy's *Lesson* focuses on horrors of the outmoded educational systems at the school level, her *Ohio State Murders* (1988) highlights the hidden racist violence in the American universities. Largely autobiographical, the protagonist Suzanne Alexander enacts the travails of an African American student in a White university. The play conflates the narrator with the writer. It is set in the campus of Ohio State University where the dramatist is lecturing on the "roots of violent imagery in her works" (Kennedy, *In One Act* 63) which reflect her mental state that is vitiated by the multiple forms of violence that have affected her psyche. Gerald Freeman comments on the fusion of time in the play. In an interview with Paul Bryant Jackson he remarks: "The play exists in the present and past" (Bryant-Jackson and Overbeck 135). Such a merger gives an aura of timelessness, thereby focussing on the ever-present racial hatred which torments them from time to time in the citadels of learning.

Suzanne Alexander is a young Black girl, who, despite securing an "A" grade is still denied a seat in English literature. Memories of Ohio State University are not very pleasant but a "series of desperate dark landscapes" (Kennedy, *In One Act* 27). Every section of the university campus remains green in her memory: "the oval, behind the green, the golf hut, behind zoology, the tennis courts beyond the golf hut" (Kennedy, *In One Act* 27) are all alive in her thoughts. The culturally diverse and receptive community at Cleveland did not prepare Kennedy for the hostility she had to face at the university. The classrooms, dormitories, restaurants etc., were all segregated. Her self-esteem could not easily accept the tertiary position designated to her by the racist White society. When Prof. Hampshire reads certain passages from Hardy's *Tess*, Suzanne's ability to empathise with Tess is so intense that she weeps. This is rather significant for an African American student, since her love of literature transcends cultural, racial and colour boundaries. Moreover her paper on Tess is commented upon by her White professor as "an extension of Hardy's own language" (Kennedy, *In One Act* 35). Despite her brilliance, she's denied a course in English literature. She yearns for the imagery, the marvel and the imagination of English literature. Suzanne is also agonised by the fact that while Hampshire has the power of empathising with Tess (because she is a White woman), he fails to show any sympathy towards Suzanne since she is Black. It is a deliberate attempt by the White society to stifle the intellectual brilliance of African American women and underrate their performance. In her personal life, Kennedy had been initiated into the classics early and her mind had been conditioned by western studies.[24] Kennedy's present predicament is a consequence of her early indoctrination into English studies. Not only has this instilled a deep love for an alien culture, but it has also given less space for the understanding of her own ethnic roots.[25] Suzanne Alexander is thus left with little choice. Her mind was "conditioned" even before racial awareness dawned on it. But later, when the awareness grows, there is a war between the native and the White-nurtured values. It leads to violence that torments their lives.[26]

Kennedy acknowledges that "violence is just beneath the surface in most human beings" (Lehman 45). It transforms the mind of the characters into veritable battlefields. Apart from the racist attitude of the White teachers and students, it gives the Blacks a shock of recognition. The African American girls were only twelve against six hundred. Not only were they prohibited from walking on High Street, but they were also not invited to the parties of the White girls. Suzanne's problems are further compounded by her pregnancy through Prof. Hampshire and his subsequent abandonment of her. The feelings of isolation and her single motherhood pose enormous psychological anxieties in her mind. To overcome this, she winds pink plastic curlers in her hair till her head bleeds. The White doctors examine her, being careful not to touch her. Ironically, Suzanne is dismissed from the dorm (on account of her pregnancy) on the day of Easter. While even the crucified Christ can be resurrected on the day of Easter, the Blacks in America know no redemption. Towards the end of the play, Kennedy mentions that the racist tribulation experienced at Ohio State University was the "main source of violent imagery in my [her] work" (Kennedy, *Alexander Plays* 63).[27]

Kennedy's interest in French impressionism especially Cezanne has added to the depth of her imagery. Impressionism, as a reaction against realism, attempts to lay bare a deeper psychical reality. Kennedy uses this White artistic medium to lay bare the turmoil and agony of a Black woman. The use of colours, the deliberate mutation of forms and the blurred figures in her plays are of a deeper significance. Impressionistic art attempts to portray a deeper, inner psychic reality which calls for a probing participation from the spectators too. Its cumulative effect on the spectator is much more than superficial. It affects their entire sensory perception. It is as intense to them as it is to the creator. Suzanne transforms agony into art when she makes drawings of the dormitory: "with the doors of each room outlined in red ink and muttered definitions of rooms, stairs, colour, skin." (Kennedy, *Alexander Plays* 61). Impressionistic painting makes a symbolic use of colour. In Suzanne's art, the dormitory is outlined in red to symbolise the racial violence inherent there.

The innate violence is also depicted through powerful imagery. The plays are full of cataclysmic images like "bludgeoned head," "gnawing rats," "black ravens," "wild black beast," "night owls," "attic beams," "worms," "cursing boys," "empty swings," "darkness," "steel wire," "axe," "beasts, "blood" etc. It is therefore vested with psychic and literary functions such as the ability to condense states of mind, feelings and emotions. Thus presenting "an intellectual and emotional complex in an instant of time" (Wellek and Warren 170). In Kennedy, the images are further surcharged with violent experiences.

Like Kennedy, Sonia Sanchez also inquires into the problem of campus racism in her play *Sister Son/ji* (1969). Elizabeth Brown Guillory calls it as "one of the most significant portrayals of the Black Power Movement of the Sixties" (Guillory 153). The play opens with the protagonist made up to appear in her fifties. She regresses to her youth and then gradually progresses through her life until she returns to her fifties. During her youth, she recalls a painful experience at a White college where the professor invalidated her along with two other African American students by refusing to learn their names. In a moment of resentment, she leaves the classroom. It is a typical Ellisonian predicament wherein the protagonist of Ellison's *Invisible Man* mentions: "I am invisible, understand simply because people refuse to see me" (Ellison 2), encapsulating the nullification of the Black race. The most crippling effect of racism is at the psychological level. This is best dramatised in two of Kennedy's plays *The Dramatic Circle* (1992) and *She Talks to Beethoven* (1992). Highly autobiographical, the former play highlights the psychosomatic symptoms in Kennedy, caused due to her separation from her husband who was away with Frantz Fanon in Ghana in the cause of the race. In penetrating into her psychological disorders, Kennedy identifies herself with similar aberrations present in the patients of Fanon. Like the trepidations caused among Algerian prisoners (as described in Fanon's *The Wretched of the Earth*), Suzanne Alexander also develops fits of psychic anarchism. Kennedy uses her individual psychosomatic symptoms to understand the greater psychic agony present among the Algerian patients of Fanon.[28] It also acts as a pretext for her projection of the turmoil that her race had experienced in America. The irony lies in the fact that while the Algerians suffered under the French rule, the African Americans suffer despite their professedly free conditions. Colonialism, with its systematic negation of the "other" against the "self" not only denies all human attributes of the individuals, but also alienates them from their own selves. Fanon pertinently questions in his book *The Wretched of the Earth*, "In reality, who am I?" (24). Such an estranged self at times loses its psychic balance. In Kennedy's play *The Dramatic Circle*, Suzanne Alexander loiters in the streets of London, develops breathlessness and psychic tremors. Dr. Freudenberger, her psychiatrist, makes her read crucial passages from Bram Stoker's *Dracula*. Animal imagery teems the passage.[29] Put together, these images connote the devastating experiences of the American Blacks whose vitality has been sapped out by the White race. All forms of feeble resistance are easily enmeshed. The individual loses all forms of personal identity. Albert Memmi in *The Coloniser and the Colonised* (1967) mentions how the colonised is never individuated. The identity is only one of a herd: "The colonised is never characterised in an individual manner; he is entitled to only drown in anonymous collectivity" (Memmi 88). What is required is immense resistance. Fanon points out how when the excessive "harmful nervous stimuli overstep a certain threshold," they are admitted into "mental hospitals" which is consequential of oppression. (Fanon, *The Wretched* 201). In such an overwhelming state of subjugation, Suzanne Alexander has little consolation. Dr. Freudenberger[30] not only restores normalcy in Suzanne, but through the sessions of literary reading, he prepares her mind for the ghastly events of the future. The play is also presented in the form of a monologue entitled *The Film Club* (1992). While the monologue probes into the interiors of the dramatist, the dramatised version has a better impact on the audience as it facilitates the trauma of the protagonist being re-enacted on the stage. Kennedy, like Fanon, also opines that the devastating wounds of colonialism are hard to efface.

The "wound" becomes a major motif in Kennedy's *She Talks to Beethoven* (1992). In this play, Suzanne Alexander is hospitalised on account of a fracture in her hand. The setting is Accra, Ghana, 1961, soon after the independence of the nation. The festering wound in her hand refuses to heal till the end. The fracture itself looms as a significant image in the play, since it is a symbolic representation of the split lives of the Blacks in America. Sandwiched between two diverse cultures, which are hard to reconcile, they face a midway existence. The room contains a photograph of Nkrumah,[31] and a diary of Beethoven,[32] representing diverse cultures. The fractured existence of Kennedy is elaborated upon in her autobiography *People Who Led to My Plays* wherein she refers to the statue of Beethoven and a photograph of Hatshepsut: "I did not understand then that I felt torn between the forces of my ancestry [. . .] European and African. [. . .] *These were my alter egos*" (Kennedy, *People* 96; my italics)

The passage refers to the conflicting cultures which indeed tear her asunder. Points and counter-points being re-concluded in harmony in his symphony, Suzanne Alexander herself becomes ultimately a metaphor for the African insurgence. Her kinte robe is a testimony to this fact. The diary of Beethoven reveals the negative side of his personality, with his minor eccentricities and deficiencies. He is deeply engrossed in the process of composing his Fidelio. The play moves from the physical plane to the spiritual one. Bryant-Jackson, while tracing the genealogy of Kennedy's plays, point out that Kennedy's *Beethoven* is like the Egungun, a ritual that involves the worshipping of the dead. By referring to Ola Rotimi's *Traditional Nigerian Drama*, Bryant-Jackson discusses the traditional theatrical practices in Nigeria which provide an intriguing lens through which *Beethoven* could be understood (Bryant-Jackson 49). If the play is read as an Egungun ritual, it offers at least three possible connections. Basically the music of Beethoven's Fidelio is compared with the drums which are usually used in an Egungun. Secondly, the radio announcer's statement about Suzanne points at her mixed ancestry and is a source of solace during David's absence.[33] Thirdly, the ritual involves a ceremony of ancestral worship which includes a masquerader.[34] Kennedy's stage direction indicates that "David's voice [is] not unlike Beethoven" (Kennedy, *Alexander Plays* 258).

Apart from the Egungun ritual, Bryant-Jackson mentions that Rotimi also describes a variation on ancestral worship that the Kalabari and Yoruba tribes employ. Jackson feels that this comparison transforms the character of Suzanne into that of a "cult priest" in comforting the entire community with regard to David who is missing. The African perspective further helps us in our enhanced understanding of Kennedy's complex images. Kennedy's plays incorporate the Egungun rituals and the ancestral worship of the Kalabari and Yoruba tribes. While Kennedy had been nurtured in European literature, her nature had searched for its native roots. In this context, her trip to Africa in 1960 had a tremendous impact on her writings wherein she "discovered a strength in being a black person and a connection to West Africa" (Kathleen and Koenig 250-51). It was during her stay in Africa that she had received a letter regarding her first formal publication. Kennedy exults in her bond with: Chinua Achebe, Amos Tutuola, Wole Soyinka, Efa Sutherland, Lawrence Durrell and is elated over the fact of her joining the band of writers (Kennedy, *People* 180). This process of being sandwiched between two cultures, argues Chinnosole, is one of the unique predicaments of African American diaspora. The culturally contradictory self is fragmented in an apathetic society. Therefore as

Chinnosole argues, to understand the Black diaspora necessitates an "acceptance of fragmentation and adaptation as critical to survival." Both Beethoven and Nkrumah are equally important icons for her emotional survival. In her autobiography, she mentions how Nkrumah was a great source of inspiration for her. At Accra, she stood mesmerised by his statue. She purchased African cloth since it symbolised her racial roots. When she wore it, she felt that she had "sealed [her] ancestry as a West African" (122).

A major symbol used for this purpose is the mask. It is an important device used in African American drama, and of immense significance to its socio-cultural ethos. It is a crucial link between her Western and ancestral heritage. The ancient Greek dramatists used the mask to differentiate between tragedy and comedy. W.B. Yeats developed a complex theory of masks to account for human character. In many of his plays, he borrowed the ancient Greek and Japanese styles of masked acting to bring about the role of artifice in life. O'Neill also revived the use of masks in his plays like *The Great God Brown* (1926). In Africa, the masks were generally made of animal hide (a pun also intended). It basically connotes the intimate relationship between human beings and animals in the cosmic scheme, which has always been at the centre of the African world view. It has deeper implications too: "[the] struggle with chthonic presences, the goal of the conflict being a harmonious resolution for plenitude and the well being of the community" (Soyinka 38). While mask in the African culture is viewed as an equaliser that resolves the conflict between the individual and the cosmic forces which loom large against him, it is used by the African American women dramatists to explore their schizoid existence. Kennedy mentions how it was initially the works of Picasso that had inspired her to amplify the appearance of her characters. But it was after that she had purchased an African mask at Accra that she finally detached herself from "realistic looking characters" (Kennedy, *People* 121). The mask not only reminded her of her African origin, but it also made her explore new forms in art. Art being a hyper-reality, her use of masks made her reveal their nuances of her characters' emotions through exaggeration. Her shift from realism to surrealism actually helped her probe deeply into the splintered African American psyche of her protagonists. In *Funny House*, a dark faceless man appears in the centre of the stage, holding an ebony mask. The figure slowly repeats (Sarah's own earlier telling) her mother's loss of hair. The apparition-like figure later slowly identifies itself with Lumumba, one of the selves of Sarah. This is significant, since Lumumba is ultimately transformed into a crucial link between Sarah and her father. He embodies the African American man's frantic efforts to save his race and his blackness, which is a stern, inescapable reality. The mask, the traditional symbol of power and mystery, is used to develop what Michael Goldman calls "the double movement of dramatic elation—both escape from self and self-discovery" (Meigs 175). It also acts as a signifier of Sarah's Black-White conflict. Being a "mulatto," she is denied the opportunity of wearing the masks of both Black and White women. She is thus unacceptable to both the Black and White races.

Kennedy's next play *The Owl Answers* makes subtle use of masks. Clara, a "mulatto" is harassed by three masked figures who resemble Shakespeare, Chaucer and William the Conqueror. Masks are used here to conceal their deeper, darker intentions. Not only do they imprison Clara in the tower of London, they also assault her with questions on her lineage: "If you are his ancestor why are you a Negro? Yes, why is it you are a Negro if you are his ancestor? Keep her locked there." (Kennedy, *In One Act* 28) The peeling White skin of her father reveals a shockingly darker skin inside. Here, masks are used as a device to camouflage the real selves of the characters.

Kennedy's use of masks becomes more complex in her later plays, especially *A Movie Star has to Star in Black and White*. It becomes more complicated when the movie stars wear the masks of their respective film roles. They metaphorically don the roles of Hollywood icons like Marlon Brando, Paul Henried, Montgomery

Clift and Shelley Winters. It symbolises the contrast between the "real" and celluloid selves of the popular Hollywood icons of the Sixties.[35] Towards the end of the play, Montgomery Clift does not heroically help Shelley Winters who is drowning (as he does in his movies). He stares impassively at her who cannot even raise a voice for help. Much against the glitz and glamour of their Hollywood roles, these masked characters are rather pallid figures who cannot transcend their monotonous existence. Like her White contemporary Sam Shepard, Kennedy also uses icons of popular culture to give her plays a greater sense of contemporariness. At the same time, as an African American woman, she's also acutely aware of the sanctions imposed by a racist culture which would prevent her race from becoming one with the White Hollywood icons. Although Kennedy's autobiography suggests that she was fascinated by the Hollywood figures, her use of these idols in the play is to project the unacceptability of the Blacks in the dream merchant world. Deborah R. Geis rightly focuses on the contrast between the romantic aura of the film stars and the "oppressive" "unassailability" of the tinsel world (Geis 171) which may make the emotional identification of the race with Hollywood almost impenetrable. Along with the mask, Kennedy also uses the "camera" to project the unknown dimensions of the Hollywood personalities speaking through the Columbia Pictures Lady. Clara compares the smooth looks of her photographer Joel with the way he really looks (Kennedy, *In One Act* 81). Ultimately, the camera becomes a metaphor for the human eye, which can sieve the false from the real. Both the mask and the camera together aid not only in the self-recognition of the subject, but the falsity of the object of comparison.

While Kennedy uses masks to contrast the apparent and the real, Sonia Sanchez makes a symbolic use of masks to contrast the White and Black cultures as in the third section of *Uh! Uh! but How Do it Free Us?*. There are two women in this section of the play: one Black and another White. On the side of the White woman, the stage props include a phone, a phonograph and a butterfly chair. As a counterpoint to this, on the side of the Black woman are African masks and stools indicative of her African origin. The Black woman in the play is loyal to her ethnic roots. With firm faith in her race, she works hard for its upliftment. She delivers speeches on "The Black Experience" and renders a few poetry reading sessions for her race. Her loyalty to her roots is emphasised through the mask, symbolising the resilience which the women of her race possess in facing the perils of their existence in the White man's land.

The mask remains in the room throughout the play, constantly reminding her of the tertiary position that the American society has relegated her to. It is a constant reminder of her Blackness, with which she falls in love. She refuses to give up the glory of her colour and basks in it with joy. She prefers to "rock" herself in "sweet sweet Blackness." As a Black woman, she prefers to "get blacker by the nite." During her pregnancy, she has a significant dream of "delivering twins," one White and the other Black.[36] Among them, the White baby is "ugly" and "deformed," and so she refuses to have it although she is forced with it. Contrary to the general notion that the Blacks consider their race ugly and the White race beautiful, the Black woman considers whiteness as disease, ugly and deformed. This is an integral part of the Black Arts Movement and the Black Power Movement which glorify their dark complexions. It throws a significant light on the colour-psychology of the Blacks. Like the White race which considers everything Black as being ugly, the Blacks associate the colour White as being anaemic, pale and a sign of festering disease. The dream is further indicative of her animosity towards the White race that has stampeded her being. Like the camera which forms an interesting accompaniment to the mask in Kennedy's *A Movie Star*, the dream forms an interesting accompaniment to the mask in Sanchez's *Uh! Uh! but How Do it Free Us?*. The dream reveals her latent thoughts and commitment towards her race. The mask is a silent spectator watching the events in the life of the Black woman. Thus, the mask turns into a sort of fetish from which the Black woman draws her power. Although the mask is not even touched by the Black woman, its very presence in the room probably wields a strange sense of power over her. Technically, the masks act as a signifier of the times past and present.

Shange uses masks to revive the lost theatrical traditions of her ancestral heritage as mentioned in her foreword to the *three pieces*. The dominant theatrical practices made "primary statements with somebody else's life and somebody else's idea of what theatre is" (Shange, *three pieces* x). Minstrelsy along with the use of masks is one way of authentically penetrating into their deepest lives and lending a greater validity towards the evaluation of African American theatre. In *spell #7*, she suspends a large minstrel mask above the stage as a counterpoint to films and movies which misrepresent Blacks in popular arts and culture.[37] Shange is against such minstrel and coon shows as they represent "somebody else's idea of Black existence" (Shange, *three pieces* xx). Her foreword to *spell #7* states that "the minstrel may be banned as racist but the minstrel is more powerful in his deformities than our alleged rejection of him" (Shange, *three pieces* 7). She uses this device to symbolise the domineering influence of the Whites in the area of culture and arts. It is also used to make the audience forcefully "face the mask and unmask the face underneath the mask" (Cronacher 178) helping them to probe the unprobed. The three dramatists have thus creatively explored the conventional dramatic device.

In the process of inquiring into Black life, Shange uses an interdisciplinary approach. Music is the soul of African life. To her, the African American artists have a "resurrecting" mission to connect themselves with the lives of the living and the lived (Shange, *three pieces* ix-x). Like the ancient Indian theatre, the African theatre also integrates poetry, music, drama and dance in order to "demolish the notion of straight theatre." (Shange, *three pieces* x) African American theatre transcends the spoken word which indeed confers a special responsibility on them. She is closer to her Afro-centric view of life/theatre. W. Carlton and Barbara J. Molette in *Black Theatre–Premise and Presentation*

(1992) mention that one of the major functions of African theatre is to "create a total spiritual involvement, sometimes referred to as emotional environment" (145). This is because the African American aesthetic disapproves of the fact that all human behaviour operates only through rational motivation. Therefore, the arbitrary classifications of "fine" and "coarse" behaviours do not fit in here. A holistic approach towards human behaviour should be the forte of African-American theatre if it is to be modelled on its original art forms which place immense value on "emotionally motivated behaviour" and the "soul" which form a contrast to the rational and objective motivations of Eurocentric theatre (Carlton and Molette 145). It is the antithesis of the western notion of theatre which according to Artaud is "static." In *The Theatre of Cruelty* (1938), Artaud mentions that this theatre would no longer subject itself to the text, which was hitherto considered "definitive" and "sacred" and instead recover a unique dramatic language which was "half-way between gesture and thought" (Artaud 55). Such a function cannot be carried out in the limited possibilities of spoken dialogue. The aim of *The Theatre of Cruelty* is to transcend the boundaries of words and aim at "dissociative and vibratory action upon the sensibility" (Artaud 55). The effect of such a theatre is cumulative. It shreds and sinks into the layers of the spectators' consciousness. Shange is nearer this view of theatre since she opines that "theatre is an all-encompassing moment/a moment of poetry/the opportunity *to make something happen*" (Shange, *three pieces* 21; my italics). It is to this effect that Shange uses music, dance, poetry, lights, voice etc. As a dramatist, she prefers to "address the space" in order to "create an emotional environment/ felt architecture" (Shange, *three pieces* xi). Her *colored girls*, makes a vibrant use of colour schema; her *spell #7* uses music, dance, magic and acrobats. Her *boogie woogie landscapes* uses music, dance and lighting to project the predicament of the protagonist Layla; her *From Okra to Greens/ A Different Kinda Love Story* uses the metaphor of food to describe the intriguing relationship between

Okra and Greens. The metaphysics of such a theatre is total. Such an inter-connected approach of the African American artists is essential for us to fully comprehend their racist predicament.

The crippling effects of racism are rather overwhelming in these three dramatists. It pervades their whole being. The power exhorted by racism has simultaneously distorted their culture, values, religion and changed their total perception of life. No longer is racism uncountered. It is the first mountain that the African Americans have to transcend in the White land. The effects of racism are felt by both the sexes, but unfortunately they have been projected as exclusively male. To eradicate this imbalance, women dramatists from Angelina Grimke to Ntozake Shange have used their plays to project the multiple levels of oppression that continue to torment the African American women.

Notes

1. Oppression in one form or the other had always been a part of human history. The ancient Greeks had slaves; so had the Arabs.
2. Georgia Douglas Johnson's *A Sunday Morning in the South* (1927) is also about lynching wherein a young black boy is unduly lynched significantly on the day of Sabbath. Similarly her *Blue-Eyed Black Boy* (1928) is also about lynching.
3. "Protest" and "Revolution" were the key terms of the early African American men's theatre. Even renowned male writers like Amiri Baraka and Ron Karenga have not attempted to probe into the so-called religio-cultural sanctions bestowed on racism.
4. In probing into the supposedly biblical sanctions given to racism, Zora Neale Hurston delves deep into the roots of racism, which had been unthought of by her male counterparts.
5. Human beings, especially women transformed into birds on account of unbearable pain, have been existing in literature since Ovid's *Metamorphosis* wherein Philomel was transformed into a nightingale after being raped by her brother-in-law Tereus. Although both the women are transformed into birds, the difference lies in the fact that the nightingale while accepting its grief transforms sorrow into songs. But the owl, as a bird of wisdom has the

penetrating vision to see through its enveloping gloom as does Clara. The particular racio-gendered experiences of a poor young woman like Clara endow her with the power to probe into the oppressions that surround her. Moreover, the African view of life with its close connections with nature sees little difference between human and animal lives, the two being a part of the cosmic scheme.

6. Owl is a bird, which is traditionally associated with wisdom. It is also a bird of ill omen, associated with death. Apart from this, it is a nocturnal bird which can see through the enveloping darkness. As an African American woman, Clara is an evil portent in the dominant culture who is able to perceive the stifling circumstances that surround her.
7. Indeed, it does involve an act of mimicry, since the colonised blindly mimes the ways of the dominant culture. The act of mimicry also produces a certain amount of ambivalence, since the colonised subject "is never simply and completely opposed to the colonizer" (Ashcroft et al, *Key Concepts* 12). On the other hand, it suggests that "complicity and resistance exist in a fluctuating relation within the colonising subject" (*Ibid.* 13-14).
8. Shange deliberately reverses the western notion of "Midas touch." Like his golden touch which transformed every object into gold, her dark complexion creates a complex which makes her imagine that all she touches is transformed into darkness.
9. Frantz Fanon in *Black Skins, White Masks* mentions that "the black man's alienation is not an individual question. Besides phylogeny and ontogeny stands sociogeny" (9). Thus, the solution to his blackness is also according to him, "socio diagnostic" (9).
10. Michael Vannoy Adams in *The Multicultural Imagination* (1996) analyses a film called *School Daze*. The film, which is a commentary on the internalised racist attitude within the American Blacks, includes a song and dance number called "straight and nappy." Two groups of African-American college students exchange insults about each other's hair. They label it as either "good" or "bad." Towards the end they connote hair with spiritual and psychical realities. One's hair may be straight, but it's of no use when one's soul is crooked. When psychoanalysts like Kathy Russel, Midge Wilson and Ronald Hall discuss the term "colour complex,"

it also includes "hair complex." It is a form of inferiority complex which has sunk into the psyche of the African Americans since, many a times, even if their skins are nearly White, their hair alone is unmistakably frizzy. It acts as a painful reminder of their race to many of the African Americans who would like to escape from their "stigmatised" racial features. It is significant that Kennedy had dramatised the issue of "hair-complex nearly twenty years before Spike Lee.

11. Jesus in this play is one of the selves of a black girl. Far from an expected religious piety, he is also extremely obsessed with his hair. (16)
12. Malcolm X comments: "This was my first really big step toward self-degradation: when I endured all of that pain [. . .] to have it look like a White man's hair, I had joined that multitude of Negro men and women in America who are brainwashed into believing that the black people are "inferior"—and White people are "superior"—that they will even violate and cultivate their God-created bodies to try to look "pretty" by White standards." (54)
13. See "Was Jesus Black-Skinned?" in *The Hindu*, March 29, 2001 (16). True or false, the news, however startling it may be to the White Christian view, definitely gives greater religious credential for the Blacks. It provides a scientific base for a greater religious affinity with Christianity. The emotional identification with Christ and Christianity will therefore become easier and less ambivalent for the future African American writers. No longer need their Jesus be hunch-backed and dwarfed. Christ need not be a White father, but a Black one. This would also have to transform the perceptions of the White writers, for their God need no longer be projected as being with White skin and norcisized features.
14. See Adrienne Kennedy, *In One Act*, 30. The idea of sex and virginity as mentioned here is a Christian one. Primitive African societies do not brand sex as a taboo. It is an integral part of human life. Couples often got married only after they had lived together for some time. Clara's mother (and subsequently Clara also) lose their virginity before their weddings. Their minds, which have been conditioned by the Christian notions of "sex" and "virginity" against their racial inheritance are thus confused and therefore mourn for it. But ironically, while they accept the White man's faith, the faith refuses to accept them.

15. A study of Kennedy's autobiography *People Who Led to My Plays* reveals the fact that Kennedy was deeply attached to her family. In the section "Elementary School," she mentions how her family remained well-knit and tight. Kennedy enjoys her Sunday drives with her father, the games of swinging with her brother, her mother's story-telling sessions and the warmth of living together. For a person with an immense concern for the domestic peace, the divorce which occurred between the parents must have come as a shock. Kennedy's struggle against the shattering of the family as an institution and her futile struggle at domestic harmony is projected through her female protagonist.
16. It is a stern historical fact that the White races of both America and England do integrate on numerous destructive missions. Both of them have always looked down upon the Black races of their nations as being inferior. They have allied during the first and the second world wars. The most recent example could be their alliance in their war against Iraq. Their common Anglo-Saxon blood makes them power-thirsty or to put it rather blatantly, bloodthirsty.
17. The father seeking the daughter's companionship could also mean the *animus* seeking the *anima* for the completeness of personality. These two are not antagonistic to each other as they happen to be, but complementary to each other which is revealed in the desire of the male (father) to establish contact with the female (daughter). It could also be that the father having been rejected by the mother is seeking a sexual satisfaction by using the daughter as the surrogate, and the girl having been raped herself by a male, mistakes the father's gestures of affection as sexual overtures and runs away from him. Fondling a child is a form of sexual act. Signing lullaby is one way of fondling. The dead father does it to the dead child and its replication of it in the living world is the Beast Man's attempt to come closer to his daughter.
18. It is significant that the rape of the Beast Girl takes place in the fields. Fields are a symbol of fecundity in both the men and women. Sanskrit literature labels fields as "Kshetram" which is a female principle, whereas "Beejam" or the seed is a male principle. Anthropological studies reveal the fact that the sexes influence vegetation to a great extent. James Frazer in *The Golden Bough*

(1967) devotes a chapter "The Influence of the Sexes on Vegetation" to this purpose. A number of customs are mentioned globally wherein the ancients have personified the powers of vegetation as male and female. To cite a few examples:

(a) The Pipiles of Central America were kept away from their wives for four days, "in order that on the night before planting they might indulge their passions to the fullest extent" (179). At times, certain people were even appointed to perform the sexual act at the precise moment when the first seeds were sown.

(b) In some parts of Java, the men and women mate in the fields to promote the growth of the rice.

(c) The Baganda tribes of Central Africa believe strongly in the intimate relation between the intercourse of the sexes and the fertility of the ground. While a "barren" wife is sent away as her presence may not permit the flowering of the banana tree, a fertile couple with twins are supposed to be endowed with the power of increasing the fruitfulness of the plantain trees (178-84).

In this play, Kennedy does not use the idea of the union between the man and woman as positive. It is rather negatively portrayed. But the point of comparison remains that the conception takes place in the fields. Kennedy is using a number of anthropological references to infer to the specificity of the Beast Girl being raped in the fields and the resultant conception. Apart from its anthropological significance, the conception which takes place in the open-air atmosphere is a strong contrast to the dimly-lit interiors of their house.

19. The darkness that follows the "strange" sunlight is indicative of the relentless gloom that surrounds the play. The characters may try frantically one form of consolation or the other. But nothing gives them succour in the truest sense of the term.
20. Shange says to Ann Levine in "Bein' a woman, Bein' Colored" (23) "I think it is unfortunate that we [blacks] buffaloed ourselves into thinking that the black children who were integrated had a good time because that was the worst period of my life."
21. Such a form of segregation is also found in Langston Hughes's play *Simply Heaven* (1956). He presents a segregated bar where

Blacks take refuge from White racism and find strength and freedom to probe into their own culture.

22. In India also, English education was often used as a means to serve colonial interests. In India, Thomas Babbington Macaulay, the architect of English education in his famous *Minute on Indian Education* (1835) suggested that he would train natives who were "Indian in blood and colour," to be transformed into "English in taste, in opinion, in morals and in intellect" (Macaulay 249).
23. The influence of Lorca in her plays cannot be undermined. She mentions his profound influence among others like Tennessee Williams, Eugene O'Neill, Anton Chekhov, T.S. Eliot. There are numerous instances of her references to Lorca. In the section entitled "Marriage and Motherhood," she mentions a friend called Florence who majored in Spanish having given her a book, *Poet in New York* to read. The book suited her temperament: "My unhappiness with the racial climate at Ohio State and the drafting of my fiancé into the army left me feeling dark. Lorca's dark and complex vision was thrilling and comforting to me" (72).

    At yet another place in the same chapter Kennedy mentions how Lorca's book showed her that: "imagery is multilayered that it comes from recovering connections long ago lost and buried" (98). Again she mentions the influence of Lorca in the course of her dramatic career:

    > After I read and saw Blood Wedding, I changed my ideas about what a play was. Ibsen, Chekhov, O'Neill and even Williams fell away. Never again would I try to set a play in a "living room," never again could I be afraid to have my character's talk in a non-realistic play [. . .] *it was a turning point*" (108 my italics)
24. That Kennedy had been influenced by the White English classics even during her elementary school days, is evident from her autobiography *People Who Led to My Plays*. Not only was she aware of her English racial connections with relatives at Montezuma, she was also familiar with a number of British/White classics. The works of Jane Eyre, Charles Dickens, and the fairytales had all made indelible impressions on her mind, which is evident in her works.

25. Ngugi wa Thiong'o in his *Homecoming and Other Essays* (1972) calls upon the African universities to abolish departments of English studies and make them departments of African studies. This, he feels, would help his people go back to their traditional roots of art and literature and get properly oriented in their native culture. This would further enable them to avoid "orientalism" and develop the African perspective. These feelings have spread elsewhere too. Gauri Viswanathan's *Masks of Conquest* (1990) analyses the negative impact of colonial studies in India. It is used as a mask for economic and political control. Such an inordinate love for the literature of the oppressor is a form of intellectual bondage. Spivak makes this point in "Three Women's Texts and a Critique of Imperialism" (1985): It should not be possible to read nineteenth century British literature without remembering that imperialism, understood as England's social mission, was a crucial part of the cultural representation of England to the English. (Spivak 43)
26. Apart from *Homecoming and Other Essays*, Ngugi reiterates the same idea in his "The Language of African Literature" in *Decolonising the Mind: The Politics of Language in African Literature*: "A central fact of Kenyan life today is the fierce struggle between the cultural forces representing foreign interests and those representing patriotic national interests" (42). The conflict present in African culture is more complex among the African Americans since they remain caught between multiple forces which are indeed hard to reconcile.
27. The purpose of images is always metaphoric. Kennedy in her *People Who Led to My Plays* mentions how she had learnt the immense value of metaphors from Aristotle's *Poetics*: "The greatest thing by far is to be a master of metaphor [. . .] it is also a sign of genius since a good metaphor implies an intuitive perception of the similarity in dissimilar" (105).
28. In the chapter entitled "Colonial War and Mental Disorders," Fanon describes a number of psycho-pathological disorders among the Algerian patients (which could most probably occur to any oppressed group). Some of the psychosomatic symptoms he catalogues in this section are: impotence, homicidal impulsions, anxiety psychosis, depression, murder instinct, accusatory delirium, suicidal conduct, sadistic tendencies, periodical enuresis. Among women, the most common problem was puerperal psychosis and

menstruation trouble. Apart from these specific symptoms, the general ones were: nervous depressions, loss of appetite, motor instability, electricity phobia, stomach ulcers, insomnia, hair turning white early, paroxysmal tachycardia, muscular stiffness and the like. (Fanon, *The Wretched of the Earth* 227-28)

29. Kennedy significantly chooses certain sections of Bram Stoker's *Dracula* for this play. Like the innocent Lucy who is sucked to death by the Dracula, the Black race has been killed by the Americans. Horror-filled imagery like "blood," "wolf" and "vampire" evoke a sense of horror not only in the mind of Suzanne, but also in the audience, as it helps them have an authentic perception of the terrors of racist experience in America.
30. It is a therapeutic process that Dr. Freudenberger undertakes. His name is significant, a portmanteau of Freud and Swedenborg. By preparing her mind for the ghastly events of the future, he is actually inducing mental strength in her.
31. Nkrumah is an important figure who had helped Kennedy in terms of a personal renaissance, during her trip to Ghana. In her *People Who Led to My Plays*, she mentions the fact "In front of the House of Parliament in Accra was a statue of Nkrumah. To see a man and to see a statue of him in the same space of time broke through boundaries in my mind" (22). In another unpublished interview with Margaret B. Wilkerson, Kennedy mentions her trip to Africa during 1961. Ghana had gained freedom from colonial rule only seven years earlier and was struggling hard for economic and political stability. Unrest prevailed in Zaire: "One thing that was important was the whole psychological thing [. . .] Nkrumah was president, so we used to go to the airport and would watch Nkrumah when he'd fly in—this is what people did on Sunday afternoon. [. . .] They'd go and watch Nkrumah come in from somewhere" (Bryant-Jackson and Overbeck 71-72).
32. Kennedy's *People Who Led to My Plays* shows how she was acquainted with music at an early stage of her life. During her high school days, she recalls Miss Eicherbaum, a Polish woman who taught her piano: "The top of her piano was filled with photographs of her family and statues of Mozart, Beethoven and Chopin" (42). Later in life, when she was a wife and a mother, Kennedy brought in "foot high ivory statue [. . .] at Pellenbergs on

Broadway and put it on [my] desk for inspiration and reread Sullivan's books on the life of Beethoven—his spiritual development, his music, his lukewarm Danube baths and his growing deafness—and I listened to the quartets" (108). Moreover, in 1956, when Kennedy was twenty-five years old, she remembers, "I ordered all his string quartets from a record club. Each record was wrapped in delicate paper and the record covers were in romantic pale covers. How I treasured them" (86).

33. It is significant that Kennedy hears news about her husband over the radio. It becomes an important symbol in the play. The information broadcast over the radio is through space where spiritual elements reign. Therefore, the communication between the living and the dead is assimilated through the radio. At another level, Philip C. Kolin, in an article entitled "Orpheus Ascending: Music, Race and Gender in Adrienne Kennedy's *She talks to Beethoven*," feels that Kennedy has inscribed the Orpheus myth into her play when he compares the film with Jean Cocteau's film *Orphee* (1950). One modern addition common to both is the use of the radio. In *Orphee*, the poet of Orpheus hears mysterious poetry and coded messages over a car radio. The transmissions come from: "[t]he Zone—the land of the dead [. . .] Suzanne, like Cocteau's Orpheus, must lift out and respond to messages about love and art from a world beyond her control or consciousness" (Kolin 299).
34. According to this ritual, a member of the cult is fully masked. He represents the dead house. Accompanied by drumming and chanting, he moves from the groves to the home of the dead. The cult leader constantly evokes him with the name of the dead. When the masked person ultimately speaks, it is disguised to sound like the dead. (Bryant-Jackson and Overbeck 50).
35. Apart from a cultural and anthropological use of the masks, Kennedy also uses it as she was influenced by the movie "The Seventh Veil," wherein the heroine Ann Todd wore veils "to mask her hidden thoughts and feelings" (Kennedy, *People* 49).
36. This dream, if interpreted in Freudian terms, gives a greater scope to probe into her hidden thoughts. In his seminal work *The Interpretation of Dreams*, Freud mentions, "Dreams are brief, meagre and laconic in comparison with the range and wealth of dream thoughts. If a dream is written out, it may perhaps fill half a page. The analysis setting out the dream thoughts underlying it may occupy six, eight or a dozen times as much space" (312-13).

37. Critics like Hans Nathan and Robert Toll have made an extensive study in this form of art. J.R. Edith Isaacs in *The Negro in the American Theatre* considers the Black minstrel theatre as their "first authentic American theatre form" (Isaacs 27).

Chapter 3

Being Coloured, Being Woman and Being Loved

This chapter initially traces the evolution of a distinct African American women's movement, and delves into the issues of gender like rape, motherhood, menstruation, clitorectomy, infibulation, sexual autonomy, pregnancy and abortion. The chapter ends with a discussion of the uniqueness of the African American feminist discourse wherein they use language as a tool of empowerment.

Racial discrimination has always been defined in terms of the larger racial interests, but never with an eye on dividing the larger community itself in terms of gender because the foremost concern of the struggle was the liberation of the community as a whole and the discrimination within the community had been overlooked. Therefore, a gendered dimension in the ethnic strife had not been given serious thought until the women intellectuals sought that racial as well as gender discrimination must be addressed simultaneously.

Calvin Hernton in "The Sexual Mountain" (1990), probes into the "backburner" status accorded to the African American women in all domains during the early part of the century. Hernton bemoans the fact that *The Black Scholar* (1969) had articles authored by men alone because they sought to strategically enforce control (Braxton and Mc Laughlin 197).

Undoubtedly, the African American woman's tertiary position is not easy to grapple with, on account of the multiple oppressions she faces. Often, her sexist struggle is viewed merely as an offshoot of racism. Although a dialectical relationship between the two cannot be ruled out, it is not merely an extension of the racist strife. bell hooks in her *Killing Rage: Ending Racism* (1995) contends that such an equation would "deflect" their perception of the White male privileged position while also underplaying the seriousness of the sexist issue and insisting "that the problem is ultimately and always, only racism" (87). Therefore, racism is an integral part of the gender struggle (though not vice-versa) and also much beyond that. Even at the turn of the century, a number of men and women writers were immensely concerned with the nexus between racism and gender. This is because, the "colour complex" is an innate aspect of not only the African American male psyche, but their female psyche too. Frantz Fanon in his *Black Skin, White Masks* (1967) calls the psychic enslavement of the African American women based on colour as one of the indices of the "black weltenschaung" (47) while also being an indication of her alteristic perspective.

Therefore, the hegemonistic culture in which the African American woman remains enmeshed has established hierarchal values based upon colour, with its apex being White Europe and Africa its base. Spivak's "Three Women's Texts and a Critique of Imperialism" (1985) focuses on the "unfortunate" nature of feminist criticism which reproduces "the axioms of imperialism" wherein the female subject of Anglo America is placed in the category of "high feminism" when the "Third World" literature is often deliberately interpreted in "non-theoretical methodology with self-conscious rectitude" (45). A point that Spivak seems to have forgotten is that despite the power binarisms, such an interpretation also prevents Third world literatures from being stereotyped with the ideological hegemony that is often involved in interpreting native literatures from purely Eurocentric norms which would distort their native bearings and act as impediments from original interpretations. But the colour-blindness of White feminist movements is an undeniable reality.

It is yet another intrinsic factor which helped the African American women charter out an indigenous course of action. For instance, works on feminist studies by western White feminists like Simone de Beauvoir's *The Second Sex* (1953) and Betty Friedan's *The Feminist Mystique* (1963) have ignored the particular predicament of African American women. The Black Liberation Movement, the Black Arts Movement and organisations like the Black Panthers hardly showed any sensitivity to the particular needs of their women who were described by President John Kennedy as "the nation's greatest untapped resource."[1] The Combahee River Collective Statement (1974) therefore sought the establishment of a Black feminist approach. The foundations were laid in the late nineteenth century and early twentieth century by a number of African American women activists like Harriet Tubman, Sojourner Truth, Frances E.W. Harper, Ida B. Wells, Mary Church Terrell and the like.

A growing sense of autonomy is a major factor which has also contributed to the growth of the African American women's movements since they no longer see themselves as mere appendages. Basically, the African American women would prefer to use Alice Walker's term "Womanism" as it does not exclude males. Walker's *In Search of Our Mother's Gardens* (1983) mentions how the term is used as being opposite to "girlish," and refers to a "black feminist or feminist of color" (xi). This is indeed a significant remark since, apart from "appreciating and preferring women's culture, woman's emotional flexibility [. . .] and women's strength" the term also includes not only "love for women, but love for "individual men, sexually and/or non sexually." (Walker, *In Search* xi). Therefore, the African American women's liberation movements do not exclude men. bell hooks in *Killing Rage: Ending Racism* (1995) rightly contends that although male domination is a serious problem, it is not the sole focus of the African American Women's Movement. To her, it is basically "revolutionary" since it simultaneously wages a war against racism, capitalism, imperialism and sexism. It is *not* antimale. Rather, she is concerned with her men's "uncritical absorption and participation in patriarchy" (hooks, *Killing Rage* 63).

hooks, of course, condones the idea of equating Black liberation with Black patriarchy, since, the post civil-rights era witnessed a massive unemployment which necessitated ideological re-definitions of manhood. Men were no longer seen as "benevolent patriarchs, protectors and providers," but manhood was "proved by one's capacity to coerce, control and dominate" (hooks, *Killing Rage* 67). So, the relationship of the African American women with their men-folk is both paradoxical and dialectic, since they work *with* them against racism and *against* them for their gender liberation.

Another major tenet of the African American sexist struggle is their refusal to see themselves as mere victims. bell hooks puts forth this argument both in her *Feminist Theory: From Margin to Center* (1984) and *Killing Rage*: *Ending Racism* (1995). She beckons her women to refrain from embracing the mantle of victimisation. To her, such an ideology is a serious blemish because it is psychologically both "disempowering and disenabling" (hooks, *Killing Rage* 57). hooks acknowledges having borrowed this idea from Martin Luther King Jr., who in his 1965 speech "Where Do We Go from Here" insists on pursuit of equality and empowerment, rather than basking in empty feelings of victimisation. Moreover, the image of the victim calls forth negative feelings since "despair and feelings of hopelessness are central to the formation of a psychology of victimisation" (hooks, *Killing Rage* 57). Therefore, a victim-focused feminist identity has been rejected by the African American feminist movement.

One of the unique features of African American women's movement is its broader base. It does not cater to the needs of the coloured women in America alone. It moves a step forward to include the oppressed women of colour in the other third world countries and other parts of the globe. Shange has significantly named her debut play *for colored girls who have considered suicide when the rainbow is enuf* (1976) for, the rainbow emerges as an optimistic symbol of hope, faith and conviction to not only the Black women in America, but also the coloured women in all parts of the globe. Alice Walker refers to the "colored race" as a "flower garden, with every color flower represented" (Walker, *In Search* xi). Therefore, a truly African American feminism while being opposed to the Euro-White imperialistic feminism also counteracts their colour-blindness. In this connection, Michelle Wallace mentions in "A Black Feminist's Search for Sisterhood," that "being on the bottom, we have to do what no one else has done: we would have to fight the world" (Hull 13). Wallace's allusion to the classic isolation of the African American women's struggle also implies the fact that if the African American women were free, then everyone else would be automatically freed since her "freedom would necessitate the destruction of all the systems of oppression" (Hull 13).

To view the African American women's oppression as a mere reactionary movement against the interlocking systems of racist, gender and class, struggles would be myopic, since the movement also draws some of the basic tenets of the African view of life. Sojourner Truth is an instance to prove the fusion between two cultures. Gloria I. Joseph labels her as an "Archetypal Black Feminist" (Braxton and Mc Laughlin 35). This revolutionary woman's life reflects the integrity and commitment to oppose the forces that deny the fundamental human rights of both the Blacks and all oppressed groups. She is a prototype for a number of African American women in their struggle against racism and gender bias. Her deeply religious perspective is undoubtedly based upon the organised, White, western, patriarchal religion. At the same time, her ideologies were also conditioned by the African cosmological framework which has a "fundamental belief in an indivisible and inexhaustible relationship among God, mankind and the cosmos" (Braxton and Mc Laughlin 39). Another important trait in this revolutionary woman is her holistic perspective that does not permit dichotomies like "material" and "spiritual" which is reflected in every facet of African life since all is intricately connected and "everything becomes spirit manifest" (Braxton and Mc Laughlin 39). Along with a unified "wholeness," the idea of "sacrifice" is also important in the African culture, which is different from its western connotation. In Africa, it connects a "redistribution of the life force that permeates all living things" (Braxton and Mc Laughlin 42). In a way the African American women are trying to establish what could be labelled as a "collective consciousness" and are also trying to repossess the strength of the basic ethos of the African culture in the American sphere. Hence, the African American women's struggle is firmly grounded in the African world view too just as it has effectively combined with it the methods of the Judaeo-Christian world.

In forging new paradigms for their liberation, the African American women had to encounter a number of negative stereotypes like Mammy, Aunt Jemima, Sapphire, Jezebel etc. These images collectively depict African American women as the antithesis of the American concepts of beauty, femininity and womanhood and this is one of the strategies adopted by the dominant culture to subjugate her. In Gramscian terms it is a "systematic engineering of mass consent to establish order" (Gitlin 253) and to shape cultural images since it controls the production of ideas and their perpetuation in order to establish their power and authority over oppressed groups.

If this is the position of the African American women today, what had been their position in their ethnic roots? Where were they placed in their ancestral continent? Studies reveal that African women enjoyed power, prestige and position in their native soil. There prevails a theory that the earliest brown human ancestor, the African mother of all mankind was "Lucy."[2] Larry Williams and Charles Finch mention how women's rule seems to have first evolved in Africa.[3] The African woman who was once the repository of power now stands debased with the advent of colonial powers and the rise of patriarchal values. Slavery and forced transplantation have further demeaned her intrinsic value as a human being. Women's bodies in general have always been analogous to territories which remain to be conquered.[4] Women and gender occupy an important place in colonial discourse. The situation is more deplorable in the case of the African American women since their bodies occupy meagre positions in the diasporic political spaces as also negating their agonies, in an inimical setting.

From the earliest anti-lynching plays like *Rachel* to the present ones by Sanchez, Kennedy, Shange and beyond, the psychosexual dimensions of the violence inflicted upon the African American women's bodies has been of central concern. One of the basic forms of sexual abuse that has continually terrorised the African American woman is rape. Susan Griffin in her "Rape: The All American Crime" calls it "*The most frequently committed crime in America today*." (Freeman 12, my italics). The African American woman's body is transformed into a veritable battleground for the play of imperialistic powers in America. Angela Y. Davis in *Women, Culture and Politics* (1989) disagrees with the fact that rape is a consequence of the male anatomical construction. She adds a political dimension to it mentioning the fact that "sexual violence often flows directly from official policy"[5] (Davis 46). In America, the Ku Klux Klan and other racist groups have also used rape as a weapon of political power.

Rape as an act is a hard thing to define, since it is not merely the forceful penetration of a man into a woman. It involves the entire gamut of physical and psychological mutilation that the act brings about. The world's first rape could be viewed as the first battle between a forcible man and an un-accepting woman. This led man to understand the power of his penis: "Man's discovery that his genitalia could serve as a weapon to generate fear must rank as one of the important discoveries of prehistoric times along with the use of fire and the first crude stone axe" (Miller, *Against Our Will* 115). On realizing his structural capacity to rape, man has therefore adopted a conscious process of intimidation and violence through which he keeps the woman in a perpetual state of fear.

Rape in America during slavery, was not just a tool of terror adopted by the White man in order to keep the African American woman in a continuous state of fear. It was "an institutional crime, part and parcel of the White man's subjugation of a people for economic and psychological gain" (Miller, *Against Our Will* 153). The White man's exertion of power on the African American woman's body also benefited him economically, since more propagation meant increased production of cheap labour to work on his farms. His easy access to numerous submissive female bodies incidentally gratified his libidinal impulses. The African American woman could not refuse, since, apart from physical bondage, instruments like knives, whips and guns were used against her. The White man had therefore a total control over her reproductive system. Miller mentions how in the lexicon of slavery, the terms "breeder woman," "child-bearing woman," "too old to breed," and "not a breeding woman" were used to signify the slave woman's ability to procreate (Miller, *Against Our Will* 23). These terms indicate the power of the ruling class to commodify the woman's womb for their economic gain.

The exploitation of the African American women's bodies, which was a norm during the times of slavery, has not been nullified in the post abolitionist times. Feminist creativity is usually gyno-centric since the themes centre around the physical and psychological realities of being women. This idea is explored in the plays of Sanchez, Kennedy and Shange who present protagonists, who are raped in the seemingly free urban settings.

In Sonia Sanchez's play *The Bronx is Next*, an unnamed "Black bitch" is a victim of physical exploitation. When she refuses to move out of the ghetto, Charles threatens her with rape. It is ironical, that in the play, set as it is in the nineteen sixties (during the Black Arts Movement and the Black Liberation Movement), an African American woman continues to be threatened by rape, and that too by a man of her own race. Sanchez spares no efforts in lashing out at the exploiters of the African American women, who masquerade as the champions of their race. Labelling herself as a "smart-assed-black-bitch," the African American woman adds that she is only too happy to be away from Black men who uninhibitedly change their women (Sanchez, *The Bronx* 82). Subject to sexual exploitation and the resultant psychological harassment, she has lost faith in all men, even in her own racial counterparts. The anger should be justified since, while the plight of the African American males slightly improved following the abolition, that of their women continued to remain the same. The shift from an agrarian economy to an industrial one only modified their problems, but never eradicated them. All her pleas initially fall on deaf ears since Charles continues to threaten her with sexual assaults. Apart from being a sexual prey to a Black man, the woman also serves the same purpose to a White man who has been regularly visiting her during weekends for a couple of years. Yet she understands that she finds no place as a human being in his scheme of thoughts since his heart lies with his "White wife and kids and reality" (Sanchez, *The Bronx* 82). The word "reality" significantly projects the unrealistic predicament of the African American women in a White man's land. While the women of the dominant White culture form the "reality" of the American territorial space, the African American women with their multiple stigmas can hardly make such claims. Although the White cop uses her to satisfy his biological urges, he fails to understand and recognize her autonomy as a human being and the painful psycho-gendered reality of her existence. In her, he enacts all his deeply-embedded sexual fantasies. But even during such intimate moments, his dreams are centered on his White folks. The "Black bitch" is therefore nothing beyond an instrument for gratifying his fleshly desires. That she finds no place even in his dreams (leave alone the reality) signifies her invisibility in the American social domain.

The issue of rape is deeply probed by Kennedy, whose plays, to use Rosemary Curb's phrase "abound in heterosexual terrors" (Bryant-Jackson and Overbeck 142). Curb prefixes the word "hetero" within the word "sexual" as a "signifier of the mainstream conflation of sexuality into heterosexuality" (Bryant-Jackson and Overbeck 142). Rape is the major form of heterosexual terror that predates the female protagonists of Kennedy's plays. The African American women inherit a dubious heritage of institutionalized rape by White masters since the times of slavery in both the fields and in the homes (hooks, *Ain't I a Woman* 24). The rape of the Black women did not stop with slavery. In fact, during the whole suffragist movement, the African American women perceived the vote as a means to ending their gendered exploitation (Giddings 121). Rosemary Curb refers to Jacquelin Dowd Hall's regret that the rape of Black women received only a secondary treatment when compared with the lynching of the Black men (Curb 143).[6] The assaults on their person are both racist and gendered. Despite its magnitude of the issue did not receive due attention.

The situation has improved very little for the female protagonists of Adrienne Kennedy like Sarah in *Funny House* (1962), Clara in *Owl Answers* (1963) and Beast Girl in *A Beast Story* (1969), since they are all products of rape. In fact, many of the characters speak obsessively about their own births and deaths. Numerous monologues focus on rape, incest, miscarriage and infanticide leading the characters to a state of psychological paralysis. At the other extreme, they are also constantly enmeshed in vortices of stormy emotions. The play *Funny House* is actually set in Sarah's room as suggested by Kennedy's note at the beginning of the play. (Kennedy, *In One Act* 1-2) The room actually becomes a symbol for the subconscious existence of Sarah. It is an attempt to project the protagonist's interior reality which remains tormented on account of her past. The play opens with a fear of rape. Robert Scanlan mentions how the protagonist of the play "suffers the continual reappearance of the dead father in an unending ritual suggesting incest and violence" (Scanlan 97).

The after effects of the rape are clearly visible on both the raped and the product of rape. Throughout the play, Sarah's mother appears to be in a delirious state with fits of somnambulism. The event has transformed her life. She can never be the same again. The rape negates her very existence as a human being since she lives with a shining skull. (Kennedy, *In One Act* 4) As an aftermath of the harrowing experience, the mother walks in a state of trance. She "mumbles something inaudible to her self" (2). She carries a "bald head" and later a "bludgeoned head," symbolically indicating the violence inflicted on her life. The rape that follows her marriage, paves way for psychosomatic tensions which cause her hair to fall, leading her to a state of baldness and emotional delirium. In fact, Scanlan's "Surrealism as Mimesis" focuses on the dense sexual atmosphere which is evident from the beginning of the play. Commenting on the queen, who, holding a mirror is attended by the Duchess of Hapsburg, who stands at the foot of the bed, Scanlan comments, "It is a page taken out of the sexual history of western women, awaiting the arrival of the male who, for whatever reasons, is entitled to conjugal rights" (Scanlan 97). The fear is akin to the fear of women in Gothic romances and horror stories. While the White western women at least had royalty and power, the African American women like Sarah merely assume these. With sheer detestation, Sarah hopes that her father was dead since he still continues to get closer to his daughter. Although he approaches her with due apologies for having raped her mother, she continues to detest him. The father still pleads "forgiveness" as he understands that she is a "nigger of torment." (Kennedy, *In One Act* 21). These words focus on the moment of her being conceived. The violence inherent during the moment of her being conceived is also echoed by the other selves of Sarah: "before I was born he haunted my conception, diseased my birth." (Kennedy, *In One Act* 4)

In a way, like Hamlet, Sarah also considers birth a "disease" and not a healthy lease of life. The Duchess also speaks in a similar tone: "He haunted my conception. He was a wild beast who raped my mother." (Kennedy, *In One Act* 10)

Later, while describing her paternal grandmother's vision of her son, Sarah describes how the dream stood deflated when he suddenly raped his wife. The fear psychosis of rape is genetically inherited by the daughter too, since she dreads the presence of her father even when he approaches her in an apologetic manner. Consequently, her single self is split, creating a terror in her psychological space.[7] James Glass, while quoting Putnam mentions how there prevails a complex process of "layering" which bewilders the individual. The layering phenomenon is described as a "defensive process of dissociation that binds pain and horror by dividing it into little parts and storing it in such a way that it is difficult to reassemble and to remember" (Glass 50). Both Putnam and Glass feel that around 96% of the patients suffering from multiple personality disorders have suffered a history of prolonged child abuse and child sexual abuse. Moreover, they contend that 90% of such patients are women. Claudia Barnett mentions how Kennedy's characters adopt a "paranoid-schizoid position." According to this theory, the life and death instincts which remain present in infants from birth gradually gets integrated when the individual learns to deal with life in an integrated manner (Barnett 374). But in the case of Kennedy's characters, they hardly reach the point of integration, for they continue to wallow in their "paranoid-schizoid" positions. They continue to remain in a world which is disordered, irrational and also irrevocable.

In 1896, Maeterlinck published "The Tragical in Daily Life" that rejected external action in drama and instead believed in a static element which would keep the audience in touch with the invisible and the unknown forces of the universe or the "ominous silence of the soul and of God" (Maeterlinck 8). Despite its intensity, a static element in Kennedy's theatre cannot be missed. The characters are haunted by the past, which remains as enigmatic as the future. Therefore, the stage presents less action in the conventional sense of the term. Kennedy's theatre goes against traditional theatrical models and conventions like a dramatic plot and character development. Robert Scanlan mentions that "What is dramatised in the performance is something that is done as *a result of the story*" (Scanlan 95; my italics). The dramatic tensions and changes are presented by the mood and tone of the stage. The objects like "bludgeoned head," "fallen hair," "flying ravens," the "bed resembling an ebony tomb" (Kennedy, *In One Act* 2) are all symbolic representations of the "paralytic stasis" (Scanlan 78) which is central to Kennedy's early plays. Nothing happens and nothing can happen except death in *Funny House*, bombing in *A Rat's Mass* (1966) and self-immolation in *The Owl Answers*. The highly charged atmosphere only permits an endless repetition of their massive conflicts. The repetition gives the plays a circular movement, imbuing them with an incantatory quality which is a feature of the oral tradition in the African theatre. The sources of Kennedy's repetition are many. In an interview with Lois More Overbeck, Kennedy mentions the influence of spirituals in her works as being a major cause of repetition. Moreover, critics like Herbert Blau consider Kennedy's language as being akin to "litany" and prayer" (Fuchs 83). Rosemary Curb on the other hand finds in Kennedy's repetitions "[m]agic spells and incantations towards an infernal pit filled with unspeakable horrors" (Fuchs 83). The repetition is also enhanced by the different selves of Sarah who remains forever split on account of the various racio-sexual conflicts.

Among the four selves of Sarah, the Duchess of Hapsburg and Queen Victoria are the figures of White female power with which she longs to identify. Queen Victoria embodies the White women's power to rule. While the Black women in their native lands had the opportunity to rule, in America only White women were given some power and privilege. Kennedy in her interview with Lisa Lehman mentions how she had always been fascinated with Queen Victoria: "It always seemed to amaze me that one person could have a whole era named after them [sic]. I find the obsession with royalty fascinating" (Kennedy, "The Growth of Images" 45-46). Therefore, Sarah remains the antithesis of Queen Victoria since she remains bereft of both the power and the White skin. Sarah simultaneously admires the statue for the power and the beauty and also detests it, since the two remain unattainable for the African American women.

Claudia Barnett mentions that choosing the Duchess is "an odd choice for a figure of female power" (Barnett 379). This is because, although the Duchess was beautiful and also powerful, she remained issueless, and on account of various political reasons she ultimately turned insane. But Kennedy could have made this choice because she realised that like the life of the Duchess, the African American woman's life is also thwarted by misery which could ultimately take a toll on her psychic existence. While the Duchess has suffered a schizophrenic death, Sarah too faces a psychic annihilation with her different warring selves not attaining a cohesive unity till the end.

Like Sarah, Clara in Kennedy's play *The Owl Answers* is also a product of rape and troubled ancestry. As in *Funny House*, this play also explores the psychological terrain of its protagonist who is ravaged by the conflicting desires of acceptance in the White world, her mixed ancestry, and her ultimate desire to move into the kingdom of God. She is conceived through the rape by a rich White man of someone who cooked for him. The cook who is also the Reverend's wife cherishes her virginity and that of her daughter too, since she wants to live up to the ideals of the Virgin Mary. But this seems a hard task indeed in a land where the African American woman is merely perceived as a sexual commodity. Therefore even the ideology of the Virgin Mary is a sort of burden to both Clara and her mother since no efforts are made on the part of the patriarchal forces to thwart that dream. The sacred and the profane, the mundane and the spiritual are all deliberately conflated into each other for highlighting the particular predicament of the African American women in the land of promise. A major religio-sexual idea which haunts the play is the idea of "conception." Clara J. McDonnough in her "Gods and the Owls: The Sacred and the Profane in Adrienne Kennedy's *The Owl Answers*" (1997) focuses on the double meaning involved in the term "conception" which means conception in the biological and ideological senses (McDonnough 386). According to this idea, one's biological conception determines one's cultural and social image, ultimately affecting one's psychological space. Like *Funny House* which takes place in Sarah's room, this play is set in the mind of Clara, blurring the distinction between fantasy and reality. The reality is closer to expressionism as used by Strindberg's definition of it in his *Dream Play* (1974) wherein all things can happen in an arena wherein time and space do not exist. In such a dramatic space, the imagination creates new patterns wherein there is a strange "mixture of memories, experiences, spontaneous ideas, impossibilities and improbabilities." (Strindberg 575).

Like Sarah, Clara is also splintered into several selves, as she is both a product of rape and also a victim of one. She is simultaneously Clara Passmore, the Virgin Mary, the Bastard and the Owl. Similarly, her mother, a victim of the rape also has several selves. She is the Bastard's Black mother, the Reverend's wife and also Anne Boleyn. Along with them, the rapist has also multiple selves. He is the Goddam Father, the Richest White man in town and also the Dead White father. Though not proclaimed by Kennedy, this play is also clearly set in the multiple levels of the protagonists' psyche. The splintered selves present in the rapist, the raped and the product of the rape are a proof of their emotional tempests. Consequently they taunt each other in a hostile universe.

Among the three fragmented personalities, the multiple selves of Clara deserve a detailed consideration not only because she forms the central character of the play, but also because her existence irks and forms the main concern of the other characters too. Her mother is genuinely concerned with the future of her daughter; her father develops a love-hate relationship with her while her boyfriend remains obsessed with her physicality. Yet, none of them has touched the core of her inner being which yearns for spiritual love. Being an unwelcome product of an unexpected relationship, she encounters innumerable barriers in her life which stifle her progress. The experiences of Clara are actually Kennedy's very own. In an interview with Lisa Lehman, Kennedy has commented that Clara is a mixture of her mother,

her mother's half-sister aunt Martha and also herself.[8] Martha was also half-White and therefore she failed to fit into the Black and White worlds like Clara. Clara's acceptability into the White patriarchal world and her longing to be amalgamated into the English culture are actually the dramatist's own yearnings and her mixed heritage as revealed in her *People* (22).

Kennedy's urban upper-middle-class background, her exposure to English films, her English education and her Catholic upbringing had all firmly rooted in her the love for English culture and education. Despite these facts, "heritage" continues to be a troublesome issue for Clara. "THEY" refuse to accept her, since they represent White patriarchal power. Amongst them, William the Conqueror represents political power, while Shakespeare and Chaucer represent creative power, who deny her a place in the English land and letters, despite her Anglo-Saxon features. This is proof of the fact that however Saxonised a racially Black woman's features may be, she is denied entry into the White male world both on account of her race and gender. The ideas of "inheritance" and "ancestry" are cleverly twisted so that THEY taunt her with questions. Immediately after uttering these sentences, they bring out the corpse of the Dead White Father and say to her: "Here is your father" (Kennedy, *In One Act* 28). By deliberately confusing the ideas of "inheritance" and "ancestry," Kennedy focuses on the ever-repetitive ideas of history which continue to undermine the position of the African American women that denies their history, past, present and future.

Clara McDonnough examines the term "Dead White Father" from a gendered perspective and calls it an endearing term for the contemporary audience since it connotes the "multicultural literary attitude that tries to avoid too much emphasis on the works of 'Dead White Males' [. . .] in favor of recognizing the importance of those who are not male, white or already dead" (McDonnough 393). But Clara still continues to love London, Shakespeare and English life. The inordinate love for an alien culture is itself a product of an intellectual rape, since not only has the English education conditioned her mind to an alien culture, but it has also simultaneously failed to authenticate her existence. Therefore, when both the mundane and the spiritual worlds fail to respond to her needs, she turns to the world of animals, thereby being transformed into an owl which is also ultimately immolated, thereby negating the very existence of the African American woman into a state of nothingness.

Clara's transformation is to a great extent because of her invisibility in the powerful White patriarchal world. She is seen in the play both as a virgin and a whore. The loss of virginity pains her and her mother. The mother's idea of virginity is closely akin to Foucault's "sexual morality of Christianity" which is sharply contrasted with the "sexual morality of ancient paganism." Elaborating upon the idea of sex in Christian terms, he mentions how "Christianity associated it with evil, sin, the Fall and death, whereas antiquity invested it with positive symbolic values"[9] (Foucault, *Use of Pleasure* 14). Further, contrasting it with Greek and Roman sexual values, he mentions how: "Christianity, unlike Pagan morality, accorded to strict abstinence, life-long chastity, and virginity" (Foucault, *Use of Pleasure* 15). Seen from this perspective, the mother's idea of sexual knowledge is closer to the Christian view of sex which is a sin. As a symbolic representation of the damnation, she also carries a vial of the blood, which she had lost during her rape. It symbolises loss of maidenhead. Frequently she repeats: "when I see Marys, I cry for their deaths, when I see brides, Clara, I cry for their deaths." (Kennedy, *In One Act* 36) The Madonna/whore antithetical ideologies are embodied in both the mother and the daughter. The opposed views of Mary Magdalene[10] and the Virgin Mary[11] are also deeply implied in them. The Bastard's Black Mother is also the Reverend's wife and also Anne Boleyn.[12] As the Reverend's wife, she struggles to live up to the image of the Virgin Mary, but as Anne Boleyn she is viewed as a whore as did the Catholics during the divorce issue. Moreover, like Anne Boleyn who had been deceived by Henry VIII towards the end of her life,

Clara's mother also finds little compassion from her partner throughout.

The surrealistic mode of the play's locale is indicative of the play being set in the psyche of Clara, the tower of London, a subway car, St. Peter's Basilica and a Harlem hotel. The conflation of the political, spiritual and the mundane is a consequence of the surrealistic setting of the play. Also the technique of superimposition of one setting upon another is the consequence of Kennedy's viewing of the French impressionistic films as a student. The deliberate intersection is essential to lay bare the inherent confusions that Clara faces in a hostile patriarchal setting like America. Moreover it also projects the wide chasm that lies between Clara's expectation and reality. While she longs to become a White dove in the Basilica, she is reduced to her sexual parts as she is a call girl in a Harlem hotel room. Although the play begins on a realistic mode, it transmutes into the surreal, thereby syncopating time, place and character. As Richard Watts mentions the "past and present merge, characters shift from being one person to another, and time is telescoped" (Bryant-Jackson and Overbeck 27). Seemingly caught in the present, the characters are actually entangled in timeless situations out of which they find little escape. The characters are thwarted by racio-sexual problems, being basically guided by the events of their "biology" and their "consciousness."[13] The racio-sexual trauma faced by the women characters in Kennedy's plays are both biological and a product of their "consciousness." It is biological in the sense that their intense awareness of their biological vulnerability and power of the phallus forces them through a series of sexual experiences. The prowling predators inflict the violence with a consciousness of the power vested in them and an awareness of the weakness of the sufferer.[14] The rapist whom the women feared "was usually a dark man"[15] (Freud 604). The racist-cultural myth stereotyped the African American man as a rapist who lusted for female flesh. Curb mentions a prevailing myth that "the darker the man, the more likely he is to rape and the lighter the woman the more likely she is to be the victim" (Curb 145). The sinister association of darkness with rape is also at times instilled into the psyche of not only White women but also Black women. Sarah in Kennedy's *Funny House* fears that her father would rape her.

The fear of rape is the most explicit in Kennedy's *A Lesson in Dead Language* (1968). The seven adolescent girls, dressed in White organdy, repeat the lesson "I bleed," while there are enlarging circles of blood on the backs of their dresses. They express immense apprehension over the onset of their first menstruation since it signals their biological ability to procreate and also their potential to become victims of rape. Lois More Overbeck in "The Life of the Work: A Preliminary Sketch" mentions how in *Lesson* "Sexual maturation is treated as a trauma" (Bryant-Jackson and Overbeck 31). Overbeck mentions how in a performance of the play by Gaby Rogers, the movement included actors as religious sculptures. Kennedy also used gospel music in the background, indicative of the religious rape which they undergo. In the play when the White Dog says "I bleed," the pupils also repeat "I bleed" (Kennedy, *In One Act* 48). Kennedy's stage direction which pinpoints the dark circles of blood indicates the onset of their menstruation and the resultant confusion. The circle is an important symbol signifying the menstrual cycles of women and the gynaecological trauma. The young girls stand confused as the White dog/mother fails to instruct them regarding their passage from childhood to womanhood.

The onset of menstruation gives them unknown phobias, wherein both the young girls and the mothers feared a possible rape. Eldridge Cleaver calls it "the ultimate physical threat by which all men kept all women in a state of psychological intimidation" (Cleaver 254). To combat this fear, young girls needed the guidance of mothers. They perceive the biological act as a curse and therefore experience horror at the first sight of menstrual blood. This is more in consonance with the Biblical idea of menstruation which views it as a curse laid by God on Eve on account of her act of disobedience.[16] Modern feminist critics, while rejecting the notion of "sin" associated with it, do not rule out the inherent confusion arising during this period, since, apart from the hormonal changes in her physique, the woman is also a victim of a number of taboos surrounding this biological event since patriarchal times.[17]

The speech of Maxine in Shange's spell#7 also lays bare the pain that young adolescent girls undergo during puberty. As a child, she was free, with trees growing in her room and birds flying through. But the moment she became a woman, she is made to feel threatened by the outside world. Maxine moves on to mention how she was prohibited from meeting the trolley driver or every young man because it meant trouble. On account of the excessive concern for her, Maxine's mother and grandmother do not understand that they were questioning her autonomy. The phobia against menstruation, along with the unfavourable socio-cultural milieu often left young African American girls in baffled state. True, that slave mothers would have often educated the young girls against the sexual hazards that they were likely to encounter, but the young girls ultimately remained as defenceless as their mothers and were also prone to rape. To consider slaves as "objects of pleasure" is not unique to the African American culture alone. Foucault in his second volume of *The Use of Pleasure: The History of Sexuality* (1981) mentions a principle of "isomorphism" which implies the presence of power as an inherent factor in sexual relations.[18]

The young girls in *A Lesson in a Dead Language* feel a sense of shame on account of their menstruation. Comparing the menstrual flow with spermal fluid, Adrienne Rich points out how: "Men often exalt and romanticize the spermal fluid (one man I know compared it to the scent of chestnut blossoms) while degrading menstrual blood as unnatural and distasteful" (106). The lack of such logical questioning and reasoning gives the pupils a sense of fear and guilt. This is further reinforced symbolically by the lesson which is taught in the class regarding Calpurnia's dream and the death of Caesar. The connection between the two is deeper. Like Calpurnia who could not use her foreknowledge to avert Caesar's death, the mothers can also do little to prevent the ultimate catastrophe that may befall their daughters in an inimical setting. To Curb, the pinnacle could be symbolic of the "phallic" principle "which is capable of being toppled" (Curb 150). Moreover, for the first time, the girls understand their own vulnerability and the advantages of being male (since they are spared of the trouble). The theme of the tumbling pinnacle has been borrowed by Kennedy from Plutarch and not Shakespeare.[19]

To Kennedy, rape need not be feared essentially before marriage, but also after it. Marriage is no passport for men to legally exploit women. Havelock Ellis remarks that there are certainly more rapes committed "in marriage" than outside it. According to this report: "among six intelligent middle-classed women, all said that their first marital intercourse came as a shock; two were ignorant and the others were physically injured nonetheless" (Beauvoir 461). The theme of post-marital rape which Kennedy has touched upon in *Funny House* is elaborated in *A Beast Story*. The play presents a death in life situation, as the four members of a family, are haunted by a fifth member, an innocent babe killed by murder. The Beast Man rapes his wife the Beast Woman, after their wedding. The product of the rape is a Beast Girl who is in turn raped by her husband on their wedding night. While the Beast Woman has not killed the Beast Girl, the latter kills the girl child (the product of the rape) and subsequently also her husband who sings lullabies for his dead child. The post-marital rape of the Beast Man has triggered a chain of harrowing events, since the cycle of rape-conception-death is again re-enacted in the life of his daughter too suggesting an archetypal experience. Therefore the dividing line between the different characters is very thin. Walter Kerr calls them interchangeable: "All roles blur, divide and recombine [. . .] the heavens light up with finger painted child's pictures of houses, robins, blood stains and ebony suns. Sounds, sights, gestures occur as in a dream that won't move forward" (Overbeck 28). George Oppenheimer feels that the characters are enacting an allegory (Overbeck 29). The play may appear to be a bit too elusive and baffling to us but it is inevitable as Richard Watt that Kennedy is "giving us important and moving insights into the minds and emotions of deeply tormented people" (Overbeck 28).

The play abounds in surrealistic images of death like "floating corpses," "dead toad,"[20] "dead blue crow,"[21] "dead human" and the like to suggest the bleak picture of life that follows the rape of the Beast Woman. Perceived in these terms, the word "beast" in the title refers to the carnal appetite in human beings, the unfulfillment of which leads them to adopt violent means of gratifying it. Throughout his writings, Freud concedes how the libidinal instinct in human beings is the most powerful drive. When the id is not guided by the super ego, it may result in rape. In *A Beast Story*, the lives of all the four characters are enveloped in a state of gloom symbolically suggested by the candle as the only source of light on the stage. Nearly all the plays of Kennedy take place in darkness. In an interview she mentions: "I do see black things all around scenes. It's true, it's really true" (Bryant-Jackson and Overbeck 9). The blurred conversation is the effect of the traumatic aftermath of rape which leaves four alienated individuals existing in a house. The Beast Girl explains how the wedding itself started on a note of discord, since, when her father the Beast Man performed the wedding, it was shrouded by evil portents like "crow," "black sun" and "a red sunrise morning."[22] (Kennedy, "*A Beast Story*" 200). The violence-filled imagery is suggestive of the latent violence in their lives. The music in the play aptly lacks harmony. The dense and powerful images suggest the complexity in their lives. The play was originally published under the title *Cities of Bezique*. With regard to the production of that play, Gerald Freeman mentions the difficulty of re-creating on the stage the dense images. Since "bezique" is basically a card game. Kennedy's text actually had pictures of the cards turned over. Freeman points at the practical difficulties of finding a theatre company that could financially afford to create such costly stage settings (Bryant-Jackson and Overbeck 27).

Abiding by the dictates of her mother, she refuses to enter into a sexual union with her husband. She adopts artificial means of maintaining her virginity, like pretending bleeding.[23] Therefore, the final act of copulation takes place forcibly through a rape in the fields. With vindictiveness, she kills the infant born of this union with quinine and whiskey while later slaying her husband too. Both the mother and the daughter undergo an "elemental sexual struggle" (Benston 244). The act, when perceived in sexist terms, does signify the emergence of the African American woman as an individual, unhindered by familial bonds. But it leaves little room for joy, for she remains more devastated after it. She is exposed to greater nightmarish experiences since, the ever-present wild beasts like the crow, jackal and the toad continue to predate her. Still, she shows little signs of repentance, as she accepts her acts to be final and therefore feels no obligation to seek an outside force, or a deeper spiritual force for consolation. As Kimberley Benston puts it, "her conscience will not allow her an artificial martyrdom" (243). The play deals with numerous births, deaths, sublimations, rapes, forces and frustrations. Therefore, even after the crow is killed with the axe the light is only temporary, since, "the strange light of failure envelops her once again" (Benston 243). Kennedy's discussion of rape is ultimately at a deeper, metaphoric level which is different from that of her counterparts.

Like Sanchez, Shange outrightly discusses the issue through her female protagonists. The basic theme of *colored girls* is the girls' coming of age which is looked upon with both apprehension and celebration. Shange's rapist is not a predating, prowling man who battles for/with the female body. He is closer to Marie Fortune's description of a modern rapist who need not be a stranger but one who may be familiar to the raped (Fortune 147). Shange's idea of rape also bears a close semblance to the Freudian theory of "seduction." Feminists question Freud's "silence" on rape. Shange is closer to the Freudian theory of it. John Forrester mentions that Freud used the word only once, and that too for an "attempted rape" but he does frequently refer to the word "seduction" (Forrester 63). Freud contends that the perpetuator of this form of offence may usually be a closely known person who may indulge in the crime both physically and psychologically.[24] Like Freud, Shange also contends that though rape has become more "sophisticated" in modern urban-settings, its aftermath has been little altered. (Shange, *colored girls* 17-18) Her warnings are not meant to brand every male a rapist nor does she create a male phobia amongst women, her aim is actually to educate the latent sexual violence which women have to cope with at all times and places. Whether attacked by a stranger or a friend, the anguish of the raped can never be under-estimated.[25]

The agony of being a woman, especially a Black woman in a hostile environment, forms one of the themes of Shange's *boogie woogie landscapes* (1979). Layla's anguish is both over being "colored" and being a "woman." Throughout, Layla moves towards different planes of awareness. Her name in Arabic means "born in the night" (Shange, *three pieces* 113) and therefore her life is filled with night-life companions. Shange contends that the music in the play throws light on the nuances of Layla's inner life. The title "boogie woogie" is a style of jazz, which describes the musical character of the play as also incorporating the elements of dream, fluidity and temporal qualities associated with this musical genre. Memory is yet another crucial jazzian quality which informs the play throughout since Layla is obsessed with the past.

Music becomes an integral part of the play wherein the psychological topography as well as the physical growth of Layla are explored. Shange uses the terms "landscapes" and "geography" in a rather significant manner. Her introductory note to the play clarifies that terms like "might," "suggested" etc., lay bare the fluidity of the setting as in a dream play, since Layla dreams that particular night. Through expressionistic settings, Shange focuses on the entry and exit of her nlcs. The stage direction indicates the permeability of the walls for the entry of the nlc's (dream memories) and their exit. (Shange, *three pieces* 113) It may appear that the dream-like setting makes the play deficient in terms of lacking a firmly grounded locale, but it is crucial to remember that Shange is using the dream motif as a structural device since dreams are a world which seemingly lack coherence and continuity. The nlcs actually enhance her self-understanding. It is with a renewed perspective that Layla starts examining her body wherein she optimistically discovers new "horizons" and "different dawns" which suggest her growth beyond the present dimensions. (Shange, *three pieces* 118).

Layla's examination of her body, the growth of hair on her pubic areas and the fullness of her lips suggest the sudden awareness of her physical changes and a fear of sexual victimisation. Although she voices every American woman's fear of rape as expressed by Susan Griffin,[25] the feminist thinker, she is also voicing the particular trepidation of the African American women in a hostile milieu since the times of slavery to the present. Layla's night life-companion #4 who masquerades as a lover is actually interested in her body. Words like "scarlet wine," "lips," "brazziere," "sleep near you," "caressed," "full of love," "a kiss," "red goblet" and others reflect his physical obsession for Layla. Through his seductive language, he arouses her sexual instinct as depicted in the episode of undressing. Cleverly does he brand himself a mere "accomplice" implying Layla alone as being the prime cause of the event while he projects himself as a mere passive partner in the sexual act. She realises that her once-hated body is now an object of male lust, and therefore becomes intensely aware of the ever-predating potential of rape. Throughout, the night life-companions 1 and 3 chart out their own means to prevent rape, at the same time cautioning Layla against it. They think of a "rape prevention month"; they envy women in Cuba who are free of rape, advocate that women do not walk alone, counter rumours of close-companionship between women as only being lesbianism, want the idea of self-defence classes to be made mandatory for all coloured children, plead for parading of rapists, and also want the closing down of porno-houses. The insecure environment gives place to the wishful thinking of constructing a world where even the "fear of rape" stands little chance to exist. But the reality exists otherwise, since even children are victims of rape.

Apart from adult rape, Shange also protests against child rape in her *From Okra to Greens/ A Different Kinda Love Story* where both Greens and Okra raise a voice against child molestation. (Shange, *From Okra* 40-41). Child rape becomes Shange's metaphor for the larger sexist issues that plague the African American women. In her *boogie woogie landscapes* she openly expresses her disgust for societies which play with women's genital organs. Nearly all the patriarchal cultures place excessive value on women's chastity with an intact hymen as a test of it. To protect it, women have to undergo a number of painful experiences. The nlc # 3 catalogues the other forms of physical mutilation that women have to undergo, apart from rape like "infibulation" "excision" and clitorectomy which act as "virginity insurance." (Shange, *three pieces* 135) Infibulation is a process which women have had to encounter in various cultures since ancient times. Many cultures, while ensuring a woman's chastity, ironically do little to preserve the virginity of men. These are modes of patriarchal constructs meant to alter the biological destinies of women to suit their own needs. Graphic details like "oozing pus" and female genitals shock traditionally complacent minds when her women unhesitatingly speak about their sexual encounters in order to vindicate their sexual rights and legitimate joys.

colored girls can be seen as black women's defiance of social expectations both thematically and linguistically. Both Lady in Orange and the Lady in Purple admit their inabilities to live up to the idea of "ladies" on account of the multiple battles they have to wage. The Lady in Yellow's memories of graduation night is actually a double movement for, it not only deals with her transition into the high school, but also with her change from girlhood to womanhood. The graduation night is therefore a night of sexual initiation for her. In the same night she both graduates and loses her virginity. The Lady in Yellow describes her first sexual experience as being "wonderful" in explicit terms. (Shange, *colored girls* 9). It cannot be branded as "rape" because it is actually a woman's conscious decision to act upon her sexual stirrings. Moreover she remains a willing and an active partner in the act while at the same time "there is no indication that this woman wants lasting romance with this man or any other [. . .] she is just as capable of moving on [. . .] as men allegedly are" (Lester 38-39).

The idea of female sexuality and its affirmation is further developed in Shange's *From Okra to Greens / A Different Kinda Love Story*. Shange has drawn upon this collection of poems from an earlier anthology entitled *A Daughter's Geography* (1983). Music is an integral part of the play and "functions in much the same manner as the Greek chorus." (Lester 225) It is with music as background that we meet the modern couple who establish a relationship based on sexual compatibility. Their sexual encounters are devoid of gender prescriptions and power play. It is an intimate relationship whereby they disclose their mutual feelings, dreams, hopes and fears. Their conversation is laden with eroticism. Phrases like "take my tongue outta my mouth," "dew between yr. legs," "poured wine down my throat," "seduced sound," "animal sounds," "my body loosens for you," "you wet yr. fingers / lay it to my lips" (Shange, *From Okra* 12) and the like, form a vivid description of the sexual compatibility that the partners enjoy. Shange vividly describes Okra's vaginal wetness as a response to Green's ejaculation. In fact, it is Okra who remains more sexually expressive than her partner. Greens is also a distinct male who is not interested in the power play between the sexes during moments of intimacy. Therefore, her achievement of orgasm is a moment of both emotional and physical fulfillment.[26]

While elaborating on women's autonomy and sexuality, Shange makes an apt distinction between freedom and license.

The Lady in Blue's abortion experience in *colored girls* depicts how a hedonistic pursuit of pleasure not only produces a negative self-image, but also leads to a sense of disillusionment. Lester mentions: "Whether a pregnancy results from a consensual or coerced sexual encounter, abortion itself is a metaphoric rape that can also leave deep and lasting scars" (Lester 51). The abortion and the resultant psycho-physical turmoil could have well been averted had the Lady in Blue been aware of the distinction between sexual liberty and license.

At no point does Shange encourage women to become engaged in sexual power games in order to vindicate their stance as women. Sechita and Passion Flower in her *colored girls* are examples to prove this point. Sechita is a young dancer in a cheap bar at Mississippi. Her gaudy dress reminds one of the stereotypical prostitutes. Her "red garters," "thigh," "yellow threads," "black stocking" and the "Orange color" suggest a gaudiness associated with omen involved in the profession of flesh trade. When the White men throw coins on her genitalia, this is a symbolic illustration of the White men perceiving the Black women as objects of sexuality. In a mood of despondency she mentions "god seemed to be wipin his feet in my [her] face" (*colored girls* 25). As the conventional White masculine God remains rather cold towards her sufferings, she moves inwardly for solace and fulfillment. Dance is yet another tool through which she finds a satisfaction, since, apart from asserting her racial memory, dance and music form an alternative for the oppressed Black women's survival since through these, she is transported into a different realm internally by transforming herself into a "goddess of love." (*for colored girls* 25).This is the empowerment that Sechita finds even in the oddest of the circumstances, since an ordinary bar-dance is transformed into one of power over the lustful men wherein she is no longer vulnerable to exploitative strategies. Instead, all men remain controlled and she imbibes her performance with "cosmic proportions." (Lester 46)

The idea of creative fantasy as an act of liberation is further elaborated in spell#7 (1979). It highlights Shange's ability to merge African aesthetic forms with the western ones for a complete celebration of the African American women's creativity. As a foil to Sechita who converts the oddities into her favour is Passion Flower who plays power games with men through her sexuality. She juggles men who are vulnerable to her feminine charms. Attractively dressed, she checkmates every man to make him a potential victim. Like Sean in Shange's *A Photograph: Lovers in Motion* (1979) she uses men as her sexual pawns, and ultimately discards them. Every move of hers is intended on sexual conquest. But in the long run, her own life remains uncontrolled, thereby leading her to an ultimate state of disillusionment. Therefore, a ruthless pursuit of physical pleasure will have far-reaching consequences, whether it is a woman like Passion Flower or a man like Sean.[27]

Like Kennedy, Shange also focuses on the biological determinism that impregnates women in the post-rape scenario. Motherhood is conferred on them by force or choice. It may lead to abortion at times. The "abortion cycle #1" in Shange's *colored girls* highlights this uniquely female suffering in poetic terms. Terms like "metal horses" touching the womb, the "eyes rolling" on the thighs, and the "steel rods" that hurt her are in fact less agonizing when compared to the destitution that she faces during such emotionally distressed times. (*for colored girls* 72-73). The select diction is suggestive of rape, coerced sex, pregnancy and the painful process of abortion which the women face alone. The turmoil of the woman is highlighted through the imagery of blood, shattered bones, "steel rods," "scream" and the ultimate word used to sum up all the pain: "hurt." To top all this, the woman suffers alone since biological and socio-cultural norms spare men.

The issue of pregnancy and abortion has been adopted by Kennedy in a highly metaphoric manner in her play *A Movie Star Has to Star in Black and White*. The protagonist of the play, Clara, tries to identify herself with the icons of Hollywood cinema like Bette Davis, Jean Peters, Marlon Brando, Montgomery Clift and the like. All her attempts to recreate the romantic aura of Hollywood films remain abortive since these fantasies originate in a culture that is ultimately oppressive to her creativity. She is seen in the play wearing a maternity dress, but she is haemorraging and she has also had a miscarriage earlier. She bleeds Black blood on White sheets (a symbolic re-enactment of her intellectual conception and its abortion). Deborah R. Geis mentions how there basically exists a subconscious division between her Bette Davis identity and her African American identity[28] (Geis 172). Therefore, her attempts to erase her "dark" thoughts through an identification with the oppressive culture only reveal the stark reality of her existence to herself. In fact it is the re-enactment of Lacan's "mirror stage"[29] wherein Clara moves into a symbolic realm only to discover her "otherness." She continually bleeds as Marlon Brando pulls White sheets with Black blood under her. But it still remains a source of power since what she creates is something that emerges from her insides. (Geis 177)

A similar idea is voiced by Shange in *From Okra to Greens*, wherein she lashes at men who think that their manhood is determined on the basis of their ability to impregnate women and alter their life styles. Shange is actually laying bare the emotional and biological realities of motherhood. While the biological fathering of a child only needs providing a sperm, motherhood is an intense physical and psychological bonding rarely understood by many men.

If not abortion, women undergo the experience of forced motherhood. Motherhood is a traumatic experience which women alone have to endure. Adrienne Rich in *Of Woman Born* (1976) mentions how while the terms "barren" and "childless" are used to refer to childless women, the term "non-father" does not find a place in the human lexicon. In *The Black Woman: A Historical Overview* (1987) La Frances Rodgers and Rose mention how the role of the mother was vital in African societies where they were viewed on par with Gods: "No other person has [. . .] the ability to give birth, to ensure the ever-increasing number of ancestors, to link the past with the present" (126). Many slave narratives and autobiographies like those of Martha Browne, Harriet Jacobs and Amanda Berry are in fact moving sagas of the woes of African American motherhood. It has posed special burdens on them on account of the multiple jeopardies of race, gender and class. Daryl C. Dance's "Black Eve or Madonna? A Study of the Antithetical views of the mother in Black American Literature" (1979) mentions how the symbiotic nature of oppression in America has cast the African American mother in two particular images: "Eve" and "Madonna." As "Eve," she is responsible for the destruction of mankind and has been the cause of God's curse on her progeny too. Daryl Dance also concedes that there is simultaneously a redemptive figure of "Mary who gives birth to the saviour who brings redemption and salvation to man" (Dance 123). The negative picture of the African American mother can be seen in Baraka's morality plays *Mad Heart* (1969)[30] and *A Black Mass* (1969)[31] and also for instance in Jimmy Garret's play *We Own the Night* (1970).[32] Black women dramatists in America have countered the Eve-like stereotyping of the African American motherhood. Not only have they projected them in realistic and positive light but they have also been cast as revolutionary. For instance, in Grimke's play *Rachel*, the protagonist's ultimate denunciation of motherhood is quite revolutionary since she vows not to bear children only to sacrifice them at the altar of the White man's bestiality. The mother figures in Lorraine Hansberry's *A Raisin in the Sun* (1959) and Elaine Jackson's *Toe Jam* (1971) are instances to prove the specific resilience of African American motherhood which is remarkable despite the multiple burdens borne by them. Chinnosole uses the word "Matrilineal diaspora" to describe the connection between African American mothers and daughters. It is:

> The capacity to survive and aspire, to be contrary and self-affirming across continents and generations. It names the strength and beauty we pass on as friends and lovers from foremothers to mother and daughters allowing us to survive radical cultural changes and be empowered through differences. (Braxton and Mc Laughlin 379)

Chinnosole's use of the word "diaspora" is rather revolutionary. While it is conventionally used to mean dispersal and scattering, it is used here as a term of empowerment. The Black race itself with its firm faith in the past and with their forms of ancestral worship always had an acute sense of the past. The women in particular needed greater emotional strength to surmount the multiple barriers they faced. Psychologically it ensures a greater emotional bonding which sustains the women during troublesome times. Chinnosole goes on to mention how this concept is meant to form an intricate network among Black women globally. It simultaneously enables them to "experience distinct but related cultures while retaining a special sense of home as the locus of self-definition and power" (Braxton and Mc Laughlin 379). Patricia Bell Scott in *Double Stitch* (1991) uses the metaphor of "quilt" to describe this relationship since it is an important metaphor of the African American culture: "As an essential element of women's culture, quilts offer a framework for conceptualising mother-daughter relations" (Scott 1).

The African American mothers' unique sense of vision allowed them to provide a strong physio-psychological strength to their daughters which propelled them for ascension. Sonia Sanchez also voices the same idea in an interview with Zala Chandler wherein she sees her source of power as emanating and being transmitted from her grandmother and other ancestors. (Braxton and Mc Laughlin 354)

Another reason for the mothers being a reservoir of strength for the African American women could be the worship of the manes in their homeland.[33] Adrienne Kennedy explores the mother-daughter relationship in three of her plays. They are

Funny House, *The Owl Answers* and *A Beast Story*. But none of these mothers provide their daughters the power and emotional courage needed for their struggle. They are themselves haunted by a doomed past. Sarah's mother does not have any dialogue or a voice of her own, Clara's mother does cherish a spiritual vision for her daughter, but remains helpless in the overwhelming circumstances; in *A Beast Story* the mother instigates infanticide to her daughter, hardly providing a positive solution to the enveloping gloom. The characters are actually thrown into a vast universe, which is full of conflicting forces that enfeeble them. Such a universe knows no ideologies like optimism or pessimism. Moreover, as Margaret B. Wilkerson mentions, there is a basic difference of perception between Kennedy and dramatists like Hansberry. In the latter, there is an intellectual attempt at "consciously imposing order on the chaos of experience" in spite of her deep awareness of the "absurdity and irrationality of human beings." (Wilkerson, "Diverse Angles of Vision" 74). The positive vision of Hansberry transforms the gross realities of life into a deeper vision. Kennedy, on the other hand, remains quite comfortable with the latent violence in African American lives and "works against the censoring intellect." Far from being "affirming beings," they "explicate the mysterious and primeval fears of humans" (Bryant-Jackson and Overbeck 74-75). It would be fallacious to consider one perspective right for, each of these visions remain authentically rooted in their modes of cognition.

Whether seen in relationship with their daughters or as mothers establishing special bonds with their children, the African American women spare little efforts to nurture their children. Sonia Sanchez's play *The Bronx is Next* presents a "Black bitch" who hates men, especially her own men on account of her feelings of betrayal. Impregnated and deserted by a man of her own race, she hates them since the man has ruthlessly deserted her with her two sons. Since men lust after her flesh, she is forced into the trade for the sake of economic needs. She regrets that she could hardly find a Black man who would love her and her sons. Although her body is forcibly engaged in the act of flesh trade, her inner self is in search of an ideal companion who could fulfill the inner emotional yearnings of her family. The unfulfilled longings pave way to frustration and therefore she rebels when Charles and Roland threaten her with sexual assaults. She is considered a sexual pawn, an instrument of pleasure on whom a White cop enacts his sexual fantasies while he dreams of the "reality" of his white wife and kids. (Sanchez, "The Bronx" 82; my italics) The word "reality" is significant here. As an African American woman, she is not a part of the White patriarchy's real space. Rather she remains a passing middle-passage with which he has no connections the moment he leaves her. Historically, the term may relate to the passage of slaves from Africa to West Indies across the Atlantic, but practically, the African American women have always been used for specific purposes like child-bearing, labour, sexual gratification etc. and then discarded as if they had no human value. She confesses that even the White man's dreams are not about her as they are about his White wife and children, thereby indicating her almost invisible status, since even his unconscious self does not ruminate about her. Despite such stifling circumstances, she continues to cherish a dream as a mother. She hopes to raise them as men of substance who would know how to appropriately estimate a Black woman. Though cast in the Jezebel image, she still vows to raise her sons with a high esteem for all African American women. Similarly, the African American woman in the third section of Sanchez's *Uh! Uh! But How Do it Free Us?* nourishes a spiritual vision for her unborn child. As the mother of a child in its foetal stages, she realises the need for a well-ordered universe into which her child needs to be born, to give the child "lights" and not "madness" (Sanchez, *Uh! Uh!* 213). She never allows the trauma of her life to ever impinge upon her duty as a mother.

Among the mothers of Kennedy, it is Suzanne in *Ohio State Murders* alone who strives hard to endure the multiple assaults inflicted upon herself, to take care of the twins born out of campus rape. The music in the play is suggestive of the central theme of seduction, abandonment, impregnation and infanticide. Two significant songs: "Don't go away mad" and another piece of music from the film *A Place in the Sun* which is based on Theodore Dreiser's *American Tragedy* (28), are indicative of the tragic mood of the play wherein the protagonist is in for a series of horrors. It is actually a trip down memory lane of Kennedy wherein the present and the past are subtly interpolated in order to lay bare the horror of the past to the present audience. The play is dense with horror-filled imagery. The university itself is depicted as a "vast dark structure" (27). Apart from this, Kennedy also uses the technique of superimposition wherein "sections of the stacks become places on campus during the play" (27). The playwright also subtly builds up the violent atmosphere through films like *Battleship Potempkin* dealing with the 1905 Revolution. The speech of Hampshire wherein he reads a passage from Arthur's vow to revenge is laden with words like "blood," "beasts, "bitterwoe," "grief," "sank," "destroyed," "hunt," "hound," etc. (48), indicating the agony that Suzanne faces on being brushed aside like a fly after being sophisticatedly raped. Although the mothers and daughters in *A Beast Story*, *The Owl Answers* and *Funny House* are engrossed in mutually destructive relationships, this play presents a comparatively positive image of a mother who strives hard to maintain her twins. This highly autobiographical play presents Suzanne Alexander, a Black student who strives hard to bring up her twin daughters. The poetic quality of the play is highlighted through the condensation of a number of symbols, images, rhythms, colours and the existence of the play both in the times past and present. In the director's note book to the play, Gerald Freeman mentions to Paul K. Bryant-Jackson how he is struck by the: "Mystery, imagery, flights of imagination, lack of cliché and structure, the unexpected and the surprise of it" (Bryant-Jackson and Overbeck 207). In a condensed medium, Kennedy equates Suzanne with he predicament of Tess who is also jilted by her lover. When Suzanne confesses her pregnancy to Prof. Hampshire, he refuses to acknowledge his role in it. Though the White Professor condescendingly appreciates her intellectual capabilities and establishes sexual liaison with her, he refuses to acknowledge his fatherhood, having made her a mother. Kennedy mentions in her *People* how from the story of Hester Prynne in Hawthorne's *The Scarlet Letter*, she realised that "severe punishment lies ahead for a woman who commits a sin" (Kennedy, *People* 61). Expelled from her family and dormitory she suffers like Tess in the vale of Blackmoor. She is forced to take up odd jobs for the sake of nurturing her twins. But all her efforts prove futile when Prof. Hampshire kills the twins in a gruesome manner since "he had never been able to forget their existence." (Kennedy, *The Alexander Plays* 60)

Suzanne's predicament as a mother is comparable with Crystal in Shange's *colored girls*. The violence she experiences as a mother is more blatant since she is a mute witness to her children being thrown from the fifth floor of an apartment by their father. Shange argues that while much discussion has been generated to an analysis of Beau Williams' character, little has been done to probe into the agony of Crystal. Shange is in fact throwing a deeper insight into Crystal's plight as a powerless mother. She continues to love him despite his torment. He kills the children to prove his masculinity and his power over her. Shange deliberately conceals the action of dropping the children in ambiguity because it could be emotionally overpowering and a gruesome spectacle on the stage. Crystal's loss is therefore emblematic of an ultimate powerless Black woman who has been raped, battered, mothered and ultimately destroyed in a tug of power.

At times, women also engage themselves in power-games. *for colored girls* presents Sue Jean who desires power over the males. Maternity is her chosen way. She wants to bear a son without a family, a son to "smile suckle & sleep" (*for colored girls* 28). She prefers to have a son since she views him as a representative of the male world which she hates. She manipulates her relationship with Ray for this purpose. She seduces him not for the sake of sexual pleasure, but to attain her goal of a power-filled motherhood. To her, it is an effective means of gaining identity and establishing power over a male infant's life. But things turn adversely for Sue Jean after the delivery. The severing of the umbilical cord also leads her to a greater awareness over her limited ability to control the life of her son. Realising her limitations, she commits the gruesome act of infanticide, and by drinking the blood of the child, she symbolically incorporates the child into herself. The deed done, she turns delirious. Like the narrator of Ellison's short story "King of the Bingo Game," she too turns insane by trying to control the lives of the others. As a mother, her madness is the consequence of her inability to realise that the path towards self-empowerment is constructive and not destructive. Toni Morrison in *Beloved* (1987) also presents Sethe murdering her infant, which is ultimately an act of sacrifice, but Sue Jean's act leads her to a state of devastation. The violence that fills the lives of Suzanne, Beast Girl, Crystal and Sue Jean is actually a symbolic re-enactment of the larger violence that has predated the lives of the African American woman ever since she was brought to the land of promise.[34]

Violence has thus sunk into the psyche of the African American woman which is ever-present in her life. Sonia Sanchez explores the theme of physical violence inflicted on the body of the Black woman in her plays: *The Bronx is Next* and in the third section of *Uh! Uh! but How Do it Free Us?* The continuous doses of violence to which the woman is subjected instills a sort of defiant attitude within the "Black bitch." In her *The Bronx is Next* Charles continuously engages himself in acts of sexual violence to prove his power over her and to actually conform to the image of masculinity which makes a man resort to violence. His oppressed condition does not allow him to exercise his power over the Whites. The extreme passivity to the White race imposed on him makes him exercise his innate violence on his women who are the only creatures at his mercy. This idea also runs through the third section of Sanchez's play *Uh! Uh! but How Do it Free Us?*, where a Black man, while living with a woman of his own race, also has a secret liaison with a White woman. When his intellectually accomplished Black woman questions him over it, he slaps her as also uses immense verbal violence to further demean her status as a Black woman.

Kennedy's presentation of violence is more complex. She is immensely concerned with the deeper and latent violence that has shaped the psyche of the African American women. In her depiction of violence, Kennedy's theatre is closer to that of Artaud who in his *Theatre and its Double* (1970) compares the stage with plague. They are synonymous to him on account of their potential to disturb large groups at a time: "A real stage play upsets our sensual tranquillity, releases our repressed subconscious, drives us to a kind of potential rebellion [. . .] calling for a difficult heroic attitude on the part of the assembled groups" (Artaud 19). Plague-like, Kennedy's plays also continue to torment the spectators, long after they have visualised them. The violence may not be as blatant as in Baraka, Bullins or Sanchez, but its power can never be undermined since it disturbs our inner beings. Like plague, "theatre is a powerful appeal through the illustration to those powers which return the mind, to the origins of its inner struggles" (Artaud 20). In fact, Paul K. Bryant-Jackson in an interview with the director of Kennedy's *Ohio State Murders* acknowledges that he could not but marvel at Kennedy's ability to understate action. "Three hours after I was walking in the park, and all of a sudden the images started baring themselves" (Bryant-Jackson and Overbeck 215)). As an African American, she understands that violence is deeply entrenched in their lives and therefore it is an integral part of the African American psyche. To her, playwriting is an act of projecting her real self on to the stage. In "On Becoming a Playwright" Kennedy mentions Albee's advice to her: "Well, do you know what a playwright is? A playwright is one who lets his guts out on the stage and that's what you've done in this play" (Bryant-Jackson and Overbeck 27).

The universe of Kennedy is rather an absurd one, wherein the characters are haunted by the fear of an "absent presence."[35]

The world undergoes a process of imbalance: "God is the linchpin suddenly discovered missing from the machinery of living and the moment the absence is noticed, everything flies apart, nothing coheres and the world collapses into anarchy and madness" (Killinger 25). In such an insecure world, there is little scope for certainty. Everything remains uncertain including life. Thus, towards the end of *Funny House*, Sarah is both dead and alive. The only certainty is death. The idea of death haunts many of Kennedy's characters. Elinor Fuchs, while comparing the plays of Kennedy with those of Maeterlinck mentions how like the latter, Kennedy's plays are also enacted in a world of madness and internal gloom. Dèath is hinted at symbolically also. For instance, in *Funnyhouse*, the stage direction calls for an "unnatural Blackness" (Kennedy, *In One Act* 2) for most part of the stage, to highlight the dominant gloom that symbolically shrouds the protagonist's life. In *A Rat's Mass*, the only light is that of candles, whereas in *The Owl Answers*, the light is scant as much of the action is set in a subway car: "All the three project stifling and fatalistic universes where central characters are doomed by their own guilt, the crimes of earlier generations, and a sense of extrusion from the normative world" (Fuchs 78). Death pervades not merely in the atmosphere, but is transformed into an innate part of the structure, imbibing a sort of "paralytic stasis" (Maeterlinck 98) a feature found in Maeterlinckian theatre.[36] Living in a fatalistic universe, haunted alike by violence and death, Kennedy's female protagonists make all attempts at transcending the static violence to escape this predicament. Therefore, despite the stasis, her plays implode violently, thereby distinguishing it from a Maeterlinckian drama: "Her stasis has the quality not of the void, but of an impacted wound that can never heal. The pain expressed in them is far more violent and tragic [. . .] than Maeterlinck's own metaphysical ache" (Fuchs 80). The power of great drama according to Maeterlinck stems not from external action but from "psychological action." The eternal vitality of the plays stem from the inalterability of their protogonists' predicament. Sarah is forever sandwiched between the White and the Black worlds. The rat children will forever be tormented by their own guilt.

One of the effective means through which Kennedy depicts the violence in her plays is through her use of imagery. Apart from a number of other negative images, blood is the major sexist image that runs through her works. In her *A Rat's Mass*, it is used as a symbol of guilt since it represents the incestuous relationship between the Brother and Sister rats. In *A Lesson in Dead Language*, the widening circles of blood in the White organdy dresses of the pupils symbolise the rites of passage for the adolescent African American girls. The white organdy dress of the students is a symbolic reference to the White culture, which makes the African American women bleed in multiple ways. Apart from the women's natural process of bleeding, the White culture has also been responsible for the various forms of violence inflicted upon the African American women, symbolised by the "ever-enlarging" circles of blood. Kennedy's symbolic use of the colour schema is effectively used in that it highlights the contrast between the proclaimed "purity" of the White race with the actual sense of guilt that it carries. Jeanie Forte sees blood as evidence of "history," since Kennedy's women are haunted by the geography of location and their histories. Sarah and Clara long for historical identities and when the struggle turns violent, there is a flow of blood. Forte mentions, how in this play, though the obvious reference is to menstruation it has a wider historical connection wherein it is linked with the violent histories of Caesar, Pompey and even Christianity. It is deeply rooted in their education. "The girls are literally taught to menstruate [. . .] learning the requisite social stigma [. . .] of being female" (Forte 165). Therefore, blood is converted by Kennedy as a metaphor of multi-layered definitions, wherein it assumes historico-cultural significance, as well as a biological process within a female body over which she has no control.

The latent violence in the lives of African American women and its psychological consequences are best highlighted in Kennedy's *The Dramatic Circle*, (1988) and *The Film Club* (1998). The latter is a monologue detailing the shuddering experiences of Suzanne as she waits for her husband David Alexander who has been to London. *The Dramatic Circle* is actually a dramatised version of the monologue *The Film Club*, its theme being the apprehensions of a young African American woman who waits for the return of her husband. Her psychic ailments like somnambulism, nausea, breathlessness, trepidations are similar to the ones experienced by Frantz Fanon's patients in *The Wretched of the Earth* (1961). Suzanne also quotes from the historical letters of Napoleon to Josephine to highlight the pangs of separation. Dr. Fruedenberger gives reading as a therapy to test the nerves of Suzanne. They are made to read from Bram Stoker's *Dracula*, which further gives a minute depiction of her delirious state of mind. The fifteenth chapter of the book abounds in animal imagery like "rat," "bats," "vampire" and "wolf." These images have an overwhelming effect on the audience, for they help us to have a glimpse of the intensity of the turbulence that surrounds the lives of Black women. The entire play is highly charged with emotions of latent violence. Napoleon's plans for an attack on Egypt are read. Dr. Freudenberger's reference to the passages where Lucy and Vincent remain punctured by the Dracula are also metaphoric representations of the violence which plagues the lives of African American women.[38] Their lives continue to remain in a state of tenterhooks, for, they hardly know what follows. Dr. Freudenberger's reading is loaded with images of violence like "puncture," "bite," "animals," "rat," "bats," "malignant species" "vampire" "wolf" (91). Suzanne even goes to Windsor Palace in the rain since it was there that Queen Victoria grieved for Albert. The troubled nerves of Suzanne are attempted at soothing with different music like "African music" (93), "piano Chopin" (100) and "Wagner chorus" (89). Along with these, the character's psychologically distressed condition is depicted through subdued background music like "breathlessness of Ocean" (88) "sound of rain" etc. which indicate her psychological stress. Violence in Kennedy is therefore deep and inbuilt. It may assume multiple connotations, but its presence cannot be denied. In Shange, the violence is apparent and more open as in the case of the Crystal episode or the sexual violence of Sean in *A Photograph: Lovers in Motion*.

Despite the tormenting violence and perils in their lives, the African American women continue to place deep faith in religion. In this way, Cheryl Townshed sees them as "agents of traditions" (Townshed 223). Sanchez, Kennedy and Shange all think on similar lines. In the third section of Sanchez's *Uh! Uh! but How Do it Free Us?* the Black woman is subject to multiple abuses. She feels crippled temporarily. The patriarchal White Christian God, for a moment seems to be unmoved by her condition. But realisation dawns on her slowly and she dreads to imagine her children groping in a spiritually anarchic universe. She is no longer only the mother of her unborn child. She is also the "mother of the sun" (213). Like her child, the sun also dawns out of darkness. The mystery of birth lies in darkness.[39] Sanchez's faith in God remains stable. Born into a Christian family, she had a short tryst with Islam and is back again into her previous faith, which runs through her works.

In a similar vein, Kennedy's autobiographical work *People Who Led to My Plays* stresses her Catholic upbringing. Apart from her references to Jesus and Mary, she strongly believes in the deeper racial memory of religion: "I learned that I belonged to a race of people who were in touch with a kingdom of spirituality and mystery beyond my visible sight" (82). It is true that the Africans come from a land of a religious past however "heathen" it may appear to the White people's eyes. The forced uprootment into an alien land had made them adopt the religion of the oppressor, which they have done with great fervour and zeal. This has been possible only on account of their ability to adapt religion as an integral part of life since times immemorial. In the same book Kennedy also mentions how she had always nurtured a hope that God, the protector always in his heaven took care of her, a faith akin to Browning's Pippa. (Kennedy, *People* 14)

The adoption of Christianity in an oppressed condition has therefore established a common bond between the race, and their Christ-suffering. Like Jesus having borne the sins of the world, the African American women are forced to bear the triple burdens of race, gender and class. Therefore, religion plays a major role in her plays. The Jesus in her *Funny House* may be dwarfed and hunchbacked; in her *The Owl Answers* Virgin Mary may be juxtaposed with Mary Magdalene, in her *A Beast Story*, the picture of the Virgin may be "doleful" and it is an ideal which the two women want to live up to, but still religion prevails. Kennedy undoubtedly questions it, but still at no point of time does she lose faith in it.[40] The faith that she reposes in Christ gains its strength from the fact that she had been initiated into Christianity since childhood, as revealed in her autobiography.

Shange's spiritual vision is clear from her debut piece *colored girls*. Despite the common woes of all coloured women, they move inwardly in a pyramid-like existence and the play also thematically moves from mundane to a higher level of spiritual existence.[41] For the first time, Shange spells out religion in Christian terms in her spell # 7, which probes deeper into the psychological existence of Layla who temporarily undergoes a phase of low self-esteem for having been born a Black woman. Home, mother, the printed media and even food offer her little solace, since her existential angst continues to predate her. Transformation comes to her in the form of religion when she hears a radio evangelist. As a contrast to her earlier colour in her life, there is the "brilliant" sun, a "brilliant" glow and she feels "bathed in gold," since, she feels "cleansed" and reborn spiritually, on the lines of baptism. While the seven women in *colored girls* move towards a greater emotional bonding through their pyramid-formation, Layla in *spell # 7* feels alienated from her own folks. Despite the contrast, Shange is sure of the fact that religion alone can serve as a panacea for all the travails of coloured women.

To counter the battering forces which have been tormenting them for centuries, the African American women have turned to myths to present an ideal vision of the universe. Kennedy has adapted the Greek myths of *Electra* and *Orestes* (1980) since they chronicled women's power.[42] Various forms of art and creativity are also used as a positive outlet for their pains. The transformation of agony into art has sustained them in an alien land. To the Africans, art is not basically divorced from life. It is an integral part of their lives. Benjamin Brawley in *The Negro in Literature and Art* (1930) mentions how aesthetics form the core of African American existence. The instinct for beauty, contends Brawley, being an innate part of the African psyche, has been transplanted into the new soil too. It may not confirm to the Eurocentric ideal of beauty but it is still beauty in its own right.[43]

The strength arises from the deep love for beauty adapted by the African Americans. It is "something deeper than the sensuousness of beauty [. . .] and that is the soul of the race" (Brawley 7). This innate love for beauty and art forms can also be clearly seen in the African American old melodies which have a plaintive quality. Suffering has added to the dimensions of depth and poignancy in their art. The sweetness of their songs is born out of their sad thoughts, sorrow being an integral part of their lives, especially for their women.[44] Painting, poetry, plays music, sculpture and every other art form has been created by them as an outlet for their pains and creativity.[45] The African American world of arts is replete with models who both enrich and guide the African American aesthetic life. Alice Walker highlights the crucial position occupied by models in the aesthetic lives of artists in *In Search of Our Mother's Gardens*: "The absence of models in literature as in life [. . .] is an occupational hazard for the artist, simply because models in art . . . enrich and enlarge one's views of existence" (4). Models, therefore, enlarge the horizons of the artist's inner life which form the core of the artist's creative genius. Walker mentions that unlike Van Gogh, the artist who suffered on account of the lack of artistic models, the African Americans have a plethora of models to choose from. She also reproduces Marilow Awiakto's poem on creativity.[46] The

Black poet here highlights the unseen turbulence involved in the process of creativity. Pain, agony and vicissitudes form an inseparable part of the process of the poet's imaginative vision which only enhances the quality of the work of art. Therefore, the African American women's turmoils in the new land have in fact, strengthened their capacity to create.

Unfortunately, the African American energies were born to blush unseen and waste their sweetness in the desert air of White America. Walker cites the instances of artists whose creative capacities were undermined. To Walker, poets like Toomer are "exquisite butterflies trapped in an evil honey, toiling away their lives in a century that did not acknowledge them except as the mules of the world"[47] (Walker, *In Search* 232). These "exquisite butterflies" had always been engaged in the process of artistic creation like spirituals, songs, lullabies, painting, drama or poetry which validate their inner lives and widens their public and private worlds' perspectives. (Walker 5). The medium may be songs, speeches, novel, prose, drama or poetry, but the deep pain in their works can never be questioned. When the existence of the African American women is in a continual state of peril they resort to various mediums of art to both highlight their grief and also ameliorate it through art.[48]

Poetry is one of the mediums through which Sanchez, Kennedy and Shange present their creative perceptions. This is because the cryptic nature of the medium is apt for them to highlight the multiple forms of oppressions and their macabre experiences. The charged language is actually in consonance with their harrowing experiences. T.S. Eliot in his essay "Poetic Drama" mentions how poetry is the best medium through which deeper emotions could be spelt out.[49] The multiplicity of the Black oppressive experiences and the intensity of their turbulent emotions find an expression through a fusion of the dramatic and poetic mediums. Moreover, the native African theatrical mode cannot be divorced from poetry, as successfully practised by writers like Soyinka, Ngugi and others. The African American women being the oppressed among the oppressed have therefore instinctively fused the two creative modes to lay bare their intensely abrasive experiences. In an interview with Zala Chandler, Sanchez acknowledges the influence of Nella Larsen and Jessie Fauset in her works (Braxton and Mc Laughlin 355)

Therefore, a synchronising of both the artistic mediums can be progressively traced in her three plays undertaken for the current study. From *The Bronx is Next* (1970) to *Uh! Uh! but How Do it Free Us?* (1975) she has moved towards the poetic medium with increasing intensity. As early as the 1960s, Sanchez like Kennedy was fusing poetry with drama to highlight the predicament of the African American women. Lois More Overbeck refers to the "concerto" like quality of Kennedy's poetic theatre which is blended with number of complex visual elements (Bryant-Jackson and Overbeck 65). Kennedy's plays attempt to shred the layers of the protagonists' consciousness. This needs a highly charged language and therefore poetry is the right mode. Whether the protagonists/audience is White or Black, none can actually deny the probing power of Kennedy's poetic theatre. The condensation of Kennedy's theatrical medium is not easy to grapple with feels Michael Kahn, a director of Kennedy's plays: "Every word for Adrienne counts. But when people ask me to describe her I always think of a poet with roots in our own unconscious and everyone's [. . .] I think that's the power of these plays" (Bryant-Jackson and Overbeck 197).

Elinor Fuchs feels that the unique poetic medium of Kennedy adds a sort of "dialectical tension" with which she projects a complex "layers of consciousness." Theatre materials are used by her to shred complex emotions and the multiple layers of "time and reality."

As creative writers, both Sanchez and Kennedy use symbols. Sanchez uses symbols like ghettoes, masks, costumes and stage setting to depict the ulterior motives of her character. Kennedy uses symbols like crows, ravens, corpses, blood, bald heads, and predatory animals like wolves, jackals, toads, worms etc., to depict the horror that shrouds the lives of the African American women. Although Sanchez experiments with different forms of plot and character,[50] Kennedy eschews them both and the plays reveal themselves through intense and cryptic situation which only intensify the sheer density of the characters' psychic states. Through her symbols, Kennedy's plays form an amalgam of the autobiographical, the archetypal and the mythic, like Strindberg's *To Damascus* (1898-1901), Strindberg being one of the earliest influences on her. As a poet of the theatre, her plays remain pregnant with symbols and her dense language conveys multiple levels of meaning. Although Shange also uses poetry on the stage, like that of Sanchez, her plays are more performance-oriented. According to her, poetry is aimed directly at a particular effect. In her foreword to *three pieces* she mentions how "they are theatre [. . .] which is an all encompassing moment/a moment of poetry/the opportunity to make something happen" (Shange, *three pieces* xi). Her plays are called "choreopoems" where words play a vital role, not only textually but also help in establishing a special relationship between the actor and the text. It transcends the mere organic existence and the physical utterance of the words. Robin McCauley sees the necessity of the actors to personalize their relationship to the text in order to facilitate an experiential and imaginative involvement with the text. (Lester 3-4)

The actress moves on to mention how Shange's works demand "that inner rhythms be physicalised" (Lester 6). The choreopoem itself has its roots in Africa. It is actually "an ancient [African] form—words and movement happening simultaneously [. . .] the uniqueness [. . .] is that the words are not separate over there and danced to [. . .] become one—intertwined" (Lester 4). The intertwining effect is necessary for the emotional internalisation of experiences. The power of her plays lies not merely in the act of consciousness raising, but in their ability to emotionally charge the audience to empathise with the plight of the African American people. Shange's plays are therefore extended moments of poetry. She considers this as the most authentic and creative medium to legitimise the collective problems of the African Americans and to highlight their psychological survival despite testing times.

Music is one such aid which has helped them to survive in trying times.[51] It permeates the plays of Sanchez, Kennedy and Shange. Music is one of the legacies of the African Americans. Despite the internal variations of their musical inheritance, music did serve as a unifying factor where men and women musically rendered their common sufferings.[52] Music and poetry have been so naturally integrated into the lives of the Africans that the West African people's speech was "full of figures [of speech]; hyperbolical and picturesque" (Southern 22). Although slavery modified their modes of existence, they still retained the innate love for music. They were different from the White settlers who first brought their Bible and then cultivated arts to compensate their aesthetic impoverishment.

Although the Whites curbed the African Americans of their rights to speak in their mother tongue and forcibly made them speak the English language, music still served as a primary means with which the African Americans could at least imaginatively bind themselves with the ethnic roots. As Angela Davis mentions in her *Black Women and Music* (1990), music was the only area which "escaped the devastating cultural genocide wrought by the slaveocracy on the lives of Africans who were involuntarily and forcibly transported from their homeland to the shores of North America" (Braxton and Mc Laughlin 4). The wretched conditions of the women made them freely vent out their griefs through songs. Davis mentions how "[a]side from lullabies [. . .] one discovers few gender distinctions in the songs of the slaves" (Braxton and Mc Laughlin 7). Given the prevailing conditions of the African American society, it is not surprising that women needed a creative outlet to voice their grief while simultaneously fulfilling their genetically inherited aesthetic longings. The continuous toil in the fields and homes of their White masters, the total conquest of their bodies by the Whites, the incessant turmoil caused to their psyche are all reflected in their spirituals,[53] the greatest among them being Ma Rainey. Gender oppression is also one of her major themes: "Moreover, the language of sexual love in Ma Rainer's blues metaphorically reveals and experiences a range of economic, social and psychological difficulties which Black people suffered" (Braxton and Mc Laughlin 13-14). As the African American women had both inherited and fused music within their inner selves, it is of little surprise that dramatists like Sanchez, Kennedy and Shange meaningfully integrate drama with poetry, music and dance.

In her *People Who Led to My Plays*, Kennedy refers to her seventh grade music teacher, Esther Clements from whom she learnt "the power and rebelliousness in music, words that burned [her] twelve year [. . .] old mind" (42). Poetry and music are structurally intrinsic to a study of her plays. The Paris production of *Funny House* on March 8, 1968 highlights the condition of Sarah along with music. Music throws a more penetrating light into the tormented psyche of Sarah since it shows "a young black [woman] imprisoned in the complexes and conditioning that the American society has created in her" (Bryant-Jackson and Overbeck 26). Kennedy's plays are ultimately as powerful as that of Le Roi Jones. The support of jazz rhythms only enhances the African American women's predicament, since "music plays in counterpoint to the role of the broken and cruel world in which we live" (Bryant-Jackson and Overbeck 6). Music was interfused with Kennedy's adaptations of *Orestes* and *Electra* (1988), the two plays also being important for the reinstatement of the patriarchal order after the Trojan War. Michael Kahn's direction of the play amalgamated music with the primitive and feathered costumes the predominant colour being orange, to create a cumulative effect of ancient drama. But, the most significant use of music arises in Kennedy's *She Talks to Beethoven* (1989). Beethoven is the White, male musician who attempts to give Suzanne some consolation in the absence of her husband and the festering wound in her hands which refuses to heal. The play is different from the bizarre, horrendous, fragmented world of a typical Kennedy play. The festering wound, the agony of separation and pain are all amply shared with a White male. Instead of frenzied language and horror-filled metaphors, *She Talks to Beethoven* offers calmer words of consolation and a soothing touch to the tormented protagonist. Rhythm, harmony, poetry and music pervade the play along with Ghanian stringed music, Beethoven's Fidelio and the sonorous beats of African poetry read by David on the radio, sound euphonic and not cacophonic. Kennedy's identification with Beethoven is both socio-political and psychological.[54] Like the photographs and cards of her private collection which Kennedy calls her "alter egos" (Kennedy, People 96), Beethoven also becomes Suzanne's alter ego, thereby rendering himself both male and female, Black and White, assuaging a Black woman in times of distress.

To Shange, music is necessary for the inner sustenance of the battered African American women. It is an affirmation of their racist and gender claims. Moreover music, song and dance are integral aspects of Shange's choreopoem. *for colored girls* opens with a song motif, woven intricately into the poem, until it culminates in the final pyramid scene. Shange admits of typing and composing verse to suit her conscious and unconscious rhythms since she admits of hearing "very particular rhythms underneath whatever" she types that affects the structure of the piece. "For instance, you'll get a poem that looks like a rumba on the page. So the structure is connected to the music that I hear beneath the words." (Tate 162)

Music authenticates the lives of coloured women in America and to present them in a positive light. The poem opens with the presentation of African American women as "ghouls," "animals" and "children of horror." The animal imagery is presented with the accompaniment of music, dance and spectacle. Musical terminology is also used to present the plight of oppressed women in America. For instance, the Lady in Brown defines the life of an African American girl as a "song with no singers / lyrics with no voices"; the life of an African American girl is like that of "half notes scattered without rhythm / no line" (Shange, *colored girls* 1). Music is one of the prime means through which the African American woman expresses their power to protest while simultaneously staking her territorial claim. Music and songs are also used to represent the play's movement from innocence to knowledge, from adolescence to adulthood. Childhood songs of African American women like "little sally walker sittin in a saucer" (*colored girls* 4) bring nostalgic childhood memories to these women whose lives are currently scathed by multiple oppressions. Harmony being the essential character of music, the writer employs it to blend the past joys with the present sorrows in a point counterpoint scheme. Along with music, dance as a medium transcends all barriers of communication since the vocally inexpressible emotions also find an apt expression through body semiotics. Together, dance and music sustain them. Being more spontaneous and natural, it is an effective response to the inadequacies of verbal communication and therefore a fitting reply to the culturally impoverished White Americans.

Apart from a sustaining effect, certain unique female experiences are also presented through music and dance. For instance, the Lady in Yellow's dance on the graduation night also alludes to the physical act of love making. Shange uses slow rhythmical movements to describe the moment of immense physical and emotional satisfaction and her first sexual experience.[55] Sechita on the other hand, uses dance to elevate herself to a higher level. This "Egyptian goddess of creativity 2nd millennium" is initially harassed while she dances in the bar. Men throw coins at her genitals, but she continues to dance not to satisfy male lusts, but to uphold her position as an African American woman. Ultimately, her dance endows her with a transformational power to alter the patriarchal perceptions of the oppressed coloured woman, thereby giving "her ritual performance, cosmic proportions" (Lester 46). By connecting herself with the ancient African rituals, she moves beyond the temporal and physical dimension in life.

Shange's strengthening of the position of the African American woman through music and dance continues in her spell#7.

(Shange, *three pieces* xiv) The sub-title of the play is a "magic trance manual for the technologically stressed third world people" (*three pieces* 19). The playwright contends that "music, song and dance are together of innate value to draw the most human and revealing moments from lives spent in non-verbal activity" (*three pieces* 19). In the play, the dramatist has innovatively used the minstrel mask in musical performance not only as a symbol of racist power, but also as an embodiment of the African American female power. Minstrelsy was not basically an African tradition, but a White male tradition written in a mocking imitation of Black dialect to jest about African American men and White women. The African American women were excluded from the minstrel shows even as objects of joke thereby indicating their rock-bottom status in the American patriarchal power play. Karen Cronacher bemoans the sad fact of African American women being "doubly excluded" from the scene and also "from the dubious pleasure of being on the joke." (Cronacher 178). Through the effective use of masks, Shange lashes out a fitting answer to the American patriarchal society, since it had hitherto been a White patriarchal site of domination with the Black male as its subject. Through this technique, Shange has established the absent subject position of the African American women by re-writing the legacy. In terms of its language, cultural traditions and representational systems, America continues to remain White, segregated and unchanged. Hortense Spiller's "Mama's Baby, Papa's May be: An American Grammar Book" (1987)[56] contends that the original theft of the African American body during slavery and its commodification still continues in a symbolic manner. (Spillers 67) Therefore, Shange successfully implants the missing subject of the African American women through her indigenous use of minstrel mask and music.

Along with music, magic is also used in *Spell #7* to project the triviality attached to the African American women's bodies. Lou, the magician, promises "scarlet ribbons" for women's hair, thereby subtly referring to the petty ways through which the African American women were tempted into sexual liaisons with White masters.[57] Music and dance form the core of Shange's *From Okra to Greens/ A Different Kinda Love Story*. She calls this poem "a feminist poem in motion." Music and dance prove to be commentative as in the Greek chorus since they complement in the delineation of the characters. At the same time, they are also used to bring out certain gyno-centric realities of the female protagonist. Shange calls the play "as real, as menses" since she understands that women's existence cannot be divorced from their gyno-centric realities. Most of the poems have been borrowed from her earlier anthology, *A Daughter's Geography* (1983). The term "geography" metaphorically refers to women's physicality which forms an intrinsic part of her psyche and emotional topology. Music and dance are used in this play to highlight women's realities like vaginal wetness, menstruation and sexual rights, which add a deeper dimension to the character of Okra. The play is actually a commentary on the plight of the African American women from the times past to the present. Okra dances her way out to enact the agony surrounding the women of her race. But at no point of time does she wallow in self-pity. The dance and music encapsulate to the audience the entire gamut of the painful experiences which the African American women underwent, while also simultaneously ameliorating the latent pain in her. Greens is a complementing partner who in his own way, tries to raise Okra's self-esteem. By deliberately labelling her as a "crooked woman,"[58] he provokes her to action. The crooked woman tries various forms of refuge like attempting to crawl back to the earth like into a mother's womb. Finally she chooses dance as the best form of survival, since her bodily semiotics express more poignantly her inner turmoil than the verbal medium.

The agony and horrendous experiences of the African American women, highlighted by these women dramatists are many. All aspects of their lives like motherhood, rape, pregnancy, abortion, sex and violence have been dramatised with the help of embellishments like music, dance, surrealism, symbolism, expressionism and absurdism. Language itself has been used by these women dramatists with a unique power-discourse. The language engages itself in an act of consciousness raising and dialogism.[59] It aims to usher a reformation of thought and feeling on the part of the audience who also become an integral part of the drama.

Feminist linguistic studies contend language as one of the prime means of assessing the position of women in society. Language is basically a socio-cultural mirror, reflecting the power play and the prerogatives of the society of whence it springs. Socio-linguistic studies lay bare the social control exerted by language over the weak. Women are as such subaltern species.[60]

Language is also used at times to trivialise women.[61] Moreover, even the linguistic convention to refer to both "generic man"—a word used to refer to both sexes—remains unacceptable to feminists: "Precisely because the word is used to mean both male people and people in general; being included under the rubric of man means losing their "linguistic identity as woman" (Adams and Ware 493). Feminists, therefore, protest against the patriarchal modes of using a language and the traditional role assigned to them. In her "Autonomy and Assimilation in African American and Feminist Literary Theory" (1985) Elaine Showalter discusses the need for an autonomous feminist discourse for the African American women whom Gallop identifies as the "left-hand of Feminist criticism" (Showalter 1). The freedom for women to use language to assert and voice their unique needs have also been felt by many writers like Dorothy Richardson and Virginia Woolf. When Joyce Carol Oates in her "[Woman] Writer: Theory and Practice" (1976) protested against the category of "woman" or "gender" in art saying: "Subject matter is culture determined and not gender determined, and the imagination in itself is genderless, allows us all things" (Showalter 45), many feminists rejected the notion of genderless imagination and have argued for gender-consciousness as an important criterion for women's writing. As Sandra Gilbert argues:

"If the writer is a woman [. . .] how can her sexual identity be split off from her literary energy?" Lacanian psychoanalysis also believes in the split in the female subject within language.[62] But the Lacanian idea of gynocentric discourse has been subject to much criticism since it also implies the fact that man forms the pivot of women's creativity. During the 1970s, feminist critics rejected the existing trajectories of creativity as insufficient to voice their protest and instead created a unique discourse which could both authentically present their gyno-centric realities while simultaneously making a territorial claim in the linguistic domain. In "Towards a Feminist Aesthetic" (1978), Julia Penelope Stanley and Susan J. Wolfe proposed that "the unique perceptions and interpretations of women require a literary style that reflects, captures and embodies the quality of our thought" (67). The French feminist writing of that period, while revolutionising women's thoughts to write with authority and power, also indicated women's genital and libidinal difference from men. Critics like Helene Cixous, Luce Irigaray and Julia Kristeva explore the possibility of a unique feminist discourse. This is aptly summed up by Elaine Showalter:

> Whether clitoral, vulval, vaginal or uterine; whether centred on semiotic pulsions (or) child bearing [. . .] feminist theorization of female sexuality / textuality and its funky audacity in violating patriarchal taboos by unveiling the medusa is in itself an exhilarating challenge to phallic discourse. (Showalter 26)

Poets like Anne Sexton through works like "In Celebration of My Uterus" (1969) strike a note of joy in celebrating women's bodies. Ten years later, Shange writes rather defiantly:

> I've decided to wear my ovaries on my sleeves, raise my poems on my milk and count my days by the flow of my menses. (*Nappy Edges 16*)

The obsession with bodies is deeper in the African American women since all their travails stem from their physical exploitation and whose bodies have always been degraded by patriarchal power play. It is a constant site of oppression and a permanent source of anxiety.

The power of Sanchez's discourse stems from her ability to use language with a raw intensity. While Sanchez's male counterparts in the Sixties like Baraka and Bullins were using forceful language to call attention to the racist issues, women dramatists like Sanchez explored the blatancy of the language to bring to the fore the African American women's predicament. The language may appear coarse to conditioned minds, but it is essential to lay bare the deeply embedded violence in the women's lives. Words like "Fuck you," "bitch," "Put his dick in me" may appear blatant to the mild audience, but they are essential to aptly lay bare the scum that surrounds these women's lives. The overt and covert forms of violence inflicted upon the race and the greater brutality inflicted upon the Black woman is aptly reflected in Sanchez's discourse. That nearly the major assaults on their selves are sexual is aptly summed up in the speech of the "Black bitch" who refers to her customer's phallus. The utterance may appear to be obnoxious to genteel minds, but it is appropriate to the blatant physical exploitation that the African American woman has undergone.

The language of these women focuses on the African American woman's identity being established only through the body. The Black whore in the second section of Sanchez's play *Uh! Uh! but How Do it Free Us?* mentions how she had forgotten her name since she was "just a body." Her body being the location for patriarchal power play, her identity hardly transcends it. Sanchez's language is also affected by Zora Neale Hurston, Nella Larsen and Jessie Fausset. She believes that her discourse would pave way for an oppression-free world.[63]

Kennedy's discourse may not present such a perspective, since her angle of vision is different. Her discourse is centred on the "self" and thus there is a non-linear and discontinuous form and a preoccupation with consciousness. Even her autobiography *People Who Led to My Plays* "seems [to be] driven by a search for an incandescent touchstone of [. . .] some primal image [. . .] that would heal the self's constitution" (Benston 115). The elusiveness is that of the dramatist who refuses any clear reference to a conceptual design beyond the text. Every Kennedy character is a locus of frustration, desire, expectation, pain and wounds. All these are best expressed through her powerful language. For instance, in her *Ohio State Murders*, the infanticide of her daughters by their father is narrated by Suzanne. The murder could be easily laid bare with action, but the shrouded nature of the narrative creates a deeper impact on the spectators, for, through imagination, the horror surpasses our boundaries of mediocrity.

In *Film Club*, the rendering of David Diop's poem which is laden with words like "vultures," "claws," "bloody monument" (Kennedy, *In One Act* 72) are suggestive of the horrendous psychic state of Suzanne. The poetic style of Kennedy does not permit the use of a large number of words. The utterances are cryptic and short but loaded with emotions, so that the plays continue to reverberate in the memory of the audience long after they have witnessed them. The language is further aided by the powerful theatrical effects like symbols, imagery, light and other stage props. Issues like rape, miscegenation, incest, pregnancy, abortion, menstruation, murder and infanticide all find a place in her plays.

Shange's use of language is closer to Sanchez's in its blatancy, but goes further in rejecting standard English itself in favour of Black vernacular and profanity. While Sanchez lays bare every emotion, Shange's works are charged with an emotional internalisation of experiences, while simultaneously avoiding the poetic condensation of Kennedy. With a wizard-like management of language, she aims to unearth "the richness of unconscious emotional responses to being alive" (Tate 151). In her debut piece *for colored girls*, she uses the word "lady" as opposed to "woman" in defining and re-defining her women, since, the title was hitherto referred only to women of the White race.

Their stigma and menial positions in life spring to a certain extent from their physical reality. Therefore, much of the language of the three dramatists centre around the body. In Sanchez's *Uh! Uh! but How Do it Free Us?* the two Black women Waleesha and Nefertia are obsessed with their bodies. While the big, fat and round Waleesha represents the African ideal of beauty, the slim Nefertia represents the western idea of beauty with her flat tummy. In fact, Kennedy's mythical adaptation of *Orestes* presents Clytemnestra symbolically projecting her breast to her son before she breathes her last. The body language indicates her maternal prerogative against his revengeful act of matricide.

In Shange's *for colored girls* the Lady in green is detested by her Black lover on account of her big thighs, loud laugh, manner of sitting, her un-manicured fingers and un-pedicured toes, her dark arm and imperfect voice. When she wins her freedom, she does not care to impress herself with her looks or her lady-like politeness. Her language signifies her self-actualisation:

> i want my calloused
> feet and quick
> language back in my mouth (Shange, *for colored girls* 52-53)

The Lady in Green deliberately uses the first person nominative, objective and possessive pronouns to emphasise the self and to vindicate her racio-sexist stance (Wisker 32). Layla in Shange's *boogie woogie landscapes* also initially falls victim to the fallacy of alterity. Later, she realises the futility of the act and tries to ascertain herself through her stylised body language.

For Shange's women, body language is one of the best means of communicating their pains, violence, joys and their gynocentric realities too. Okra in Shange's *From Okra to Greens* (1985) unabashedly discusses her sexual gratification and uses it as an effective means of combating male power. Indeed her language does reveal the innate contradictions associated with their gyno-centric realities. Her prologue to *See No Evil* mentions this: "Worlds like words for a woman who is a poet and a mother are confusing/overlapping, contradictory [. . .] & exciting" (iv).

Shange's contention that the difference in the male and female use of language stems from their environment and emotional make up and also the male's access to an "emotional vocabulary" which prevents them from feeling the way women do. (Tate 151-54) In the same breath she continues how men hardly communicate their feelings unless it is related to strong emotions or to "dominate" another human being. Their emotional topography being different, the language is also different.[64] Their unique use of language also gives the African American women writers, a territorial claim. It calls for a dismantlement of the earlier linguistic categories and a smothering of the King's English:

> We have to murder the King's English before it murders us [. . .] because that particular women's language can't speak for us. [. . .] I think it is important for us to never forget that language determines how we perceive ourselves and unless women and people of color take charge of the language we are nothing. (Lester 271-72)

Ultimately, her language (both verbal and non-verbal) becomes the instrument of vindicating her stance as an African American woman as it aptly reflects the histories and geographies of the bodies which had been neglected for centuries. Her spellings also have a system. Wisker points out how the habitual dropping of the final 'g' in the gerund and the contraction of auxiliary verbs and prepositions are used in all her plays like 'used te' and 'cda', 'hadda' (35). Practically, it facilitates the speed of verbal delivery.

Shange significantly uses only the lower-case alphabet in her works. She attributes this influence to Amiri Baraka and Ishmael Reed, and considers capitals as "boring" (Tate 63). But other reasons also seem to be suggestive. Basically, the lower case may infer to the inferior status of coloured women in a White world. It may also be used to eliminate power structures and therefore seems to be a move towards linguistic democratisation. Shange mentions how letters not only have a music, but also dance, thereby providing her a "visual stimulation," so that reading becomes not just a passive act but demands rigorous participation

(Tate 163). Her use of the first person pronoun "I" is rejected and instead uses the lower case 'i' which looks like "a ball dancing on a single jet of water—suggest flexibility and possibility of movement" (Wisker 36).

Through their discourse Sanchez, Kennedy and Shange lay bare, their perils and their tribulations in a multiply subjugated environment. Their present predicament which started from their racially enslaved conditions continues to be undermined by their sex and the lowest class strata into which they have been pushed.

Notes

1. Kennedy's statement "The Report on the Presidents' Commission on the Status of Women" in *New York Times* assumes significance from the fact that although he could recognise the immense potential of the African American women, not much was done to utilise it.
2. Ivan Van Sertima in *Black women in Antiquity* refers to "Lucy." In this book, the editor mentions archeological findings of Lucy—the mother of all mankind. Her age is three and a half million years, her height three feet, her weight sixty pounds and her place of origin Ethiopia. The editor feels sorry that not many facts are known beyond these.
3. In *Black Women in Antiquity*, Larry Williams and Charles Finch in "The Great Queens of Ethiopia" mention how during the centuries prior to the Christian era, there existed notable women like Ethiopian queens in Meroitic Cush known as the "Candacus," which means "Queen-Mother." Another important queen is the Falesha queen Judith who conquered and ruled Abyssinia for forty years. Makeda, the legendary queen of Sheba is said to have melted Solomon's heart to songs. Through her son Menelik, she is considered the founder of Solomon's dynasty. Diedre Wimby in "The Female Horuses and Great Wives of Hemet" mentions how women had political power. From time to time, there were a number of female horuses (a designation of a king, symbolised by a falcon). The king was supposed to be endowed with divine powers, and therefore a religious patriarch. In the absence of a male heir, the queen ruled

until a new dynasty was initiated. Queens were considered guardians of the royal lineage, and for this reason consanguinity was sanctioned. The Palermo stone lists the names of mothers since it was through them that dynasties were originated.

One of the most noted of the female horuses was Hatshepsut of XVIII dynasty, who upon the death of her father Thutmose I and because her half-brother Thutmose II was still young, declared herself a horus. She donned herself male attire, led the country on many commercial expeditions and constructed a number of architectural marvels in Egypt (Sertima 6-45).

4. Peter Hulme in his *Polytropic Man: Tropes of Sexuality and Mobility in Early Colonial Discourse* (1985) discusses a sculpture by the 16th century sculptor Stradanus. In this picture, Vespucci holds a banner with the Southern Cross in one hand and a mariner's astrolobe in the other. He stands looking at America who is a naked woman, half rising from a hammock. To Hulme, it enacts the entire drama of colonial conquest, since the land "lies there, very definitely discovered" (Hulme 17). The geographical discoveries following the renaissance and a number of art works also provided a "virgin" land to European men, waiting to be ravished by them. Sir Walter Raleigh who led the first English Voyages to Guyana described America as a country that "hath her maidenhead yet" (Loomba 78). America was meant to be deflowered by Europe. After the spread of colonialism, the native women and their bodies are described in terms of the territories to be conquered. Women perceived as territories meant to be conquered by men is also common with poets.
5. Angela Davis in her *Women, Culture and Politics* mentions how the U.S. soldiers often received instructions for their searching the Vietnamese women's vaginas with their penises. Sexual violence also existed under the fascist dictatorship in Chile when women's nipples were scorched, their genitals mutilated, and shock was applied all over their bodies. There also persisted gang rape, insects forced up women's vaginas and pregnant women were beaten with rifle butts until they aborted. (46)
6. See Jacquelyn Dowd Hall in *The Mind That Burns Each Body—Woman, Rape and Racial Violence* ed. Ann Sirtow et al. (cited in Curb 143-44). This is indeed a significant question from the perspective of the Black women thinkers since their sufferings also

usually went unrecognised like their very existence. Agony being gender-free, it is ironical that the Black patriarchal culture failed to take cognizance of their sorrow.

7. The Diagnostic and Statistical Manual of the American Psychic Association defines the multiple personality disorder:
   (a) The existence within the person of two or more distinct personalities or personality states (each with its own relatively enduring pattern of perceiving) relating to, and thinking about the environment and self.
   (b) At least two of these personality states recurrently take full control of the person's behavior. (Glass 40)
8. The words of Kennedy in the interview, "The Growth of Images: An Interview with Adrienne Kennedy," ed. Lisa Lehman, assume significance from the fact that much of her writing is highly autobiographical. Although Kennedy is not a product of a rape like Clara, her mixed heritage and the first-hand experience of the resultant confusion are highlighted through the conversation. (45)
9. Fecundity and fertility are two attributes of Nature. In antiquity, the woman was always identified with Mother Earth. Sex was therefore a positive sign of Nature's plenitude in her.
10. Reay Tannahill in *Sex in History*, mentions how around the 12th century AD, temple prostitution came to Europe. She mentions that there was a church brothel in Avignon, where the girls spent a part of their time in prayer and religious duties and the rest of the time serving Christian customers. At the same time the church was also urging all prostitutes to give up their evil ways, with Mary Magdelene as their example of a repentant whore who followed Jesus. Therefore, a number of Magdelene homes were built for foreign woman who showed signs of repentance. Moreover, Tannahill also cites that Mary Magdelene "was a composite of three women in the gospels, none of whom was a whore. However the church needed saints who could be models for the world's sinners, who could prove that penance was the road to salvation and even sainthood" (764). Kennedy uses the idea of a repentant whore to explicate the practice of forced flesh trade of the African American women.
11. Reay Tannahill traces the genesis of the Virgin Mary cult in Europe around the early 12th century. Earlier, she was just one of

the saints in the western Christian calendar. But around the twelfth century, Bernard of Clairvaux, the great French churchman reformed the Cistercian order, under whose influence, hundreds of new Cistercian abbeys dedicated to the Virgin, wearing White, were founded in Europe, honouring her purity. By the thirteenth century, poets confused the Virgin with the Lady, a stately and aristocratic figure. But in the fourteenth and fifteenth century, under the influence of the Franciscans, she was transformed as the compassionate mother of the poor. But during the counter-reformation of the latter part of the sixteenth century, the saintly Madonna and the secular Lady were two views of an ideal which in the opinion of the Church had no relevance to the human situation. The church did accept Mary as the Virgin, the Bride of Christ and the Mother. But there were certain practical problems, because, the ordinary uneducated Christians saw her as an ideal of womanhood, dictating the rightful position of women (Tannahill 765).

12. The circumstances in which the relationship between Anne Boleyn and Henry VIII grew seem to indicate a sort of an extra-marital tension because, Henry VIII was not able to officially get rid of Catherine of Aragon, at the time this relationship was prospering. This extra-marital connection could still be interpreted as a kind of rape, because what made Anne Boleyn yield to him ultimately might be his royal power. Like Elizabeth born to Anne Boleyn, the Bastard's Black Mother gives birth to Clara. Recent researches have revealed that Elizabeth was not a paragon of virtues, but had a number of lovers. That equates Clara with Elizabeth.

    In her *People*, Kennedy mentions the profound influence of Anne Boleyn on her: "How I was fascinated by her [. . .] how Henry VIII had imprisoned her, how she had walked the tower at night and how Henry had beheaded her. Soon Anne would become an image for imprisonment in a play, a confidante whom a character would discuss love and sorrow with." (118)

    Like this historical woman who was exploited to cater to the needs of the men of the dominant White race, Clara's mother is also exploited by her father who then denied any relationship with her after the rape and the turbulent conception.

13. While discussing time, Rushdie quotes John Berger who believes that man's life is shaped by two events "there is the event of his

biology and the event of his consciousness. The first is linear temporal. The second is simultaneous, multiform, protean" (385).

14. Rape is not just a matter of a stronger body violently asserting its weight upon a relatively, weak body. At the primary level, this is physical violence and nothing more. But, there is violence at a deeper level where the predator's consciousness of power inflicts violence on the victim's consciousness of powerlessness. Therefore, rape leaves a shattering impact on the victim.
15. The "darkness" which Freud refers to adds a sinister dimension to the issue of colour since the "unknown" is always bound to instill a sense of fear in the human psyche. Although Freud may not have consciously intended these ideas, his theories have been interpreted as an added factor for further enhancing racist bigotry.
16. *Genesis* 4:16, *The Old Testament*, states: "Unto the woman." he said "I will greatly multiply thy sorrow and thy conception in sorrow thou shalt bring forth children; and thy desire *shall be* to thy husband and *he shall rule over thee*" (my italics). As conception is possible only after the onset of menstruation, the menstrual blood must be associated with something horrible.
17. Simone de Beauvoir in *The Second Sex* catalogues a few taboos associated with menstruation like wine becoming vinegar and milk turning sour (180). Mary Douglas in her *Purity and Danger: An Analysis of the Concepts of Pollution and Taboo* mentions how among the New Guinea tribes, even boys fear menstrual blood since it would bring evil upon them (14). Women in the Lele tribes would not touch fire during menstruation, fearing pollution. (151)
18. Michael Foucault in his *The Use of Pleasure: The History of Sexuality*, Vol. 1, mentions how "slaves were at the master's disposition [. . .] their condition made them sexual objects and this was taken for granted—so much so that people could be astonished that the same law would forbid the rape of slaves and that of children" (215-16). Foucault contends that the Greeks defended these acts since this process facilitated the birth of children of good birth and also because the culture considered women as being passive and weak slaves.
19. The second scene of the second act of Shakespeare's *Julius Caesar* illustrates Calpurnia's pleas to Caesar based on her dreams. While Calpurnia's ominous visions of her husband's death instills a sense

of fear in her, the pupil's fear at the sight of the first menstrual blood paves way to feelings of anxiety and shame.

Kennedy, in her *People*, mentions the profound influence that Julius Caesar had made in her mind during her Latin lessons:

> Kennedy: Three years of Latin made me more interested in him than in any other figure except Jesus. Caesar, his campaigns, his armies, his assassination, the betrayal by Brutus on the steps of the Capitol. How I loved him. (63)

20. Toad: The toad appears in the play whenever the sexual instinct is rampant in the characters.

    It appears in the bedpost on the wedding night when the Beast Girl's husband makes sexual advances to her.

    It appears when her husband impregnates her in the fields.

    It appears whenever she dreams of her husband. Finally it is killed along with the husband, but its image haunts the Beast Girl. Toads as symbols of carnality and degeneration have been implied by Milton in his *Paradise Lost.* It is present when Adam and Eve first copulate in Book IV. It is also the ultimate appearance of Satan in his most degenerate state.
21. Crow: Compared to the toad it makes lesser appearances:

    It appears during their wedding service.
    In the dream along with the toad
    Ultimately when it is killed.

    The crow suggests evil, something sinister, dark, fearsome and an evil portent. On the whole, the floating corpses, toad and the crow together portend ominous visions of marriage to the Beast Girl.
22. The colour scheme of "black" and "red" suggests that the whole atmosphere of the wedding scene is vitiated by something evil (Black). The red sun suggests the knowledge of the happening. Red even suggests blood, the consequence of rape. The wedding is a metonymy for rape.
23. Like Clara and her mother in Kennedy's *The Owl Answers*, the mother and daughter in this play also cherish virginity and want to preserve it till the end. While Clara and her mother are deprived of it through pre-marital rapes, the Beast Woman and Beast Girl lose it in post-marital rapes. But while Clara and her mother would like to preserve their chastity to live up to the religious ideal of the Virgin Mary, the Beast Woman and the Beast Girl cherish it for its own sake.

24. The incidents that this theory refers to are labelled by Freud as "Miss Brauch" (abuse) or passive sexual experience. But the most frequent term he uses is "Verfuhrung" (seduction).
25. In 1971, Susan Griffin published a historical article entitled "Rape: An All American Crime." She says: "I have never been free from the fear of rape. From a very early age, I have thought of rape as part of my natural environment—something to be feared [. . .] like fire or lightning. I never asked why men raped; I simply thought of it as one of the many mysteries of human nature." (32)
26. Orgasm is an important aspect of feminine eroticism which has been discussed by both psychologists and sexologists alike citing Stekel's statistics. Simone de Beauvoir in *The Second Sex* mentions how only 4 % of women have orgasmic pleasure in the beginning while 50% attain it after weeks, months or even a year. She mentions the close connection between the mental and the organic, and the moral inhibitions in women which prevent the appearance of sex feelings. Women also resent power play and domination of men in the act of sex. Citing Stekel, she mentions how "women submit gladly when they feel that their partners do not wish to subjugate them; on the other and, when they feel that wish, they rebel" (415).
27. Sean in Shange's *A Photograph: Lovers in Motion* (Shange, *three pieces*) has inflated notions of his sexuality since he juggles with three women simultaneously. In one of his sexual pursuits, he makes Claire pose nude, indulges in various forms of sexual perversities and even threatens her with gang rape.
28. The "subconscious division" is extremely significant since it necessitates an acute awareness of Clara's menial predicament while at the same time highlighting the African American woman's inability to become like the icon of the dominant White culture.
29. According to Lacan, "The mirror phase occurs at a time when the child's physical ambitions outstrips his capacity, with the result that his recognition of himself is joyous in that he imagines his mirror image to be more complete, more perfect than the experience of his own body. Recognition is thus overlaid with misrecognition [. . .] (which) projects [. . .] itself as an ideal ego [. . .] which, when re-interojected as an ego ideal gives rise to the future genera-

tion of identification with others" (Bryant-Jackson and Overbeck 173).

30. Imamu Amiri Baraka's *Mad Heart* presents a character called mother who having caught the tree of American life turns intoxicated and feels lured to evil ways.
31. Baraka's *A Black Mass* presents a Black mother called Tiila who is predated by a horrible monster who turns Blacks into Whites. This is indeed a form of protest by the African Americans who wanted to reverse colour psychology since they wanted to depict White as horrible and untouchable whereas everything black is hailed. But the fact remains that it is the White colour which continues to be the dominant ideal even amongst a number of Blacks who prefer blonde skin and Saxonised features.
32. Jimmy Garrett's *We Own the Night* depicts a young dying Black revolutionary who does not wish to see his mother who is an Eve-like figure emasculating the strength of men.

    A traditional Blues song in the American Revolution runs so:
    I arn't good looking! and arn't got
    waist-long hair. [. . .]
    But my mama gave me something that'll
    take me anywhere. (Collins 126)
33. Wole Soyinka in his *Myth, Literature and the African World View* mentions how the Yoruba conception of life is different from that of the Europeans: "life, present life, contains within it manifestations of the ancestral, the living and the unborn [. . .] the Yoruba [. . .] fails to distinguish between himself and the ancestors. This gulf must be constantly diminished by the sacrifices, the rituals, the ceremonies of appeasement to those cosmic powers which lie guardian to the gulf. This type of ancestral continuity is the core of African American culture. The African American women writers emphasise the continuity of the ancestral presence on earth and also understand the traditionally and genetically transmitted strength for the women of their race" (59-60).
34. Violence has also been an integral part of the African American male theatre, as in Baraka and Bullins. But women dramatists from Grimke to Shange project violence but as being gender based and on account of their numerous oppressions.
35. John Killinger in *Worlds in Collapse: The vision of Absurd Drama* uses this phrase to mention how the absurd theatre derives its ab-

surdity from a discovery of this metaphysical emptiness and the resultant inner vacuum (25).

36. See, Maurice Maeterlinck, *The Treasure of the Humble*. In 1898 Maeterlinck published his essay "The Tragical in Daily Life" where he thought performance must go into internal drama and deal with the unknown and invisible forces of the universe, which forms the core of his "Static theatre." He wanted his spectators to delve into the "ominous silence of the soul and of God" (98).
37. The siblings wage a powerful war between their natural instincts which had led them to an incestuous relationship and the nurtured Christian values which prohibit the liaison. At a larger level it could also be viewed as a racial instinct at war with nurtured ideals since it was not uncommon among some African groups to marry siblings for various reasons. Also, if we believe in the Bible the first children must have been through the union of Abel and Cain with their sisters.
38. The victims of Dracula in this chapter are Dr. Vincent and Lucy, an innocent child. Like the vampire which saps the vitality of innocent people, the White imperialistic patriarchal power continues to deplete the Black women off their vitalities. In her *People*, Kennedy refers to the movie *Dracula* thus: "Even though he likes blood he was noble and lived in a castle. Because of his nobility he could turn into a tiny bat and kill and make people grow fangs" (25).
39. The book of Genesis in the Bible also associates chaos with darkness out of which arose light.
40. The ambivalent attitude of Black women towards White patriarchal faith is also explicated by Alice Walker in her short story "The Diary of an African Nun" (1970). She probes into the inevitable irony that marks the life of a recently converted African nun at Uganda as the "wife of Christ" and "a wife of the Catholic Church." Having been born in a remote village, she doubts if she is really "civilized by American missionaries." This is because, her present life serves as a contrast to her native "dance of life" she now feels "shrouded" in Whiteness. Her natural "kinky hair" is now cropped. Experiencing sterility, passion haunts her and she longs for the embrace of Christ: "Pale lover [. . .] will you not come down and take me? Or are you [. . .] less passionate than your father who

took but could not show his face" (40). She contrasts this barren marriage with her passionate nature faith, thereby making the entire process of conversion ironical.

41. The pyramid is an important spiritual symbol suggesting hope for all coloured and oppressed women. The different sides of the pyramid are fused upwardly suggesting a point of hope. Yet another perception of the figure indicates a single ray of hope equidistributed to all suffering women. The pyramid is also an important cultural symbol for the African American women as it connotes their racial links with the other world, the Egyptian mummies being kept inside them.
42. In *People*, Kennedy mentions how the Greek heroines like Antigone and Electra had special feminist connotations for her: "Their vision was chronicled for me to share two thousand years later. The conflicts in women were important. [. . .] [I] often feel the same distress and conflicts [. . .] they had felt it centuries before me" (88).

    Apart from its feminist connotations, these women present to Kennedy a universal conflict which human beings have been subjected to ages hence. Kennedy therefore presents conflicts, which are both particular and universal. In depicting conflicts, Kennedy acknowledges Tennessee Williams and Lorca as her mentors. In her interview with Lisa Lehman, she mentions her admiration for plays: "In which the person is in conflict with the inner forces, with the conflicting sides to their personality [. . .] being the greatest conflict" (47). Her plays therefore attempt at articulating such inner conflicts.
43. In *Wouldn't Take Nothing for My Journey Now*, Maya Angelou mentions how she prefers to wear bright colours, beads etc. Although her son hates it, she prefers to buy things which enhance her self-image (95).
44. That one's sweetest songs are born out of one's saddest thoughts may not be applicable only to the African Americans, but the fact cannot be overlooked that to the African Americans art had a special value in the diaspora since it not only assuaged their grief but also linked them with their ethnic homelands in a creative manner. What was impossible in a geographic manner became possible in an aesthetic manner.

45. Phillis Wheatley has addressed a poem to Scipio Moorehead, a young African painter. Meta Vaux Warric, a nineteenth century African American woman sculptor had displayed her works in various parts of America. Hazel Harrison, a pianist had held concerts in Germany and New York in the nineteenth century.
46. The poem runs thus:

    Motheroot
    creation often
    needs two hearts
    one to root
    and one to flower
    one to sustain
    in time of drought
    and hold fast
    against winds of rain
    the fragile bloom that in the glory
    of its hour
    afffirms a heart unsung, unseen.
    (Walker, *In Search* 230)
47. Honey is usually associated with what sustains, what sweetens and what liberates. But here, in a sort of metaphysical conceit something sinister is associated with it. When Walker speaks of "evil honey" and "getting trapped in it," she means that what ought to create, merely destroys. The creativity, by being denied an opportunity to blossom out is sought to be snuffed out.
48. What makes for a poet is not just an intense experience because intensity of feeling is likely to be chaotic and intractable. Therefore, when this intense experience is to be made explicit, the writer needs an exposure to the nuances of language which would effectively articulate what the creator wants to communicate. Therefore, there is a need for an African American artist to be familiar with the double tradition of the western and the African which would help him to be eclectic not only in times of experience, but in terms of expression as well.
49. In his "Poetry and Drama" (1950) Eliot mentions how certain intense situation in Shakespeare's *Macbeth* and *Othello* call for "beautiful poetry," which are "surprising, and yet fit in with the

character. Only poetry could do this, but it is dramatic poetry. That is, it does not interrupt but intensifies the dramatic situation" (81).

50. Sanchez's three plays present variations in terms of plot and character. *Sister Son/ji* for instance, uses a subtle African mode like the tom-tom and a retrospective technique to highlight the plight of the protagonist. *The Bronx is Next* uses the play-within-the- play technique, while *Uh! Uh!* could neatly be divided into three acts while using a number of elements from morality plays.
51. Eileen Southern in *The Music of Black Americans: A History* mentions how the various groups which had come to America like the Fon, Yoruba, Ibo, Fanti, Fulani and the Ashanti tribes brought various forms of music.
52. James Cone in *The Spirituals and the Blues* mentions how Black music "unites the joy and the sorrow, the love and the hate and the despair of the black people [. . .] and it shapes and defines black being and creates cultural structures for black expression. Black music is unifying because it affirms that being black is possible [. . .] in a communal context." (5)
53. A number of women earned a name for themselves in the realm of spirituals. Harriet Tubman led a large number of people through songs like: "Hail oh! Hail" or "Old Chariot" to make them realise the importance of freedom. Similarly, Sojourner Truth was also popular with her spirituals. But the greatest figure in the realm of spirituals was Gertrude Ma Rainey, popularly known as the "Mother of the Blues" (Braxton and Mc Laughlin 13).
54. It is socio-political in the sense that many writers of Kennedy's generation considered Beethoven Black, based on J. Roger's work *Nature Knows No Colour Line: Research on the Negro Ancestry in the White race* He contends that Beethoven showed traces of Negro blood (131). He further calls Beethoven's colour "blackish-brown" and devoid of Norcisized features. It is likely that Kennedy may have been influenced by these ideas. Psychologically, Kennedy's love for Beethoven was due to Miss Eichenbaum, her school music teacher, as explained in her *People*. Later, she purchased a foot-high ivory statue of the musician. Undoubtedly, Beethoven made an overwhelming influence on Kennedy's psyche.
55. Neal A. Lester mentions how bump is "a common free-style dance in the late Seventies wherein partners collided rhythmically and

usually at the hips [. . .] the word can denote thrusting the pelvis forward [. . .] as in a burlesque striptease" (43).

56. Spillers' article assumes importance from the fact that it views the body of the African American woman from the larger socio-political perspective since she was not only exploited through multiple means but also ultimately rendered invisible by the dominant White and the Black male patriarchal cultures. A re-definition of the inner spaces of the African American women through an assertion of their bodies was needed for establishing multiple identities of the African American women in both public and private spheres. When Spillers established the need for it, Shange seems to have answered it through her innovative use of minstrelsy.
57. In her *Ain't I a Woman: Black Woman and Feminism* hooks mentions how "[w]hite male slave owners [. . .] found out that slave women could best be manipulated by promises of a new dress, a hair ribbon." (48)
58. This poem originally appeared in Shange's *A Daughter's Geography*. The metaphor of crookedness is a visual representation of the various forms of mutilations inflicted upon the African American women. Social ostracism, cultural oppression, lack of understanding from men have had a heavy toll on their physical and mental health so that they are ultimately shapeless. They regain their positive self-esteem and gait through dance and music.
59. Bakhtin's idea of "dialogism" (1981) has gained immense importance in the area of feminist criticism. He contends that language is essentially "dialogic" since we always have an audience in mind when we speak or write. The term is defined as "a property of any discourse [. . .] every word is directed toward an answer [. . .] the word in living conversation is directly, blatantly oriented toward a future answer [. . .] it structures itself in the answer direction" (31).
60. Robin Lakoff in *Language and the Women's Place* cites a number of instances to prove the linguistic implications of being a woman. For instance, while both "master" and "mistress" indicate power, "mistress" also has sexual overtones (3).
61. Laren Adams and Norma Ware in their *Woman: A Feminist Perspective* cite examples like "women and children first" and "wine, woman and song" to prove that women have always been perceived as male appendages (12).

62. To quote from Showalter: "Women, because they lack the phallus, the positive symbol of gender [. . .] and the authority around which language is organised, occupy a negative position in language [. . .] women can enter into the symbolic life of the unconscious only to the extent she internalises male desire [. . .] that is to the extent that she imagines herself as men imagine her. (45)
63. Sanchez says: "I can see beyond the year 2000. I can see a period when you won't have oppression [. . .] we will be victorious. This belief comes from my understanding" (Braxton and Mc Laughlin 362).
64. Much of the emotional information of Shange's women centres on gyno-centric realities. From the graduation night in *for colored girls* to Okra's vivid description of sexual intercourse in *Okra to Greens*, every aspect of the African American women's emotional life has been vividly presented. Her women are never victims, but they try to find a voice for themselves. Like the French feminists, she sees language as reflecting the deeper gyno-centric realities of women.

Chapter 4

Class

This chapter interrogates the relationship between 'class and literature'. To analyse this is indeed problematic since it has almost become customary for researchers to probe into gender issues after the racist ones and terminate at that. 'Class' is generally a term associated with sociology, economics or politics, but few of us understand that it has a major role to play in understanding a literary work of art. A consciousness of 'class' (as distinguished from 'class consciousness', a Marxist and Weberian term) has been evident in literary creations since time immemorial. Chaucer, the father of English poetry, has in his prologue created an interesting array of characters who are conscious of their social class.

This section analyses the social class of African Americans, especially its women, its nature, formation and its nexus with issues like family, education, society, culture, value systems, mobility, conflict etc. It also probes into the issues that connect the economic form of capitalism and literary representations of the same. In situating the issues, this study will use Marxian and Weberian analysis of class since all later sociologists have been influenced and have modified one or both these thinkers. Moreover, this is not a work on sociology, rather it is a study of literature which has been primarily influenced by sociological concepts. These approaches help us to penetrate into deeper connection between "class" and the particular African American situation. "Class" remains intertwined with racism, since "colour" was a major pretext used by the colonisers to subjugate the African American race and its women had also to bear the additional cross of gender.

"Class" is a difficult term to define, since the term covers a wide gamut of disciplines like sociology, philosophy, economics, colonial studies etc. The term "Class" did not exist in ancient Greece where the general nomenclature used for such a division was "genos" meaning race or category.

This section would be initially divided into two broad sections (a) stratification and (b) class. Such a division is inevitable, since there have earlier existed modes of stratification which have been devoid of exploitative political relationships, free from mercantile and colonial modes of conflict, confrontation and hierarchies. "Class" on the other hand is a recent term used most often in post-industrialised contexts which connotes the multifarious forms of commercialism, gross imbalances, relegation of a few categories of human beings to a demeaned state and transforming them into lumpenproletariats (powerless individuals).

Stratification has been theorised by numerous philosophers in an ideal manner. The process of stratification is at least five thousand years old. But the spirit behind the ancient forms of classification is very different from the modern parochial notions of class which lead to vicious cycles of conflict, anarchy, concentration of material riches in the hands of a few and deprivation of the same for many on the basis of birth, race, gender and the like. The modern systems of classification have actually done little to practise the philosophical spirit of the systems of the classification while at the same time enforcing modes of differentiation. Historical evidence proves the fact that in between the thirty centuries which separate the recorded history of the ancient Mesopotamia and the appearance of Plato's *Republic*, societies had been stratified. So social stratification is at least five thousand years old.[1]

Although Plato was an idealist, he was also a patrician and an active member of the Athenian society, and was therefore aware of socio-economic realities. Even in Plato, a truly classless society seems to be an ideal.[2] His *Republic* states that most men are destined to follow and only a few are fit to lead. Although his ideal Republic was devoid of the extremes of wealth and poverty, social class divisions were a fundamental feature of his *Republic*. Since humanity's socio-economic life is based on an order of communes, each of these classes is expected to earnestly perform its duties. But the guardians of the states are important for promoting efficiency. In the first Utopia in literature, there is a balance between one's internal (personal) and external (social) duties and capabilities. In ancient Greece, the city states were trifurcated into three main groups: the citizens, metics (resident foreigners) and slaves. A distinguishing feature of Plato is his innate awareness of the socio-economic realities of his time and his consciousness of the idealistic nature of a truly classless society. His *Republic* contends that only a few are fit to lead, while a majority remains destined to follow. Social class divisions remain fundamental in his work, since the socio-economic life of the nation was based on an order of communes. Aristotle rejected the idealism of the *Republic*, but preferred the classical virtues of moderation, order and control, subtly defining it as the "golden mean." However, what remains curious to a modern scholar of research is Aristotle's prime distinction between "citizens" and "slaves." While the former (he believes) were ruled by "minds," the latter were ruled by "bodies." The distinction is probably enough for the advocates of social Darwinism to relegate the African American race to menial levels and elevate themselves to the position of rulers. Aristotle also makes a declarative statement that the "best political community is formed by the citizens of the middle class." (Jowett 43)

The above argument brings to our minds the issue of moderation which is undoubtedly an attempt at ameliorating the inequalities amongst the different classes and an attempt at levelling the concentration of power within a few social grids. The envisioning of the moderation of power had also been done by Biblical prophets like Isaiah, Jeremiah and Ezekiel who visualized a "promised land" which would ensure equi-distribution of wealth.[3] The biblical and religious advocacies of equi-distribution of wealth and power also assume "God" and divine order as being free from partisanship and class hierarchies. Such ideal views of a classless society also need to be doubted since the African American situation questions the justification of slavery and the power of the Whites who had subjugated, all the ethnic groups of America with a whip in one hand and the bible in the other. Therefore, the call of the prophets for the dismantling of power structures, class inequalities and hierarchies need to be taken not without a pinch of salt.

"Order" and "hierarchy" form the quintessence of Elizabethan thought. Tillyard's *The Elizabethan World Picture* (1943) focuses on the solid theocentricity of the renaissance and by extension the Elizabethan age. The idea of an ordered universe[4] is reinforced by him when he cites Ulysses' speech on "degree" in Shakespeare's *Troilus and Cressida*. The order is simultaneously "cosmic" and "domestic." The fixed system of hierarchies was modified by human sin and hopes of redemption. Some protests were also registered against such a divine order. Tillyard himself cites Machiavelli (Tillyard 16-18) to whom the notion of a divine order is repugnant.

In most probability, it is the absence of a hierarchy-free world that had led to the creation of utopias. The ideal societies of Thomas More or Bacon's *New Atlantis* envisaged a greater amount of independence. While More's work stressed on social equality, Bacon's emphasised on an unfettered intellectual freedom. The idea runs through Voltaire, Rousseau, Shelley, Godwin and the like. Rousseau has envisaged a total abolition of private property, and prefers a "general will" that foresees mass democracy. Ironically, although the French revolution successfully dismantled the aristocratic class, it could not but supplant it with the new bourgeois.

The ensuing pessimism gave rise to a new school of utopian ideals, with dreams of a classless society which was also embedded in the American folklore.[5] The American creed of classlessness has its deeper roots in the Puritan beginnings where democratic ideals have been cherished. Puritanism emphasised the hardwork ethic as the only path for ascension in America. As they believed that the place was a "Promised Land" they envisaged an ideal classless society where God's Own Kingdom could be established.** During the war of independence, the success of the Jeffersonian Republicans over the Hamiltonian federalists further reaffirmed the idea that there was really a path from "log cabin to White house" (Hodges 2). The "rags-to-riches" theme was epitomized by the successes of Andrew Carnegie, John D. Rockefeller, Jay Gould and J.P. Morgan. Ben Franklin also reiterated this theme in *Poor Richards Almanack*, so much so it became a uniquely American value system. Writers like Horatio Alger incorporated the success themes even into children's stories; but "classlessness" continued to remain a myth.[6]

The pilgrim fathers undoubtedly generated differences as is revealed in the act of marginalisation of native Americans from their own soil. The evolution of social class consciousness in America takes us to the crucial task of defining "Class." Given the practical impossibility of providing a unifocal definition of the term, a rough working definition of the same would not be out of place. "Class" is a more specific term implying deeper connections with the social and economic machinery of the nation. It acts as a prime determinant of the socio-economic status of a particular group of people:

> A class is a group of people holding a common relationship to the means of production, to the political power-structure (. . .) a relationship which necessarily brings it into conflict with some other group having divergent ideas and different interests with respect to the economic and political structures. (Loprealto and Hazdrigg 19)

The basic definition is essential to focus on the multiple issues which confront a particular group like its nexus with property, production and power while also not ignoring the inevitable conflict that the group may enter into with other groups.

The above analysis has brought to the fore a dual mode of differentiation. (a) The older concept of "order," "stratification" and "station" as evinced in Greek theology or even the Bible and (b) the later concept of "social class" with which this particular study is concerned which includes money, conflict, colonialism, exploitation and the deeper material interests of post-industrial and postcolonial societies. Its deepest concern is with economic ramifications and its impact on the society. Gary Day points out an interesting difference between the earlier term "order" and the latter term "class." He asserts that while the former term implied "an essentially harmonious view of society," "the new idiom of class was an expression of social conflict" (Day 6). The dynamism involved in the term 'class' which forms a stark contrast with the more static term "order" is clearly evident when we understand that "station" is derived from the Latin term "stare" or "to stand." It is significant to note that while the earlier concept of hierarchy emphasises division on vertical lines, the modern term "class" (especially the Marxian notion) divides horizontally.

"Class" is inevitably linked with other issues like status, economy, power, culture, mobility, conflict and other similar issues which would be delineated in the process of analysing the plays. Let us now analyse the major links established between 'class' and 'status', 'ethnicity', and its relationship with the production of literature at the general level, while focussing particularly on the African American women's situation.

The term 'class' attains special significance in the African American context since the history of the race in the White land originates with slavery. The slave condition has determined their class in a capitalist America while also not ignoring their ethnicity since their phenotypes, race, ethnicity and their economic powerlessness have culminated in the fact of the lowest status being accorded to them. Women have the additional burden of gender to bear. American power structure remains criss-crossed by a dual mode of stratification structures: one, based on economic power, political power and social status, regardless of their ethnic background and the other which also includes their ethnic and gender backgrounds.

The African Americans are exploited for the economic benefit of the White race. All forms of oppression involve both exploitation and control. Colonialism is a major political stream that vitiated greater differences between the coloniser and the colonised, deepening the class differences. Imperialism is a major system of power structure that has continued to exploit the Black race. Albert Memmi contends that the coloniser's privilege was "the essence of the colonial machine" (Memmi 1). J.A. Hobson in his "Imperialism" (1903) mentions how "the spirit of imperialism poisons the springs of democracy in the mind and character of the people" (Mac Arthur 15). He poses a powerful critique against imperialist modes of domination, by branding it as a "depraved choice of national life," which may only appeal to the "lusts of quantitative acquisitiveness" and "forceful domination" often adapted by the coloniser in his "animal struggle for existence." (Mac Arthur 15). While the dominant culture struggled to break free from the imperialist power structures of the Britishers, they adopted the same values to denigrate the African American race.

Capitalism has found a congenial soil in the White American Anglo-Saxon culture which was keen on exploiting the African Americans since they were bereft of all forms of power and position. No study of 'class' could start without a reference to Karl Marx since he has altered the twentieth century history. Marx is particularly important in having analysed materialism and its impact on human life. He had studied materialism for his Ph.D. in the writings of ancient philosophers like Democritus and Epicurus. His communist ideas grew out of his consciousness of materiality. Earlier, the communist element in the French Revolution which was led by Babeuf was suppressed by the Diggers and the Levellers. The "historical materialism" of Marx is elaborated in the *Communist Manifesto* of 1848. In 1848, Marx and Engels published their *Manifesto of the Communist Party* which altered history. They contend that "all history is the history of class struggle." Marx formulated the systematic theory of class differences. He was influenced by Hegel and Ricardo. The Hegelian idea of historical change emphasises the fact: "each stage of social life contains the seeds of the next life and that life is constantly developing in a way that could be comprehended through the abstractions of the philosophical intellect" (Durant 42). Marx felt that social inequalities paved way for human injustices. This is particularly, true of the African American situation, given the tertiary positions occupied by them in a capitalist set up. Marx remained ever concerned with the essential human capacity to move into higher levels of creativity, self-awareness and self-fulfilment. The work situation is also a domain for such growth. Erich Fromm's *Marx's Concept of Man* (1961) considers labour as "the expression of human life" since through it, "man's relationship to nature is changed, hence through labour man changes himself." (Fromm 16)

Such an upwardly transformative capacity is ironically missing in the African American situation on account of their dark histories, and it remains worse in the case of its women. The hard labour had ushered multiple modes of alienation[7] and crushed their very human identity. When the individual faces multiple levels of alienation, and when the body is the property of another, it is difficult to indulge in activities that promote inner-fulfilment. But it is also a strange historical fact that times of oppression give rise to powerful literature, like the Indian literature, African or Russian literature, to cite a few. It is of little surprise then, that African American women's theatre from Grimke's *Rachael* to Shange and beyond, has made significant strides in the direction of inner fulfilment, growth and is probably moving in new directions. Aime Cesaire's *Discourse on Colonialism* (1950) delineates the crushing effect of colonialism on Marxian lines. Cesaire's famous equation "colonialism = thingification" (Cesaire 2) is also not very different from Fanon who in *The Wretched of the Earth* contends that Marxism needs to be "always slightly stretched every time we have to do with the colonial problem" (Fanon 32). The fusion of race, gender and class issues has not found a place in Marx, but its impact cannot be undermined in the enslaved African American condition. In fact, the African culture had its native brand of communism as emphasised by Odinga in his *Not Yet Uhuru* (1967) wherein land, animals and children were viewed as not private property, but as "community property" for "the gain of the community as a whole" (Odinga 13). Therefore, much before the percolation of Marxist communism, the Black race had a native form of communism which must have facilitated its growth.

Marxism has a special significance for African American women who were worst affected by the colour-blindness of the bourgeois white women. They contend that under capitalism, the white bourgeois women will not experience the same kind of oppression that African American proletarian women will. Although poverty is not the unique problem of the African American women, the crucial point is that these women are exploited through non-economic ways also on account of the differences in structural set ups and unequal distribution of power between the Blacks and Whites. Moreover, economic vulnerability is more in African American women, as a consequence of which, the poverty is distinctly feminised, making it "the most crucial challenge facing feminism today" (hooks, *Feminist Theory: From Margin to Center* 100).

The peculiar fusion of race, gender and class issues is hard for even African American men to fully grapple with. Ann Foreman rightly feels that "men find relief for their alienation through their relations with women, for women there is no relief. [. . .] These are the essential structures of oppression" (Foreman 101-2). Connecting capitalism with the exploitation of African American women, Francis Beale throws light on the apathy of African American men. Despite the exploitation and enslavement strategies adopted by the ruling class, the African American men are slightly better placed since "they have someone who is below them, at least they are not women" (Cade 94). The crushing work domain of the African American women was much larger, since, they were exploited in plantations and in homes. The Marxist idea of alienation works at a triple level for African American women: (a) basically from the capitalist machinery (b) from the White world (c) from the Black male world. Therefore it is the material condition of African American women that decides their class. Marxian thought contends that Hegel's dialectic has turned topsy-turvy, since the Mind no longer governed the world, but social relations.

Max Weber, the German sociologist, explored the relationship between class and status. He contends that "property and lack of property are the basic categories of all class situations." To him, the relations between propertied and propertyless class was the nucleus of capitalism. An important statement of Weber seems critical to the African American situation. He contends that those groups which fail to have the chance of utilizing the goods and services that are available in the market cannot be classified as slaves in the technical sense of the term. A term better preferred by him is "status group" (Weber: 1948, 77-78). This statement has a definite influence of the theory of "alienation" as propounded by his predecessor Marx. But to label the African Americans as mere "status group" would further add to vagueness, since the race has had little status and access to power.

"Status" and "Class" are closely related. In fact, "status" predates the latter term. It was originally used as a legal term which placed an individual in a definitive status (Day 9). According to Weber, a class is a group of people who share the same life chances. He differs from Marx slightly in the sense that the individuals need not be always aware of their common situation. Only under certain circumstances do they become aware of their common situation, join together and act towards the benefit of their common interests, which Weber feels, becomes a "community." Weber also specifies the interconnectedness between class, status, economy and society, not in a mechanical way, but in a logical way with an intricate pattern of its own. Weber is also important in positing certain interesting variations in material culture. He is the first thinker to connect the American capitalist spirit with the protestant religious ethic in his *The Protestant*

Ethic and the Spirit of Capitalism (1930) and declares that it ought to have been in the "permanent intrinsic character of their religious beliefs" (Parkin 43), thus taking the American class consciousness to deeper roots.

The African American women's status was that of a slave. The politics of class becomes progressively complicated due to its increasing preoccupation with race, ethnicity and gender issues. The class situation of an individual determines one's power situation. The African Americans have been stripped of all forms of power: economic and political. Subjugation is therefore easy. The economic power acts as a prime determinant of the social, cultural and political power. Institutionalisation of power had led to hegemony and it assumes complicated revivifications since the mutuality of power operate(s) on the very bodies of individuals (Foucault, 1985: 55). The slave situation in America compounded the issue since the African American women were not the actual owners of their bodies. The literature produced by this body of women needs to pierce through the multitude of shackles to attain status, identity and exchange.

Class is also related to 'exchange relation' which, along with production is the "foundation on which the bourgeoisie built itself up" (Marx and Engels, cited in Day 12). The Marxian idea of exchange delves into the new economy based on money rather than land. Marx contends that the bourgeoisie pioneer a new form of economy based on monetary transaction rather than land. Exchange relation to Marx simply means the process by which commodities are exchanged for money. The African American women's situation forms an interesting paradigm in Marxist analogy, since they remain multiply exploited both in terms of "land" and "money." "Land" is a specific term connoting (a) the lands from which these women have been displaced and (b) the lands in which the women have tilled with little economic benefits for themselves. In the former, a limited ownership to the land was available in their ancestral homelands, ensuing a limited economic identity. But, displaced, and transported, their enslaved bodies and toil in the plantation have spurred the capital flow in a market economy.

The exchange relation has a bearing on the literature produced since as Gary Day rightly points out, both are "forms of representation" (Day 14). While money represents commodities, literature "reality" (Day 14). The modes of representation vary. If money focuses on the material aspect of reality from a utilitarian perspective triggering a greater need for it; the "reality" as represented in literature is a heightened one, sensitising its audience /reader to first comprehend the material conditions out of which the work of art is produced and apprehend the transcendental nature of the reality that art alone has the capacity to project.

This takes us to the basic relationship between class and literature. It undoubtedly has a major role to play in understanding literary works. The Marxian approach to literature throws light on the material conditions that lead to its production. Thinkers like George Lukacs, Louis Althusser, Etienne Balibar and Pierre Mackery argue from this perspective.[8]

It cannot be denied that in a world vitiated by strong economic power and print capitalism, literature also does not completely remain free from economic politics. Literature and economics are inseparably fused as against postmodern thinking that insists on their separateness.

Literature is also connected with 'exchange' since it heralds the victory of print capitalism over aristocratic feudalism. In such a process, the "self" as projected in literature undergoes a vast change. The "self" as projected in African American women's theatre is often agonised and clamouring to establish its identity at multiple levels. The various determinants of class like "status," "job," "power," "property," "mobility" and above all an identity of one's own find a place in Kennedy, Sanchez and Shange. The prime motto of the dramatists is to create a dual mode of consciousness raising both amongst the White and Black women of their respective social positions.[9]

African American women's identity was established on the basis of their arenas of work. Their work domain was larger than that of men, since they toiled in white homes too, apart from the fields. While white women were "angels of the house," and were [as Sojourner Truth mentions] "helped into carriage [. . .] and lifted over ditches [. . .] to have the best place everywhere" (Stanton 47). The sheer ruggedness of African American women's collective life is further highlighted from Truth's own life testimony: "Look at me! Look at my arm [. . .] I have plowed, and planted, and gathered into barns and [. . .] bear—lash as well and ain't I a woman?" (Stanton 48). The speech forcefully sums up the menial status attached to African American women and the tenacity of their spirit which helps them combat the challenges posed by capitalist White patriarchal cultures. Art is an effective medium for the three women dramatists to wage a war against cultural imperialism and coco-colonisation.[10] Their plays emanate from the material culture, but also transcend it.

A society's culture and value systems are reflected in the basic sociological unit called the "family." African American women's theatre since its inception has continued to grapple with this issue since its women are often the worst affected. The gruesome effects of capitalism have played havoc with the African American familial set-up. The power-politics of the capitalist society has created a chasm between African American men and women. Frances Beale in her "Double Jeopardy: To be Black and Female" (1968) mentions how "[c]apitalism had destroyed the humanity of all people, particularly [that of] the Black race" (Cade 90). Capitalism had subtly created a situation wherein the African American man was denied meaningful and productive employment, thereby leading to his frustration, violence and alienation from the members of his family.

The family has been the major theme of the African American women's drama since the times of Grimke's *Rachel* (1916). Despite the odds against their lives, we understand that Rachel, and her mother have been living together. Their lives seem to be normal until Rachel's father and her elder brother are lynched. Rachel ultimately renounces motherhood. Such adverse reactions towards the family are also seen in Georgia Douglas Johnson's *A Sunday Morning in the South* (1925) wherein a Black man is falsely accused of assaulting a White woman. The play centres not on the act of lynching, but on the family's reaction when they learn of the horrible deed. In *Safe* (1926) Johnson depicts a mother who strangles her new born baby when she hears the pathetic cries of a Black man being dragged away by a lynch mob. She chooses this way to keep her children safe. The trouble within the family at times overwhelms the characters. At times, dramatists like Lorraine Hansberry portray women protagonists made of sterner stuff since they are able to weather the hostile racio-capitalistic forces of the dominant culture. Mama in Hansberry's *A Raisin in the Sun* (1959) stands testimony to this. The play could be interpreted as a fierce struggle waged by the members of the Younger family to maintain their familial unit as well as to establish a space for themselves in a hostile milieu. The strengthening ties of affection between the parents and the offspring form a crucial emotional bonding. The play's strength derives from the courage of the Younger family to stay united, dream and achieve that dream in an inimical setting.

The children in the family not only represent a source of bonding, but also a special promise of hope to the race. The African American family continues to be plagued by the capitalistic, patriarchal White American society. While during the times of slavery, the family as an institution was thwarted by lack of stability and separation of spouses, the conditions have not turned much better in the post-abolitionist times. The families are assailed by low-income levels, unemployment, underemployment, poor health conditions, malnutrition, lack of proper shelter and assistance. To sum up, the families struggle hard for economic protection and security.

In Kennedy's *Funny House of a Negro*, three alienated individuals struggle hard to get together, but no understanding ever emerges between them till the end. The circular pattern of the play throws light on the powerlessness of these individuals to conquer the ever-thwarting forces. The symbols, the expressionist techniques and the stage direction throughout reveal their despicable positions in life. The cheap stage setting like the organdy dress, faded curtains and the faded tapestry are indicative of the weak economic status of this African American family which is also one of the major causes of their oppressed circumstances. In the beginning of the play, Kennedy mentions the cheap, ravaged curtain used that is "ghastly white" and "gnawed by rats" (Adrienne Kennedy, *In One Act* 2)

The not-too-expensive material and the gaudiness of the White colour along with the tattered finish suggest the fact that the house actually belongs to a poor African American woman who tries in vain to live up to the ideals of the dominant culture despite the squalour that surrounds her life. In the same scene, Queen Victoria and the Duchess of Hapsburg are described as being "dressed in royal gowns of White, a White similar to the White of the curtain, the material of cheap satin" (Kennedy, *In One Act* 2). These two characters being the selves of Sarah, their cheap dresses are once again, indicative of their economic poverty. The splintered selves of Sarah highlight the irreconcilable class differences between Sarah's Negro self and the White aristocratic selves with which she longs to identify. Throughout, she understands the fact that her Negro self cannot blend with the White aristocratic selves like Queen Victoria or the Duchess of Hapsburg. Still, she desperately continues to at least imaginarily associate herself with them. In one of her long monologues she mentions her imaginary life with Raymond (her White boy friend), and also with Maxmillan and Albert Sax Cohburg. At one point of time, she is unable to differentiate between the imaginary and the real.

> Negro: For as *we* of *royal blood* know, black is evil. (Kennedy, *In One Act* 5; my italics)

It is undoubtedly a clash of classes. Despite her acute awareness of the fact that she is only a poor black Negro, she cannot but long to associate herself with the powerful aristocratic White figures and their life styles. In spite of majoring in English like her mother and her father's major in social work, along with Sarah's talent for poetry, she is denied a passage into the upper White class. In fact, the agony of the entire family lies in the fact of a consciousness of the unchangeable conditions of their doomed existence.

The situation is not so different in Kennedy's *The Owl Answers* (1963) where Clara longs for an emotional identity with her father and is yet denied the same, despite her father being the richest White man in town. She inherits the status of her mother who is a cook. Her low "class" is actually a cumulative effect of her being Black, a woman and also her mother being a labourer. Race and gender also act as qualifiers of one's class apart from their economic situation. As a Black person she is denied mobility into the White culture, and as a woman she is not permitted into the patriarchal creative domains. Her intellectual progress is, therefore, stifled as is her spiritual ascension. Aiming to be Virgin Mary, she becomes Mary Magdalene and ultimately a nocturnal bird. The White aristocratic, patriarchal class refuses her entry till the end, thereby relegating her to the lowest animal status. The hierarchy of the Elizabethan great chain of being seems inevitably relevant here. As a human being, while she aspires to ascend to a higher level of spiritual existence, she is pulled downward to the animal level by the hostile racio-capitalistic forces which continue to exploit and subdue her.

The innate confusions of Clara that torment her is on account of her longing to identify herself with the culture of Chaucer, Shakespeare and Dickens, yet being denied the same. This is evident from the beginning of the play. The stage direction indicates her inner conflict when SHE carries handkerchiefs and notebooks that keep falling continuously. The external abnormality of Clara's character is consequential of an internal aberration. While she adores the cult figures of the elite White culture with the same intensity with which she would love her father, they only call her in evasion a "Bastard" (Kennedy, *In One Act* 7). They do not even permit her genetic and emotional identification with her father, since, she is diametrically opposed to their class: black, a woman and above all, only a daughter of a cook. It is not just the cult figures, but her father also remains guilty of emotional betrayal. He professes to be White; but beneath his White wig is an unmistakably kinky black hair, suggestive of his Black heritage. While he is clever enough to conceal his racial identity, Clara pathetically tries to cling to the mirage of Whiteness which he deliberately projects. THEY jeer at her. Her mother, though raped and deserted, still reminds Clara of her class:

> BBM: Clara, you were conceived by your Goddam Father who was the Richest White man in the town and somebody that cooked for him. That's why you are an owl. (Kennedy, *In One Act* 30)

Deprived and denied of any identity in the class of human beings, she is ultimately transformed into an owl.

Kennedy's *A Beast Story* also probes the lack of harmony between a Black mother, father and daughter. The surrealistic images in the play like floating corpses, dead blue crow, dead toad and the lack of proper light on the stage are all indicative of the lack of happiness in the domestic set up. The dead corpses are a metonymy for the deceased existence of the family members, since they are unable to counter the hostile racio-capitalistic forces working against them. The dead blue toad, the dead blue crow and the dead infant further reinforce their nullified existence. The play is ironically set in the "living room" since all the characters in the play lead a mummified existence. The infanticide is also a product of the actual hatred between the beast girl and her husband.

In *Funny House* and *The Owl Answers*, Kennedy presents class conflicts between the members of the same family. In *A Beast Story*, the mother, father and daughter are aware of their predicaments. All the characters are Black and of the same class. Still, they seem to be enacting the consequences of the injustices meted out to their race for generations. But *Funny House* and *The Owl Answers* presents complex class conflicts both at the external level as also the psychological level often lodged within a single human being. The only solution is transformation as in the latter play or being both alive and dead as in the former play. The continuous infliction of harshness at times saps the milk of human kindness from their breasts. Consequently, their lives are loaded with violence. The two post-marital rapes in *The Beast Story* are actually a result of the violence which is class-specific. The "discordant music" is indicative of the greater discordance among the family members. The "artificial pallor or perhaps artificially pale eyes" suggest a perennial lack of vitality in their lives.

An important metaphor used to describe their clammed existence is the "attic." The attic is the place where the Dead Human, (the husband of the Beast girl) lives, and sings lullabies for his dead daughter. Like junk which is usually dumped into the attic, the fruits of the sinful acts of the familial members are dumped here. The attic therefore symbolizes the darker sides of their personality and their confined existence. Like the mad woman who was conventionally kept in the attic, the Dead Human remains there with only the dead child as his company. As a contrast to the metaphor of the attic is the "Flat blue sky" which provides some light within the house. It is a world into which all the characters (both living and dead) yearn to escape. The Beast woman is glad that the sky is "blue," "warm" and "shallow" at the beginning of the play. At the end of the play also they rejoice in the warm sunlit sky which is only a passing phenomenon since there is "strange bright sunlight, then darkness" (201) indicative of the ever enveloping pallidity that surrounds their lives.

All the three plays present protagonists who struggle for familial identity. But the longing remains unfulfilled till the end since Kennedy's characters live in a vast and overwhelming universe out of which the characters find no escape. Like in an absurd drama, their predicaments remain unaltered till the end. Their feeble economic positions also mar their relationship which is reflected in their dialogues. None of these characters give long speeches. Their short monologues and highly telegraphic language are actually indicative of their inner fragmentation. For instance, Clara in *The Owl Answers* is intensely aware of the need for communication and the lack of it. Her father's class-consciousness and her awareness of it preclude any communication with him although she longs for it. While she longs for a meaningful dialogue, they engage in cold telegraphic discussions, indicating their apathy. The linguistic fragmentation implies their fall from their status as human beings towards a state of anonymity.

Sanchez's attitude to the familial set-up is different from that of Kennedy. While the latter allows her characters to be engulfed by the hostile forces, Sanchez's women are endowed with the courage to face the odds of the capitalistic society while not quitting the family. In *The Bronx is Next*, the Black bitch heads a household and enters flesh trade to fend for her two boys and herself. The White patriarchal consumer culture, therefore, views her body as a commodity to be exploited in a market economy. Devoid of humane qualities like love, understanding and companionship, she longs for a man who would give her all these. The woman endures all agony to give support and strength to her family. Similarly, the Black Woman in the third section of *Uh! Uh! but How Do it Free Us?* continues to retain the pregnancy, despite being jilted by her Black man and mentally prepares herself to forge familial bonds with her unborn progeny. Her weak economic position does not prevent her acceptance of motherhood. Sanchez therefore represents the resilient struggle undertaken by the African American women to maintain the familial bonds despite their poverty. Angela Davis rightly mentions that the family as a unit is never given up despite the struggle. In fact, it is a crucial "cauldron of resistance, forging and preserving a vital legacy of collective struggle for freedom." (Davis, *Women,*

Race and Class 74)

Therefore, the aberrations within the African American families are not "pathological" as described by the dominant culture but more often a consequence of the social, economic and political forces of the dominant culture which continue to wreck havoc on them. The most influential work on the study of the Black family and the role of Black woman was Frazier's *The Negro Family in the United States* (1966) which provided a historical and sociological account of African American family life. "The Moynihan Report" (1967) also blindly accepted Frazier's model and blamed the economic independence of women as a major bane among the African American families. Gutman in his "Persistent Myths about the African American Family" (1975) feels that Frazier did not explain the conditions he studied, as he had linked it directly to the nineteenth century slave experience. He felt that the "matriarchate," which developed during the slave period gained prominence after emancipation, and such families were prototypical of Black family life. Herbert Gutman's study of Black families in *The Black Family in Slavery and Freedom* (1976) suggests the breadth and more accurate details required for a proper understanding of Black families. He suggests that

i. There is little evidence of a matriarchal form of household.
ii. The typical household everywhere was a simple one, headed by a male.
iii. Sustained marriage among the slaves meant that they had role models of marriage and family which was available to the younger slaves. (356-79)

Gutman's work is important since it develops a dialectical analysis of black women and their families and also because he has minutely analysed the African American family structure at specific historical moments. The underlying contention behind all these studies (with the exception of Gutman) is that female independence of male authority and her economic control is perceived as being a destructive family norm. But the African American women dramatists have negated this norm since most of their plays present dynamic women who single-handedly face the issues confronting their families in a brave manner. The families struggle hard to fulfill their basic needs. One of the fundamental needs of any family is housing.

The African Americans were lodged in ghettoes during the post-emancipation period. These segregated territories actually did little to enhance the power and prestige of the African Americans who remained bereft of all forms of succour. These infernos of squalour give unmitigated agony to its inhabitants. The ghettoes are not actually measures of upliftment of the White power. Rather, they are also a method of patterned discrimination. The basic assumption on which the ghetto was built was that Blacks were inferior to the others. The African Americans occupy a disproportionately large segment of the bottom of the occupational structure. As Gutman mentions, "The Negro is in the service caste for many people, and they are comfortable only so long as Negroes wear overalls and a blue shirt, or an apron or work dress" (Gutman 306).

Apart from segregating them in terms of jobs and means of economic sustenance, the ghettoes themselves are places of grime: "There are more rats than there are Black people in America. The combination of inadequate facilities for [. . .] garbage [. . .] and indifferent city sanitation collection and result in fast-growing rat population" (Young Jr, 29-30). Whitney Young Jr. further mentions that when the bill came to the constitution in the 90th Congress, to check the rat menace, it was jeered at (30). If the men in such cluttered spaces felt humiliated at their desperate situation, the position of their women was worse, since, apart from trying to cater to the needs of these large families, they often had to bear the brunt of their men's anger as they were the only inferior beings over whom the men could exercise their power. Sonia Sanchez's *The Bronx is Next* dramatizes on the squalour of ghetto life. The play opens with a vivid description of ghetto life in Harlem, with long narrow streets and garbage. (79)

Sanchez has ironically set the play during Harlem Renaissance, implying that the Renaissance had actually done little to alleviate their plight and class levels. The play centres around the process of evacuation which the Black cops undertake as they get prior information of the ghetto planned to be burnt down by the Whites. The attitude of the White cop towards the filth and dirt that surrounds ghetto life is found in his description of the place as being "kinda hot and awful" (Sanchez, *The Bronx* 80). The inhabitants appear like "cattle" to him. The White cop never realises that it was his race which had created it. Charles calls these "shit houses." The 1968 report on National Advisory Commission on Civil Disorders in America highlights the White society's deeper implications into ghetto life. "White institutions created it; White institutions maintain it and White society condones it." (Young Jr. 71) It is beyond the comprehension of the cop to believe that human beings could even live in such a dismal state since there was absolutely no word of *respect* there. (Sanchez, *The Bronx* 80; my italics)

The idea of survival in this place of filth is beyond the discernment of the White race. In a place devoid of any protection, shelter and respect, lives the protagonist who practically tries to meet all her family's needs by resorting to prostitution. She is sexually exploited by both Black and White men. She is thoroughly aware of the fact that she lives only a peripheral existence, as she is a part of their unrealistic world whereas the White women form their "reality," thereby pushing her to the lowest class. Survival becomes a crucial issue for her, since, being deprived of all forms of protection, she is the sole parent of her sons. The external squalour of the place like the dim light, poor ventilation, the unhygienic conditions notwithstanding, she survives the odds with extreme tenacity. Whitney Young Jr. rightly observes that "in the ghetto it is a major effort simply to survive" (Young Jr 30). The ghetto is, therefore, transformed into a metaphor for race, gender and class in which the women suffer the most. Charles's admonition of her sums up her lowest class predicament in an effective manner:

> Charles: *you ain't got no rights here.* Just shut your fucking White mouth before you get into something you wish you wasn't in. (Sanchez, *The Bronx* 80; my italics)

The speech aptly sums up the predicament of the African American woman who continues to be silenced by the exploitative capitalistic-patriarchal forces which predate her forever.

Although ghettoes are segregated territories where the African Americans alone live, surveillance by the higher White classes continues there also as illustrated by the mock-lynching scene. Surveillance transforms the ghetto into a virtual panopticon wherein the Whites exercise their power. Role-reversal is enacted. Roland uses the language of the Whites to admonish the Blacks and to make the White cop understand the depraved status of the African Americans:

> Roland: You black, you a nigger we caught running down the street—running and stealing like all the niggers around. (Sanchez, *The Bronx* 81)

Despite their efforts to erase the distorted image of the "stealing nigger," the hegemonistic dominant culture continues to brand and subjugate them. Although lynching had been technically abolished in the post-emancipation American society, it continued to exist in modified forms. Robert Weidman's "The Anatomy of Lynching" (1993) indicates how the victims of lynching are perceived as being "culturally abject," and "thoroughly negated, dehumanized and incapable of return." (Fout and Tantillo 224) Lynching, both in the physical and psychological terms is inflicted on account of the sheer impotency of its victims. Towards the end when the ghetto is set ablaze, they realise that they have just missed death marginally. It is a historical fact that outfits like the Ku Klux Klan were involved in the acts of burning ghettoes during the nineteen sixties. The burning of the ghetto towards the end of the play signifies the ultimate triumph of the dominant class in suppressing the underlings.

If Sanchez projects ghetto life in a direct manner, Kennedy

depicts the same in a highly metaphoric manner in *A Rat's Mass*. The play abounds in metaphoric representations of the stark realities of ghetto life. The protagonists are half-rats, rats being the major menace in ghettoes. The play is set in a "rat's house" with a "red carpet" and dim twilight setting. (Kennedy, *In One Act* 55). The decadent lives of the African Americans who live in ghettoes are probed. A major metaphor used in the play is the "attic." Like the "attic" where the vermin, insects and human beings live in harmony, the African Americans are also treated as junk.

The voices of the siblings turn gnawing and they are actually "two pale Negro Children" (Kennedy, *In One Act* 55). Descriptions like "dark sun" and "worms" are indicative of the appalling life of the ghettoes which provides little privacy for the adults, and may also result in incestuous relationships. Like the rats multiplying in their holes, the African Americans are biologically productive, aggravating their woes and negating the solace associated with homes. They are gripped by insecurity when they imagine Nazi invasions and instead prefer self-obliteration. Akin to the Nazis who were triggered by notions of racial superiority, the White Americans have induced a fear psychosis which mounts in the siblings until it reaches its zenith when the Brother Rat utters: "America wouldn't be safe long." (Kennedy, *In One Act* 56). The violence and injustice meted out to their race are therefore seen spreading everywhere, in all European countries along with America. The poetic nature of Kennedy's theatre allows for a fusion of the rat's house with that of the attic beams which permits us to have a deeper insight into the life of the ghettoes.

Kennedy uses a number of images to contrast the present life of slime with that of a utopian ideal. The images of innocence like sunflower, lemons, swinging-in white birch trees, spring and Easter suggest hope and idealism. The present grimy, class-wrought existence is filled with images of dead worms, rats, blood, Nazis and dead rat babies, delineating the no-escape predicament into which they are enmeshed:

Sister Rat: I bury my face in the sand so I cannot bear the rats that hide in our attic beams. (Kennedy, *In One Act* 57)

The ghetto is a fixed structure, the creation of the imperialistic-capitalistic culture which has crippled the physical and psychological health of the African American women. They wage relentless wars to merely survive. Survival becomes a crucial aspect of the lives of African American women since they are at the vortex of numerous powers oppressing them in a concomitant manner The highly paralytic ghetto structure, therefore, becomes a battleground wherein numerous capitalistic, economic, imperialist and patriarchal forces ravage the psyche of women.

Alienated at various levels, women are forced to act as bread winners of their families. But this is not an easy process, since the dominant culture, along with their own men folk brand such women as "matriarchs" while they strive hard to make their ends meet. The "Black bitch" mentions this in *The Bronx is Next*: "Man, I am surviving" (82), hinting at the rugged existence forced on her by the capitalistic forces that work against her. Marxist feminism perceives prostitution as a class phenomenon since the economic situation of the unemployed or under-employed women explains why they sell their bodies to the economically powerful.[11] It is an aspect of the general system of prostitution which labourers undergo. Strictly speaking, the relationship "falls not on the prostitute alone, but also on the one who prostitutes" (Tong 64). Viewed from this perspective, Charles, the White bourgeois male and the Black man who desert her after giving her two children in *The Bronx in Next* are merely consumers who prefer to use her body as a commodity which creates a repulsive self-alienation in her. It is also "appalling." Since what she actually sells is "what is closest to her: her body, her sexuality. So under capitalism a woman's sexuality becomes her commodity." (Tong 64)

In Kennedy's *The Owl Answers*, Clara is forced into flesh trade despite her hatred for it. Sandwiched between the richest and the lowest of parentage, Clara is thrown into the trade by an apathetic culture which refuses to understand her inner needs on account of her low class. Not only is she raped like her mother, but her class also determines her profession as a prostitute. She is stifled not only physically but also intellectually since, despite her love for England and English literature, she is imprisoned in the tower of London and denied access into the White elite patriarchal world of Shakespeare, Chaucer and William the Conqueror. Clara's socio-economic-cultural mobility thus remains paralysed forever. Neither Black nor White, rich nor poor, powerful nor powerless, she is ultimately pushed into the oldest profession for sustenance. All her pleas fall on deaf ears. The conflict between Clara and her father is the consequence of differences in perception. While Clara claims her father at a purely emotional level, his attitude is one concerned with economic and class dynamics. When class consciousness occupies the primary position, human relationships remain ultimately oppressed. When she pleads to be identified with her father, he only reverts rather coldly and orders her imprisonment. (Kennedy, *In One Act* 32)

Conscious of his affluence, the father refuses to accept Clara because of her inferior status. By ordering William the conqueror to "lock" her, he displays the attitude of the White capitalistic patriarchal society which continues to resort to form of topological lynching since the inner spaces of the African American women continue to be constricted. The tower of London is, then, a modified ghetto, a site in which African American women are continuously lynched in multiple forms. Denied all forms of consolation, Clara turns to her Black man for understanding and warmth. But he is more interested in her body than her inner needs. The chasm in their levels of perception is revealed in their dialogue thus:

> Negro Man: And what exactly do you yearn for?
> Clara: Love or something, I guess. (Kennedy, *In One Act* 35)

Her reply is beyond his apprehension since he continues to undress her. He is the consumer who has paid to enjoy her commodified sexuality. "Love" at both the human and spiritual levels is beyond his understanding. Therefore, St. Paul's Chapel is transformed into a Harlem hotel, signifying the fall of Clara from a spiritual to a mundane level on account of the harsh economic system which makes her pursue her quest for identity. While she has longed to emerge as a Madonna-like figure she is reduced to a trader of flesh in cheap Harlem hotels.

The oppressive cultural milieu in which Clara survives makes her long for an identity with her father, thereby imbibing an Electra complex. The father emerges as an important figure for her to identify with, assuring with emotional bonding while also providing her with the socio, economic and cultural identities she badly needs in a capitalistic-consumer culture. When the human world fails, she ultimately moves into the animal world. Rosemary Curb cites Hortense Spillers who contends that slavery did not only transform the African American woman into an embodiment of carnality, but also made her "the principle point of passage between the human and the non-human world" (Curb 147). Spillers continues to mention how blackness remains vestibular to culture in the great chain of being since "the black person mirrored for the society around her and him what a human being was not." (Curb 147)

Therefore, the conscious rejection of Clara at multiple levels has urged her to escape into a non-human world which she supposes would be free from the petty class-consciousness of the human world. The tyranny of power leads Kennedy's Clara to a loss of identity, history and ancestry and metamorphosis is her chosen path for freedom from the tyranny of power and exploitation. Kimberley Benston calls the search for the familial past "genealogical revisionism" (Bryant-Jackson and Overbeck 151). This is crucial towards the understanding of the African American predicament since the dominant culture, with its overwhelming influence attempts to distort the history and identity of the helpless African American women. They overcome it through their creativity. Benston continues: "All of Afro-American literature may be seen as one vast genealogical poem that attempts to restore continuity to the rupture [. . .] imposed by the history of black presence in America" (Bryant-Jackson and Overbeck 151). The women's creative milieu of the African Americans can therefore be seen as an act of resistance against the oppressive forces which crush them and as important landmarks in Black genealogical revisionism. Both Sarah and Clara pursue Eurocentric traditions and understand the impossibility of attaining them. Jeanie Forte mentions how Clara and Sarah are actually "historicized" and not just "victims" of the White oppressive forces. In fact, they are "literal embodiments of resistance [and their] search for identity [. . .] must create new grounds for debate" (Bryant-Jackson and Overbeck 159). Whether Sarah and Clara have attained the identities they had sought or not, they have definitely generated a renewed interest in the African American women's struggle for identity.

Apart from prostitution, rape is also one of the major forms of physical exploitation of the African American woman, based on her inferior status. Susan Brown Miller insists that "all rape is an exercise in power" (Miller 267). The term power here refers to the entire spectrum of power like imperialism, colonialism, capitalism and the patriarchal forces which played havoc on the African American women's bodies. Angela Davis mentions how it would be a mistake to view the rape by the White man during slavery as an expression of his sexual urges. Rather "Rape was a weapon of domination, weapon of repression, whose covert goal was to extinguish slave women's will to resist, and in the process demoralise their men" (Davis, *Women, Race and Class* 23). Rape is one of the earliest forms of violence inflicted on the African American women since they were brought to the new land. It has been a prominent theme in many of the African American women's writings. Harriet Jacob's *Incidents in the Life of a Slave Girl* (1860), Maya Angelou's *I Know Why the Caged Bird Sings* (1969), Toni Morrison's *The Bluest Eye* (1970), Gloria Naylor's *The Women of the Brewster Place* (1980), Alice

Walker's *Color Purple* (1982), are just some of the works where rape is a major punishment meted out to African American women. Rape also involves force. Force is one of the intrinsic factors that have worked on the African American women ever since they were brought into the White man's land. Black women did not willingly submit towards being exhibited. Often lashed, they had no choice in the form of labour they were not involved in nor were they given freedom in choosing their sexual partners. June Jordan's "Poem about My Rights" graphically reveals the parallels between sexual violence and the political nature of neo-colonial violence against people and nations.[12]

Citing this poem, Angela Davis mentions that it would be difficult for us "to grasp the true nature of sexual assault without situating it within the large socio political context" (Davis, *Women, Culture and Politics* 38). The African American women's sexual politics is linked to the power wrested with the dominant culture as also with the Black patriarchal culture which has internalised the White notions on Black womanhood. Sex is a biological category while gender is a social construct. Gender is socially constructed as an interplay of both the socio-cultural factors and the individual consciousness. One of the reasons for the rape of the African American women is their weak economic and social position. Being Black and women they are bereft of all forms of protection. The women of subaltern status like African Americans, Dalits and also women of the third world countries continue to be raped since, "like their nations, their bodies are also considered fit territories to be exploited" (Davis, *Women, Culture and Politics* 37). These multiple connotations enhance our understanding of the issue within a larger economic and political contexts. For centuries, the Black women have remained as objects of pornography and also "thingified" to summarise the idea of Cesaire. A chilling instance of this is the body of Sarah Bartmann who was exhibited by the nineteenth century European men and women at fashionable parties in Paris.[13]

At the core of White consciousness is the fact that the Black women and men possess biological characteristics different from the Whites which make them inferior to them. Alice Walker in her "Coming Apart" (1981), goes a step further in mentioning how while the White women were objectified, the African American women were reduced to animal status. It is only animals which can be sold out, exploited or consumed. Such treatment being meted out to the African American women also reduces them to the animal class.

In Kennedy's *Funny House*, Sarah fears rape. Her mother had conceived her through a rape. So deep is the fear of rape which has been instilled in Sarah that she shudders the moment of her conception like her mother who detests "the black beast" who raped her. The redundant term "black beast" carries the cultural weight of bestiality (Curb 144). Strangely, both the rapist and the raped are reduced to the class of animals. This is also one of the reasons why images of beasts like wolves, toads, ravens and jackals haunt Kennedy's plays. The difference between the rape of Sarah's and Clara's mother lies in the fact that while Sarah's mother is raped by a man of her own race, Clara's mother is raped by a White man. There is an interesting variation in the rapist and the raped being referred to as animals. While the rapist is labelled so in order to highlight the unbridled carnal instinct, the raped is also presented so to spotlight on the perception of the dominant section on the more vulnerable ones. In Sanchez's *The Bronx is Next*, the "Black bitch" is threatened of rape by Charles. His forceful act of kissing is more an act of vengeance proving his masculine egoistic power. Instead of empathising with the woman of his own race, the internalized values in the Black man make him hate and commodify his women.

The theme of the African American women's coming of age as a time for both celebration and fear is also found in Shange's *for colored girls* (1976). Shange acknowledges the fact that women can fall prey to the brute force of any male "fulla his power" (39) since the rapist aims at subduing the woman and controlling his environment. Marie M. Fortune mentions that rape is only "pseudo-sexual" since it involves a higher quantum of power play which is non-sexual like anger and aggression. "The desire to dominate and control the victim is the primary motivations of the rapist" (Fortune 8). Under capitalism, the subaltern status of these women placed them at the mercy of the capitalistic patriarchal forces which exploited them to gratify their sexual needs and also for the cheap production of labour. In short, every African American woman is reduced to her sexual parts like Sarah Bartmann.

Shulamith Firestone's *The Dialectic of Sex* (1970) uses Marxist ideology to make an analogy between the oppression of workers and women. Work is crucial to workers since it shapes their personal identities; with women, their sexuality is crucial towards the establishment of their personal identities. Firestone contends that with women "what is most her own is most taken away" (Firestone 229). This may be applicable to poor White women who at least assumed the freedom of "owning their bodies." But the African American women were not allowed such a "luxury" as the bodies also belonged to their White masters during slavery and to Black men after its abolition. Shorn of status, power, money and even of their value as human beings, the African American women's bodies underwent what Toni Morrison labels as a process of "Fetishisation" (Morrison, *Playing in the Dark* 68).[14] The process of the African American women being objectified and nullified becomes complete. Black women were brought to the U.S. for two economic reasons alone: to work and to produce workers (Dill 72). When the production of labourers was not up to the expectation of the White employers, they were often raped for the production of free labourers. Ironically, many such bastard children had no claims to property and therefore it is in consonance with the American socio-political norm that Clara is also called "the bastard" in Kennedy's *The Owl Answers*. Despite her rich White father, she does not inherit his class nor is she allowed socio-cultural mobility, leaving her with nothing to inherit.

The protagonists in the plays of Sanchez, Kennedy and

Shange are acutely aware of their impotent predicament. They struggle hard to rise above the allotted class. One of the basic forces which the African American women had to combat against was the myth of synonymising the African American women with sexual promiscuity. By assuming a different level of sexuality for all Blacks and by mythicising their sexual capabilities, Black women were synonymous with sexual freedom. They contend that every African American woman was a slut, and therefore sexual exploitation of such a woman was not a sin. As Fannie Barrier Williams mentions, "Slavery made her the only woman in America for whom virtue was not an ornament and necessity" (Lerner, *Black Women* 165). The moral code of the White culture always had different scales to judge the morality of the White and Black women. As an anonymous letter of a Black Woman states: "The negro woman's immorality shows more plainly than her White sister because she is poor and ignorant. The negro girl is too poor to hide her shame" (Lerner, *Black Women* 167). Such negative notions of African American women get internalized among the Black races too. Clara in Kennedy's *The Owl Answers* is also called "bastard"; the characters in Sanchez's plays are called "black bitches" and "black whores." Even their own men consider them as objects of enjoyment. While the dominant White culture usually views the African American women as Jezebels, Sapphires or as char women, they were hardly respected on par with the elite White women. The aristocratic White women were called "Ladies," a term connoting the power, status and the class to which they belong. The African American women on the other hand were denied such a term of privilege because they were considered fit enough for menial chores alone. To checkmate the popular notions of negativity and inferior status attached to the African American women, Shange calls all her seven women "Ladies" in her play, thereby countermanding the lowly notions attached to African American women to combat the power of the hegemonistic dominant culture.

Education is a potent weapon with which they can effectively battle against the all-pervading power. This is the central theme in Archie Shepp's *Junesbug Graduates Tonight* (1969). Although the African American family present in the play is aware of the fact that America is as much Black as it is White, it is unable to assert itself on account of its poor education. The sacrifices made by the family to educate Junesbug are many. The sister even resorts to flesh trade. Still, the night of his graduation is important to all the family members, especially the women, Jessie and Celia.[15] As Celia mentions, for the subjugated Black race in America it is a "pumpkin turn[ed] into a prince" (King and Milner 35), since the African American race has a long history of being denied the privilege of education. This is one of the ironies of the Anglo-Saxon race which was always concerned with education. Even way back in the earlier centuries, Sir Thomas More's *The Book Named the Governor* (1531) dedicated to Henry VII was a plan for humanist education. Milton's "On Education" (1644) did emphasise its needs. John Eliot's *Apostle to the Indians* was a primer to teach education to the American Indians. But the same was denied to the African American race, which belonged to a lower class. The struggle for universal education in the nineteenth century bred polemics since they opposed the idea of education to the oppressed classes like the African Americans.[16]

Like their British counterparts, the Southern Whites in America also initially justified their opposition to equal suffrage on the grounds of the low literacy rates among the American Blacks.[12] The occasional educated, self-reliant African American was actually hated more than the uneducated one. This is because the dominant class is always slow to bestow power on the underprivileged as education is a prime source of privilege. Education is a potent weapon which would ultimately deliver the African American families from their confined existence towards knowledge. Amiri Baraka's *Junkies Are Full of SHHH . . .* (1968) lays bare the underground activities of the African Americans which is a consequence of their lack of education.

Sonia Sanchez's "Black bitch" in *The Bronx is Next* is forced into becoming a commercial sex worker. Still, she envisages a good education for her sons. Answering a question of Charles, she explains her maternal vision of educating her boys into formal education as well as her instillation of humane value systems that may teach them to respect their women folk. It is important to note that the African American mother does not merely aim at literacy. She perceives it as a wholesome and holistic purpose which would ultimately widen their mental horizons and make them love their women who are actually stratified as the weakest among the weak. Education to her is a cultural pursuit, since culture alone informs a society with the foundation for all facets of life.

The African American women's pursuit of education is a path littered with thorns as depicted by Kennedy in *Ohio State Murders* (1992). Suzanne Alexander, the protagonist of the play is belittled at multiple levels in the course of her educational pursuits. The play weaves Kennedy's racial and class politics in an intensely personal mythopoeic dramaturgy. It depicts the restrictions imposed upon the African American women at the Ohio State University at both the physical and intellectual levels. The territorial segregation imposed upon the weaker sections by the dominant one prohibits the students from walking on "High Street."[17] The isolation causes immense agony to those alienated. Blauner moves on to mention how the power strategies worked in these forms of segregations "to cope with the systematic restraints placed on the minority by the majority, to curb their mobility. Robert Blauner uses the term "mobility" at multiple levels to throw light on the manifold segregations they face. It is a reference "both to the mobility of individuals in physical space and collective mobility in socio-economic status. Restrictions on the freedom of movement [is] part of [. . .] all forces of oppression [and] are particularly strategic in racial systems. Perhaps this is because the modern racial order [. . .] merged from movements that were color patterned. [. . .] primary movers were Whites, people of colors were [. . .] moved" (Blauner 36).[18] Suzanne and

Iris Ann are therefore prohibited from walking on the oval, are not invited to the parties by the White girls, and also denied sharing the dining tables of the White girls. The restrictions are also intellectual since Suzanne is not given admission in the English literature course, despite the positive remarks of Prof. Hampshire regarding her abilities to empathise with Tess. By denying Suzanne the course she most prefers, the dominant culture further segregates her psycho-intellectual terrain apart from the physical untouchability that it maintains.

In post-emancipated America, the domineering cultural forces have adopted strategic measures to restrict the mobility of the African Americans. This was implemented through their economic dependency, ensured through lack of proper opportunities in education and jobs in order to cripple them forever. Suzanne needs the course in English literature not only for an inner fulfillment, but also to cater to the needs of her twins, since Hampshire deserts her after a subtle seduction. The prohibition of Suzanne into the course is therefore the basic step towards disempowering the entire family. The only courses which were offered to exploited Black women like her were elementary education and courses on teaching children.

Education then becomes one of the prime means of exploitation and control of the African American women by White capitalistic patriarchal forces. In order to generate privileges, certain sections are exploited for the sake of which they are controlled directly or indirectly. Education in the hands of the dominant class is one such device of control. When some groups are excluded from equal participation in a society and its value systems, the power-sharing groups stand automatically elevated in class. Therefore, while the students of the dominant culture enroll themselves in the courses of their choice, Suzanne is doomed to the position of a "stock-girl" in a neighbouring departmental store. Therefore, the fate of the deserted Tess and that of Suzanne almost run parallel (although Tess is poor White) so much so that Prof. Hampshire's comments on Hardy's novels actually apply to Suzanne also. The subtle contours of intellectual belittlement also affect Iris Ann, another African American girl who "could play the violin beautifully" (Kennedy, *Alexander Plays* 40). Not only is Iris Ann segregated from the Whites, but together, they are accused of stealing the watch of a co-student from the women's lavatory. The suspicion falls on them on account of their vilified class and race. The incident shakes them as they hail from educated bourgeois families. The suffocating experiences at Ohio make Suzanne long for a world free from tyranny. The Hardyian description of Wessex like the open hills and are therefore transformed into a larger metaphor of a bigotry-free world. As a contrast to the vastness of the universe, the perceptions of the educated elite at the Ohio State University are extremely narrow and intolerant, which is rather ironical in one of the world's most ardent professors of a classless society. As a reaction to the reality of existence, Kennedy feels that universities should have "sacred geographies" which remain in consonance with the doctrines that the societies uphold.

Although the American constitution promises equality and freedom to all, in practice it is much distorted since the ethnic minorities like the African Americans are denied their intrinsic rights. These covert forms of discrimination leave deep impressions on Suzanne's psyche, since she winds pink plastic curlers in her hair till the scalp bleeds. The gruesome act is not only the consequence of her physical alienation but also that of her being euphemistically branded a "whore" by Prof. Hampshire who impregnates her. She is multiply exploited for being a Black, a woman and also of a lower class. Her "honor" remains violated not only because she was Black and a woman, but also because of her menial positioning. The "consciouness" bequeathed by such acts in these women is different, since it slowly emerges as a collective consciousness of the Black feminist standpoint.

Kennedy's liberal use of words like "abyss," "bespattered," "cureless," "misfortune," "enemy," "alien host" and "battle groups" best describe Suzanne's predicament and the indignity she faces in a hostile environment. To combat these negative feelings, Suzanne hangs an impressionistic painting of the port of Marseilles in her room. The bright colours like blue, red and yellow stand a contrast to the dullness that has penetrated into her life ever since her arrival at the university. Under the influence of Cezanne, she makes drawings of the corridors in the dormitory "outlined in red ink and muttered definition of rooms, stains, color, skin" (Kennedy, *Alexander Plays* 61) which throws a deeper light on the agony she faces in the inimical surroundings. The condensation of painting as a medium only intensifies its effect on the audience since it effectively depicts the cumulative effect of the multiple jeopardies she faces in a segregated society. Suzanne is bewildered of the blood spots on her pillow cases which are symbolic of the toll taken on her physical and psychical existence by the capitalistic White culture. Thomas F. Pettigrew in *A Profile of the Negro American* (1964) mentions a number of mental illnesses like psychosis, schizophrenia and fits of laughing and crying as found among the African Americans. Although the symptoms are also found among the Whites, Pettigrew contends that the distinct differences in the mental illnesses between the two groups are "traceable to contrasting patterns of environmental triggering [. . .] distinctions of social class and poverty on the one hand and racial restrictions on the other play critical roles in mental illness" (Pettigrew 78). These two factors combined with their gender discrimination are a major cause for the psychological disturbances which many of Kennedy's female protagonists face. Suzanne is anguished over her powerless predicament. Sarah in *Funny House* (1962) is also tormented over her powerless situation. Her selves actually stand a foil to her powerless situation: while the Duchess of Hapsburg and Queen Victoria are seats of political power, Jesus symbolizes White male religious power and Lumumba stands for Black resurgence. But the irony is that a mulatto like Sarah being neither Black nor White, neither poor nor rich, stands impotent to possess any of these powers on account of her midway existence. Clara Passmore can also never pass for more since she is forever sandwiched between the two races and classes, thereby leading her to a schizophrenic existence.

Class, therefore remains an important factor in shaping one's psychological health, and the lower it is the greater is the risk of disturbances. Hollingshed and Redlinck's research on *Social Class and Mental Illness* concentrates on this factor and they mention how "psychosis, particularly schizophrenia has a higher incidence among the poor than the prosperous" (Pettigrew 78). Educational opportunities also being denied to them, they have little means to maintain their psychic balances. In Kennedy's *A Lesson in a Dead Language* the poor African American adolescent girls repeat in a monotonous fashion the lessons relevant to the powerful White patriarchal culture which is an instance to prove the futility of class-conscious, White male-centered education to the poor African American girls who seek emancipation through it. In Shange's *for colored girls*, the Lady in Yellow's graduation night is a moment of triumph for her, since it literally indicates her movement from the uneducated to the educated class and therefore a passport towards a greater class mobility. The ordeals of the African American race only begin with education. It is aggravated when they pursue jobs and placements. Brought to America as mere field labourers, they have been actually disreputed as being fit only for menial jobs which lack the refinements of elitist culture. Hence Sanchez, Kennedy and Shange present cooks, school teachers, dancers, acrobats, whores and domestic helps as characters, since these people reflect a predominant African American reality. Thrown into the world in an unequipped state with little tools of survival, they struggle hard to meet their ends.

Life for African American men and women is rather an uphill task. They are actually cast into a harsh world criss-crossed by the ideologies of consumerism, social Darwinism and hierarchal forces. The fittest and the privileged alone survive whereas the others are powerless, relegated to the position of desiccated individuals. The iron law of White prevails most specifically in the area of work and jobs since it is in the labour market that the privileges are most pronounced in a strategic manner more specifically in the industrial capitalistic scenario. Labour force is not exclusively Black. White immigrants have also entered the field but under slightly better conditions than the Blacks since it has ensured them upward class mobility, apart from ensuring their migration from the rural to the urban areas (Blauner 24). Although the Mexican Americans, Puerto Ricans and the Irish immigrants also form a considerable labour force in America, the African Americans suffer a high rate of unemployment and marginal employment. Therefore, they fit into the Marxian conception of "industrial reserve army" which meets the system's need for an "elastic labor pool" (Blauner 23). From this we can conclude that the White workers have a major share in jobs which are secure, clean, highly skilled, involving authority and the possibilities of promotion.

The class divisions in the field of employment are focused by Shange in her *spell #7* and *A Photograph: Lovers in Motion*. spell#7 (1979) throws light on the socio-economic limitations of being African American artists in a racially, sexually and economically segregated society. Eli's monologue in the beginning of the play calls for the dismantling of all forms of division and instead prefers indestructible "beauty" and "strength." The evocative quality of the monologue and its visionary nature is actually a product of the rugged realities of the African Americans' struggle for existence.

The first act of this play lays bare the stark racio-economic divisions that plague the African American society. The women in the play are denied roles like those of Mother Courage and Lady Macbeth and are instead offered menial roles of props to the main characters. Such modes of segregation from the mainstream cultural tradition make them create an ideal world which is free from all forms of bigotry. Eli's monologue affirms the claim that the African Americans have the power to create their collective psychic inscapes when the socio-economic restrictions are overwhelming. The "kingdom" is free from the Whites' dehumanizing representations of the American Blacks. Rather, they are depicted as individuals who have a sense of personal hygiene and can appreciate poetry and wine. The choice of the word "kingdom" affords a nostalgic world where imaginative powers prevail. It is like an African American utopia which is free from all forms of gradations and bias. There exists an equi-distribution of power since the territory is owned by every African American individual, thereby ushering a notion of a classlessness. Ironically this also implies the impossibility of attaining such a perfectionist state since it fails to take cognizance of certain practical realities of governance. The territorial segregation becomes totally indispensable in the psychological realms of the African Americans since it countermands the socio-economic alienation imposed upon them. They seek to establish an ideal world of peace, while they actually seem to belong nowhere even in the entire continent of America.

Having earned the citizenship of the segregated kingdom, the characters, especially the women, dream of overcoming class restriction. Lily, for instance, fantasises playing the role of Rapunzel, the fairytale heroine with long blonde hair and ivory skin or that of Lady Godiva[19] (Shange, *three pieces* 26). She is innately conscious of the fact that despite her frantic longings, she can never become a "Lady" since the term refers to the elitist status accorded to the women of the White Anglo-Saxon culture. Therefore, the luxury of being involved in activities like "disco," loitering in "local trains," being involved in telephonic chats and slow dancing with strangers are all not a part of her life. Her low economic class excludes her from such privileges. The sources of their identity are different. Rochelle Gatlin mentions how while White middle-class women generally choose "gender" to establish their identity, women of different racial group are forced to choose a "multiple identity" often involving "class," the interaction of all three contributing to the complexity of their existence. (Gatlin172-73)

The social identity of Lily in the domineering White culture is that of a low-domestic labourer or a faithful mammy. Still it is a life of vibrant activity. But the wings fantasy transports to dreams of "Chaka Khan," "chocolate from graham central station," "olive hair food" and "Posner's vitamin E" which form the routine of elitist White women. Natalie also fantasises a life of luxury wherein she longs to wake up to behold herself as a White girl and live a carefree existence of not being bothered about work. (Shange, *three pieces* 47). Therefore, even passivity remains a luxury for the African American women whose lives are constantly put to grind by the capitalist machinery. Life for them remains an endless struggle wherein they ought to be strong physically and psychologically to face the endless battles of existence. The fantastic world of Natalie therefore ironically reflects the inferior class of the African American women as she moves in the imagined consciousness of the White bourgeois women who waits for her cleaning lady to arrive. (*three pieces* 49)

In the post-emancipation society too, the sundry and menial jobs are mostly reserved for the African American women, thereby reinforcing the dictum of the days of slavery that they were "beasts of the field, destined by God to the superior Caucasians" (Bahr, et al 43). Natalie therefore destroys the myth of the Black superwoman in her monologue wherein she refutes the theory of the coloured woman being a "reutered workhorse" (*three pieces* 49). Thereby she establishes her identity as an ordinary human being sensitive to the pleasures and perils of life.

To checkmate the racist notions of an inferior status attached to the African Americans, Maxine mentions how she buys pieces of gold every time the African American tries to transcend the barriers of class through achievement. "Gold" is therefore an important signifier of the African American race, since the precious yellow metal which is found in the African mines is much courted by the White world. It becomes a metaphor of class since it suggests the mobility of the African Americans from the lower to the higher class of the American socio-economic ladder. It basically connects the race with the "earth" suggesting their vibrant nature. It forms an important link in the African American Diaspora, since it symbolizes the racial roots of the American Blacks to their ethnic homelands where they were not subjects of ridicule or symbols of inferior status. It reminds them of the wounds in the new land. Most importantly it is purchased "to protest their ignorance / their disconnect from history" (*three pieces* 51). Kennedy and Shange are particular in genealogical revisionism wherein the African Americans also need to find a place in the land's history. "Gold" is also a reminder of the sufferings faced by the African Americans and the emotional turmoil which the race has suffered in the White man's capitalist land. Therefore, while acting as a symbol of racist/class vindication, the metal is also used as a protest since Natalie bemoans the fact that many African Americans remain ignorant of their histories.

"History" is an important term, since the American history is usually depicted as "white," relegating the existence of the coloured races thereby dismembering them from historical genealogy. Re-writing histories is a major task for the African American women writers since the hostile environment in the Promised Land has violently negated their histories, relegating them to a cultural vacuum. Establishing historical connections with the land of origin and the land of existence is a complex task that imbues the struggle of African American women with particular roots, strengthening their existence. She acknowledges the fact that she also purchases gold with a vengeance during certain crucial times, when the controlling White elitist patriarchal culture tends to suppress the Black minorities in multiple ways. She buys gold each time someone appropriates her "space" or "time" without her permission and to accentuate the positive aspects of her people. (*three pieces* 51) As a symbol of protest, gold is bought with a spirit of retaliation since it forms a violent answer to the oppressive powers of the dominant culture. Above all it acts as a positive metaphor of the race which has survived the unsurvivable. It is a cumulative answer to all the emotional flogging meted out to the race. Therefore, she perceives the metal at a loftier level than the Whites.

But what pains Shange the most is the internalisation of the notions of inferiority within the African Americans who see themselves through the demeaning prism of White notions of Black inferiority. Alec, for instance, is a Black actor who refuses to do audition for roles which need no "classical training." Unfortunately, he remains unfeeling to the plight of the African American female actresses who are ping-ponged by the power structures of the White dominant culture. It is rather ironic that Alec is unable to empathise with the women of his own class. Milton Gordon labels their segregation as an "ethnic sub society" (Gordon 72) wherein it is difficult for members of the same ethnic groups but of different classes to have an emotional identification. Bonnie Thornton Dill in "The Dialectics of Black Womanhood" (1998) posits an interesting variation in this stream. When people of a similar social class and different ethnic groups share common behavioral patterns, they do not share the element of peoplehood. With their ethnic counterparts, they may share a sense of peoplehood but not the common behavioral patterns. It is only the people who belong to the same ethnic groups and class share both. (Dill 73) Since Alec and these women actors do not share a common social class status despite their sharing the same ethnicity, he remains unmoved by their plight. Bettina rightly comments that it is "a failure of imagination" (*three pieces* 45) on his part since he does not comprehend the grief that informs the lives of African American women. Typecast as being inferior and unable to meet the requisites of the dominant White culture, these women undergo endless agony.

bell hooks in *Killing Rage—Ending Racism* (1995) focuses on the process of internalised racism which ushers in all forms of casteism and hierarchies. She mentions how one's skin colour leads to one's inferior position and has a detrimental impact on one's overall performance in life. The African American women have to face the brunt of devaluation as they have been historically wronged by the "assault of White supremacist aesthetic values." On the other hand, Lily is "too light" (Shange, *three pieces* 47) to act as a Black woman. When she confesses to her director that she is "Black" he is taken by surprise, but still she is denied the role of a White girl despite being a "classically trained" actress, on the grounds that it would not be ethical to accommodate a fair-skinned African American woman for the role of a White woman. The word "ethical" infuriates Lily, since the term is not used in the conventional sense of human nature, religion or culture.[20] The word reinforces colour hierarchy. It is actually a euphemism for their imperialist, classist attitudes which further demean the position of African American women, with their Eurocentric modes of thought. Such a supercilious attitude on the part of the exploitative capitalist society which denigrates the creativity of the African American artists also runs through Shange's next play *A Photograph: Lovers in Motion* (1979). The title announces not only the ambiguity of the play, but also the tensions prevailing in the mind of the protagonist Sean. A photograph captures reality at a particular moment in frozen time. The term "reality" is also contestable, since the picture is merely an image or a signifier of that reality. Instead of motion, it captures stasis. But Sean the protagonist insists on being able to capture life in motion as it would enable him to touch a "new world" (Shange, *three pieces* 58). Despite his commitment to art, his White friend Earl with prejudiced notions of White superiority asks him for the reason behind the choice despite his weak economic condition.

> Earl: It's just i don't understand / i mean you were poor all yr life / why you wanna be a poor starving artist. (Shange, *three pieces* 59)

Sean corrects the term as a "struggling artist" (Shange, *three pieces* 59). His ambitions induce a struggle in him since he insists on being able to capture life in motion like the blowing breeze, falling stars, kneading the bread and also the process of loving. But the fact remains that a photographer can only record still images of these objects. Sean represents a talented but confused individual who tends to mix his professional identity with the gender one. While the White American society places excessive emphasis on the sexuality of the African American male, it fails to concede their talents and potential.[21] By internalising such distorted notions and by muddling his creative and libidinal urges, Sean seeks to assert himself through sexual performances alone. His language is also another medium of establishing his power over women. His use of words like "bitch," "stupid bitch," (Shange, *three pieces* 83-84) reveal the fusion of sexual and linguistic violence as being consequential of his greater impotency to prove his professional merit in an antagonistic atmosphere.

When the oppressions of the dominant culture continue to stifle him, he moves inward creating his own spaces in the form of dreams. The hero of his dreams is Alexander Dumas, a French novelist and a bohemian. He is an important figure in Sean's own perceptions of manhood. Like Dumas who ascended in life from the lowest class to the highest, Sean also dreams of moving from his position as a "niggah" to that of the world's greatest photographer. To Michael he confesses his love for Dumas and his professional dream of wanting to be like him. (Shange, *three pieces* 62) Dumas-like, Sean also defines success in materialistic terms. Like Dumas who had been sent away by his father to prove himself, Sean feels alienated by the White American class-conscious society which perceives success purely on economic terms. After carving a niche for himself, Dumas returns to his father. Sean also intends to end the psychological, self-imposed exile only on the day he tastes success. Sean's boyhood memories are of an emotionally distant father who had little respect for women. But his father was himself emotionally neglected by his father. Each of them abuse women although even this does not eradicate their emotional void. But Sean cannot be easily dismissed as a mere male chauvinist "[for] he appears to be as much a victim of his out-of-hand ambition and his bitter frustration as they [the other characters] are" (Oliver 48). In fact, Shange holds much respect for Sean the dreamer and works to refute the myth that "if you're black, there's an artificial ceiling on your ambition" (Monroe 57). She never undermines his ambition of winning the Nobel Prize. She only cautions such individuals through Michael to be wary against commercial success or failure as a criterion for self-worth and the worthiness of the entire race. Success, she believes, is never to be equated with merit. "Success is entertainment in the United States, it "is so highly transitory" (Lester 152). Instead she prefers a continuous toil.

Despite Sean's proclamation of wanting to be the greatest photographer in the world, he undoubtedly remains paralysed by his own economic and social status as a Black person, "caught perpetually in the act of becoming rather than being a great photographer" (Lester 151). When Sean thus remains lost in the quagmire of racio-sexual identities, it is Michael, his girlfriend who acts as his beacon-light, inspiring him for professional elevation. Only Michael discovers Sean's hidden photos of the Vietnam War and those of fighting children from a neighbouring African American community. Fighting, therefore, is metaphorically used in the Nietzschean term of struggle for the African American artist who has to wage endless battles to establish an identity of his own. Michael alone steers clear his path towards success. Michael's catalytic effect on Sean can never be undermined. If he wins the Nobel Prize, it would be a vindication of his race and aggrandizement of his class since violence is transmuted into art.

Violence is an integral part of the African American psyche on account of their harrowing experiences in the promised land. From the times of lynching to its modified forms during the post-abolitionist times, violence continues to haunt their lives. Women are the most affected by it as they have to bear the brunt of the White capitalistic patriarchal forces which continue to economically and sexually exploit them. Allison Davis in his *Caste, Economy and Violence* (1987) considers it a cumulative predicament of the social, sexual, economic, political, educational and religious factors (319-333).[22] This paves way to frustration and violence which indeed mar the peace of the family.

In Kennedy's plays, violence is latent, and its effects are highlighted through numerous complex images along with a deep colour-schema: exploding bodies, decapitations, executions, flying suns, orange and red suns, rapes, excessive bleeding etc. The violence is inflicted on the intensely personal, physical and the psychical sites of the characters, with little resistance. The violence being in-built, it appears in dense metaphors which continue to haunt the audience long after they have seen the plays. In Sanchez's plays *The Bronx is Next* and *Uh! Uh! but How Do it Free Us?* the violence is more blatant and open, since the women face the lashes of society which continue to undermine their position. In the former play, the "Black bitch" faces excruciating pain in the ghetto which is about to be set ablaze. The violence inflicted on her only produces counter violence, which makes her resort to a strong abusive use of language that is actually in consonance with her innate turbulence. Words like "bastard," "fuck," "slap" and "dick" are just verbal expressions of her inner turmoil.

The domestic peace of the African American families is frequently disturbed on account of their powerless situations and their weak economic positions. The problem is more complicated when the men in the household remain unemployed or under-employed. The Beau Willie-Crystal episode in Shange's *colored girls* is an example to prove this point. Beau Willie Brown is a former Vietnam veteran who is rendered jobless once the war is over. In a depressed state with his mind filled with internal vacuum, he takes to alcohol and drugs, apart from physically abusing his wife Crystal. His dejection springs from a sense of betrayal by a country for whose social and legal systems he has fought. Deprived of a job and education, his frustration paves the way to destructive feelings even towards his wife and kids whom he loves the most. He kills his twins by throwing them from the fifth floor of his apartment which shatters Crystal. But Shange has not presented him as a chauvinist who is triggered by bloated notions of masculinity. Critics argue against Shange's portrayal of Willie which they assume to be a biased view of a radical feminist.[23] But Sandra Hollin Flowers offers a balanced insight into Beau Willie's complex nature. She considers him "the quintessential black man of his generation." She is careful not to vindicate his action but instead believes that Shange's understanding of the Black man is most evident in this poem since the dramatist is also recognizing the external factors that influence the man-woman relationships. (Flowers 52)

Shange depicts Beau Willie as a victim of a racist and capitalist society that defines manhood in terms of economic self-reliance, and to act as the bread-winner of the family. The conflict arises out of the fact that Beau Willie and Crystal are unable to live up to the traditional, cultural family pattern where the male member earns and the female member caters to the needs of the family. The capitalist set up renders the black male powerless. Therefore, infanticide is Beau Willie's chosen way to overpower Crystal. During the intensely emotional moment, Crystal does not poignantly express her feelings but only whimpers stating her powerlessness over the violent situation in the family. It is Crystal who experiences a greater devastation than her man, since she loses control over her environment, her life and that of her children.

Her loyalty to Willie indicates her emotional and misplaced love for a man who is rumoured as having an illicit affair.[24] A single parent at the age of twenty-two, she is powerless to form an "ideal" family on account of Beau's psychologically depressed condition. Therefore the loss of her children provides her with the opportunity to chart her own psychological path.

One of the strategic ways through which the African American women were continuously underestimated was by labelling them as "matriarchs." African American women have to battle against this negative myth while at the same time, they positively redefine themselves. Elizabeth Higginbotham in "Two Representative Issues in Contemporary Sociological Work on Black Women" cites Jacquelyne Jackson's "Black Women in a Racist Society" (1972) which probes into the forbidding ways in which the African American women were viewed. She particularly throws light on the matriarchy theory which is mis-represented by the dominant culture. (Hull, et al 94) Scott and Peterson argue how the propounders of the theory of the "castrating matriarch" have done so based on the biased statistics of Franklin Frazier, Daniel Moynihan and others.[25] They ignore the fact that employment was an intrinsic part of the African American women since they were brought to work as farm and domestic labourers to enrich the capitalistic machinery of America. During the post-emancipatory years, when the African American men were suddenly deprived of their only source of occupation—field labour, and as they have been rendered uneducated and unskilled to handle the white-collared jobs, the women were forced to be the sole bread-winners of the family to feed their children, themselves and also their spouses. But, women acting as sole caretakers of the family were also in existence to a certain extent during the times of slavery since the men were often lynched or sold off and therefore separation became inevitable. But in the post-emancipatory industrial setting, the modified menial jobs given to the African American women were deliberately distorted by the dominant culture to disrupt their domestic relationships. Ignoring the economic facts, these women are blamed for failing to "conform" to "appropriate" gender roles and are perceived as threats to the socio-economic cultural value systems of the nation. Further, by unjustly comparing her with successful business women who have been defined out of sex, Black women have been stigmatized for denouncing their roles as women. In fact their roles as aides in family stability and security have been unjustly looked down upon. As a consequence of the bigoted values of the dominant culture and the unfortunate internalizations of these values by the men of her own race, the African American men are forcefully made to undergo a feeling of "castration complex,"[26] which is actually detrimental both to the individual and his spouse. The man-woman relationships remain strained as the unlearning menfolk feel powerlessly threatened by their own women.

Charles in Sanchez's *The Bronx is Next* labels the "Black bitch" as a "castrating matriarch" (Sanchez, *The Bronx* 82) since her presence and her violent talk unconsciously disturbs his male ego, when the Black men of the Sixties were actually embodiments of masculinity and the ultimate sexual prowess. They also considered themselves as the sole bread-winners of the family even when they were powerless to do so. Similarly, Beau Willie in Shange's *colored girls* also suffers from ravaged feelings since he unconsciously feels "castrated" by his own woman when he remains powerless to cater to the basic needs of the family. Sean in Shange's *A Photograph: Lovers in Motion* also juggles with the three women since he aims at establishing his identity sexually, in order to avoid being castrated by women.

But the "castration complex" cannot be dismissed easily since its unwanted internalization by African American men has not only spoilt the domestic harmony, but has also distorted the images of both the African American men and women. Bond and Perry probe into the theory of "emasculation"[27] and define that "an emasculated people [. . .] are a broken people, a people whose spirit, strength and vigor have been destroyed, who have been reduced to a total state of ineffectuality" (Cade 115). It cannot be forgotten that despite the irretrievable suffering which has befallen the Black race, they have not been "stripped of their virility" (Cade 115) since they have produced an array of creativity which is a proof of their inner zeal and "the nemesis of western civilization" (Cade 116). The myth continues to be perpetuated by the White race as a part of their efforts to "demasculinize" the African American women.

Women are the worst sufferers. Women like the "Black bitch" in *The Bronx is Next* and Crystal in *colored girls* represent the typical African American women who have to bear the brunt of male frustration made through physical violence while at the same time they are forced to cast away their femininity. Therefore, it is the women who are inflicted with castration and not the men.[28] The woman's job provides her the bread, but not an inner satisfaction since she is exploited in the workplace and rejected by her man and made "doubly powerless" (Cade 117), but still, she continues to face the perils in an undaunted way though she may be temporarily cowed down. The African American men are deliberately projected as being castrated despite their creative virility:

> Eunuchs do not write plays that pulverize the very foundations of American theater. Eunuchs do not refuse to fight in unholy wars, thumbing their noses at trophies and fame. [. . .] Eunuchs only do the bidding of the king. (Cade 118)

Despite all the odds that confront them, African American women continue to survive in a creative way.

One of the unique paradigms forged by the African American women is their positive move towards an emotional bonding between all coloured and oppressed women. The African American women creative writers move towards sisterhood as a means of forging a unity between them. Shange makes use of the theme of sisterhood in her *for colored girls*. Towards the end, the poem moves inwardly to lay bare the agony of the African American women who are belittled in a romantic relationship. The Lady in Blue, the Lady in Red, and the Lady in Orange are in love with the same man. But when they realize that they are betrayed, they move together towards a better understanding. The Lady in Red realizes that there is "No assistance" (Shange, *for colored girls* 13) from any corner, since the African American women are continuously being undervalued by the belligerent cultural and capitalistic forces at all times. Therefore they remain stampeded at the physical, psychological and the spiritual levels. Through shared sufferings these women move towards a realized sisterhood. When the man is ultimately confronted by all these women, he can only "smile a lot" (*for colored girls* 44) which is an indication of his own shallowness. The final pyramid scene forms a culminating movement of the poem towards a shared sisterhood and self-love.

It is crucial to understand that the essence of Black sisterhood is not forged on the basis of victimhood, since it would only be a debilitating factor. Rather it is, as bell hooks asserts, based on "shared strengths and resources" (hooks, *Feminist Theory* 45). hooks asserts that idealistic and unconditional bonding would only be futile, as it cannot be achieved without the eradication of the power structures which cause segregation among women. Bonding should never be established between a chosen group of women who strengthen their ties and also exclude other women from their group, since it would mean only a vested bonding as in the case of White feminist movements. Therefore there is a need to dismantle racist and class hierarchies for an ever-lasting bond.

The seven coloured women, move towards a higher amalgamation which facilitates their ability to understand each other's needs and to also strengthen their emotional ties while at the same time forging new paradigms of their struggle against the segregated forces. The spiritual dimension (represented symbolically by the pyramid formation) is an added adhesive which binds them with great strength. The entire gamut of the African American women's writing could therefore be seen as a positive struggle against the oppressive forces.

The struggle of the African American women is the consequence of their deep faith in God and spirituality. Converted to the faith of the power holders in an alien land, religion often turned out to be their only source of solace. But, the hierarchies of power structures operated in the religious world too. The White religion was rather condescendingly bestowed on the African Americans with convoluted notions of the superiority of the White faith and the supposed spiritual impoverishment of the Black race. It is often mistaken amongst the dominant White races that economic poverty is an indicator of spiritual poverty. Whatever the intentions of the giver, the African Americans welcomed the faith with zeal as it strengthened them to survive the brutalities inflicted on them. The women in particular were deeply attached to Christianity as it imbued into them a "psychic wholeness" which was much needed in the alien land. (Lowenberg and Bogin 8). Christianity was also a tool of empowerment for them. A crucial process which the African American women underwent is that of "calling the spirit" wherein women remained possessed by the Holy Ghost. During such times of possession the women would flout all rules of "decency" and "modesty" and exhibit their religious fervour. If probed deeper, it is undoubtedly the Black woman's arsenal against patriarchy and class since she establishes a direct connection with the divine and puts an end to stubborn schistic modes of Western practices that divides the flesh from the spirit. It is an African performance strategy that bridges the chasm between the human and divine. Religion therefore plays a modified role in the plays of Sanchez, Kennedy and Shange. All the three dramatists accept it, but with a sense of ambivalence, since they apprehend that the acceptance is only for its own sake and would actually do little to elevate their class. The Black woman in Sanchez's *Uh! Uh! but How Do it Free Us?* is bewildered by the infidelity of her man. She temporarily wallows in a world of existential anguish, since she feels like a "fool" to seek help from a White male Christian God who remains unmoved by her plight. (Sanchez, *Uh! Uh!* 213) The speech is indicative of her powerless predicament, of both her love for God and also her temporary feelings of alienation. Her anger is actually a negative expression of her faith. It is only temporary since she moves back to a state of faith.

Although the materialistic power of the dominant culture is more powerful than the spiritual power which the Whites supposedly value high, the African American women continue to place immense value upon the faith. Kennedy's plays present a mixed attitude towards Christianity. Despite her Catholic upbringing, the religious figures in her plays stand overwhelmed by the antagonistic forces of America and they actually do little to ameliorate the plight of poor Black women like her. In Kennedy's *Funny House of a Negro*, Jesus is actually one of the selves of a poor Black woman. Far from emitting an aura of angelic grace, he is hunch-backed, yellow-skinned and raggedly dressed. The conflict between the African American religious expectation and the mundane reality into which they are often pushed, is effectively summed up by Kennedy in her *Funny House*. She mentions her paternal grandmother's dream of envisioning her son to emerge as a Christ-like figure to save the race, heal them and also lift the burdensome crosses of race, gender and class. (Kennedy, *In One Act* 14) Despite such expectations, she is unable to serve as a proper role model and achieve religious elevation. At dawn, her father watches his mother rise, kill a hen for his breakfast and then continue with her domestic drudgery. Kennedy is here exploring the lofty religious idealism of the mother and the humdrumness of their lives which prevents them from living up to the ideal. Ultimately Sarah's father turns out to be a rapist instead of being a saviour. Instead of "healing" his folk's misery and relieving them of their crosses, he actually becomes a burden for his wife and daughter.

In *A Lesson in a Dead Language* Jesus, Joseph, Mary and a shepherd stand dumb witnesses to the miseducation of the young African American adolescent girls, whose irrelevant education does little to re-order their desperate situations. The same characters, Jesus, Joseph, Mary and the shepherd are also present in *A Rat's Mass.* The play presents the conflict of religious powers with the political. The polyphonic nature of the play enhances our understanding of the turbulent psyche of the rat siblings. They are placeless like Sarah and Clara, without any support structures for solace. Jeanie Forte adds another important dimension to their rat existence since she compares them to "animals in a lab experiment [. . .] analogous to cruel slavers, colonizers, missionaries, carrying out their agenda at the expense of the objectified thing" (Forte 166). Like the rats hated and feared, and as carriers of diseases, in a "high" and "pure" society, the Nazis are also represented by the cult figures of Christianity, which once again intersects the military and religious institutions and symbolises the ultimate power wielded by the dominant culture. Kennedy is clearly laying bare the fascist nature of the American religio-socialist structure which is founded on all forces of exploitation like racism, slavery and imperialism. The oppressor may don different guises, but the exploitation goes on.

The theme also continues in Kennedy's *The Owl Answers.* Clara's mother wants to be Mary, Christ's bride (Kennedy, *In One Act* 41), but she is ultimately raped by Rev. Passmore. It is a doubly signifying rape, since it is signified at the physical and religious levels. Clara also aims at religious ascension; but her Negro man's carnal appetite rules. The White Bird significantly questions.

> Bird: If you are the virgin, what are you doing with his Negro in a Harlem hotel room? *Mary*? (Kennedy, *In One Act* 41; my italics)

The White bird, which is Reverend Passmore's canary, is also God's dove. When Clara and her mother long to ascend into the spiritual world of Virgin Mary, their maidenheads are violated. The intersection of the religious and the capitalistic forces which thwart the ambitions of a creative African American woman is clearly evident in the merger of Passmore's canary with God's dove. While the White dove represents peace and the holy ghost in Christian theology, the canary is a bird of beauty sans religious connotations. The conflation of these two birds is indicative of the lack of pristine purity in the White man's faith which takes little cognizance of the physical and psychic well-being of the talented African American woman. The sardonic tone of the bird is a mockery at the poor Black woman's religious aspirations. Even her Negro boyfriend fails to understand her. She continues to remain unmoved by what happens to her body:

> She: I only have a dream of love. Open the cell door and let me go down to St. Paul's Chapel. [. . .] I call God and the *Owl Answers*. [. . .] I am only yearning for our kingdom God. (Kennedy, *In One Act* 42-43)

The speech is loaded with both religious fervour and irony. Despite being belittled by White religion, she cannot but long for that ultimate union. But the kingdom of God fails to accept her on account of the supposed spiritual impoverishment labelled to her class. Therefore, instead of kingdom, she is transformed into an owl and merges with wisdom with an "oww . . . oww" instead of an Amen. Instead of salvation and divine illumination from above, the transformed Clara merely "stares into space."[25] The White Bird only laughs at her mockingly. Towards the end of the play when the Father "rises and slowly blows out candles on bed" (Kennedy, *In One Act* 45), we understand that not only Clara, but all women of her race/class remain doomed for ever.

The religious power in the play is clearly juxtaposed to the political and creative power of the White Anglo-Saxon culture (represented by Chaucer, Shakespeare and William, the Conqueror) indicative of the intricate network of institutions which collide to both bombard and negate the physical and spiritual existence of the African American women. She is closer to Foucault who does not see power as a "general matrix" but is manifest in multiple forms in different institutions like "families, limited groups and institutions," which perpetuate hegemonic values (Foucault 93-94).

Religion in Kennedy's plays offers little consolation in traditional terms, Shange's *for colored girls* deals with finding a god within themselves. One of the reasons for the seven women finding a god within could be the fact that these women reject a White Christian patriarchal faith which stifles the position of the African American women. On the other hand, the greater internal realisation is a force which helps them to assert their selves and enables them to develop a positive self-esteem.[26] Shange rejects any traditional interpretations of religion in Christian terms in this poem. In a personal interview with Neal A. Lester she mentions:

> i found god in myself is a feminist ritual. It's feminist hedonistic awakening. [. . .] It's hedonistic in the generic sense of feminist self-realisation that allegedly occurs. [. . .] [The black woman] finds it [god] in herself; she does not find it [god] outside [herself]. (Lester 67)

But Shange does speak of religion in terms of Christianity in *boogie woogie landscapes* where Layla, the protagonist, finds positive self-esteem through religion in Christian terms. Layla resorts to dreams through which her visions and fears are disclosed since her political issues and personal issues become intertwined. Like in her *colored girls*, she realises that "bein alive & bein a woman & bein colored is a metaphysical dilemma." (*for colored girls* 48). Shange describes Layla's spiritual and existential desires with food imagery. She devours the black and white pages as well as her gothic novels to satisfy her penchant for the ever-widening horizons of the world. Undernourished both emotionally and spiritually, she receives the ultimate satisfaction in the form of the radio evangelist's voice. It suddenly transforms her charcoal-existence to one of "brilliant yellow" (Shange, *three pieces* 116). The seven coloured women in the *colored girls* turn inward in an atmosphere of communal fellowship when they chant. But Layla finds God through the voice of the evangelist and emerges with renewed self-awareness and experience which create a positive vision in her.

Therefore, with faith in their souls and an undaunted courage in their hearts the African American women struggle hard to rise above the menial status attached to them.

Notes

1. Hodges points out how stratification started even in the prehistorical periods, which is actually "more than 99 percent of the human era." Nearly 5,000 years ago, much before the emergence of the three earliest civilizations: Mesopotamian, Egyptian and Indus Valley, human beings lacked the complex economic organizations which promote stratification, as they were nomadic. But once they settled down in fertile places and established permanent settlements, an economic order was needed and slowly social stratification set in. (Hodges 17)
2. Hodges begins his book with a view to tracing the "history of classification" in the world. He rightly points out how even the father

of philosophy like Plato is not free from the unconscious processes of hierarchy and stratification.

3. Moderation of power has been vindicated by Biblical prophets like Isaiah, Jeremiah and Ezekiel. They visualised a "promised land" which ensured an equi-distribution of wealth. St. Augustine in *The City of God* idealised a theocratic state. Girolamo Savanarola practised it and was executed for it. Joha Wycliffe had (a century earlier) called for a god-ordained state. Johan Ball his supporter died in the gallows.
4. The oft-cited Great Chain of Being has the different elements of nature arranged in a particular fashion with the earth at the bottom and above it water, air, fire and ether order was also imposed on life with the gods on the top, human beings occupying, middle and animals occupying, lower position.
5. Noel Babuef aimed at social equality. His successor Etienne Cabet's *The Voyage to Icaria* visualised an industrial utopia. Saint Simon's *New Christianity* sought abolition of all private property. This work influenced Marx. In England, Thomas Spence advocated a vision of a classless society. Godwin sought dismantling of ownership of all property—both private and government. In America, classless utopias were tried by Hawthorne, Emerson and Thoreau which failed practically.
6. Whether these attempts at practising Utopias were a failure or a success is only secondary. The most important issue remains the fact that humanity has always waged a war against the establishment of hierarchies.
7. To paraphrase the ideas of Allen Wood, from his book *Karl Marx*, there are four basic processes of alienation:

    First the workers are alienated from the *product* of their labour because they have no say in the production of goods, and once manufactured the goods are snatched away from them and they have no say in determining where it should be sold.

    Secondly the workers are alienated from *themselves* since if the work is unpleasant, they undergo a major psychological crisis.

    They are alienated from other *human beings* since the capitalistic power structures make them view each other as rivals competing with each other for jobs and promotions.

    They are alienated from *nature* since their working conditions make them see nature as an obstacle to their survival. This is an impediment in the establishment of a human kind of labour. (Wood 44-45)

8. Gary Day aptly sums up a few Marxists to support such a stance. (a) Lukacs' claim that the novel especially probes into the hidden connections and may lead to revolutionary transformation (b) Louis Althusser asserts that literature can make us aware of the ideologies underpinning our conventional conception of reality. (c) Lucien Goldman asserts that literature reflects the world-view of a particular group. (d) Etienne Balibar and Pierre Mackerey argue that education instead of ameliorating, only reinforces economic differences and by restricting the access to knowledge. (Day 2)
9. Gerda Lerner, in *The Grimke Sisters: A Biography*: In this book, Lerner mentions how the lives of White women were very different when compared to those of her Black counterparts. The women with "ruffled skirts, frothy bonnets and gaily colored shawls" were a stark contrast to the large number of female slaves who worked for them. The Grimke sisters were born into an aristocratic household where a large number of Black women did sundry jobs in the plantations. They spun coarse cloth, threshed corn and did all forms of odd and mean jobs.
10. Cultural imperialism is a term used by a number of Marxist thinkers to describe the effects of the western mass media (especially of the U.S.), since they feel that it spreads bourgeois values and capitalist ideology. This makes it easy for the third world people to be exploited and prevents the formation of class solidarity. The theory is also known as "Cocoa-colonization." Chilean Marxists, Ariel Dorftman and Armand Mattelart's argue that Disney comics are ultimately instruments of U.S. ideology and cultural domination (Berger 61-62).
11. Patricia Hill Collins in "The Sexual Politics of Black Womanhood" (1993) mentions how prostitution represents the fusion of the race and the class issues along with sex. In prostitution, exploitation is fused with an economic purpose which is the "commodification of the black woman's sexuality" (Bart and Moran 97). Sex here is commodified not merely in the sense that it can be purchased, but also in the sense that the individual who sells it has no control over it. This also means that the woman is alienated from

her body. It also involves the dimension of power, since the powerful can afford to consume it. As Collins summarises: "Prostitution under European and American capitalism thus exists within a complex web of political and economic relationships whereby sexuality is conceptualized along intersecting axes of race and gender" (Bart and Moran 98).

12. June Jordan's poem runs thus:

> I can't do what I want
> to do with my own body because I
> am the wrong
> sex the wrong age the wrong skin
> [. . . .] they fucked me over because I was
> wrong [. . . .]
> to be who I am which is exactly like
> South Africa
> penetrating into Namibia penetrating
> into Angola [. . . .]
> how do you know if Pretoria
> ejaculates
> what will the evidence look like the
> proof of the
> monster jack boot ejaculation on
> Black land. (Davis, *Women, Culture and Politics* 37)

13. She was clothed meagre. She represented deviant sexuality to her audience. This was in consonance with the times since many Europeans of the nineteenth century thought that the African Americans had enlarged penises or malformed female genitalia on account of their supposedly deviant sexual practices (Davis, W*omen, Race and Class* 90-91). After her death in 1815, she was dissected and her genitalia and buttocks remain on display at Paris. Sander Gilman explains the impact that the exhibition of the woman had on the Victorian audience:

> The figure of Sarah Bartman was reduced to her sexual parts. The audience which had paid to see her buttocks and had fantasized about the uniqueness of her genitalia when she was alive could, after her death and dissection, examine both. (Gilman 213)

14. Morrison uses the word "Fetishisation" to describe the attitude of

the White patriarchal society towards the African American women. In *Playing in the Dark* (1992) she explicates the term: "Fetishisation: This is especially useful in evoking erotic fears or desires and establishing fixed and major difference where difference does not exist or is minimal. Blood, for example is a pervasive fetish: Black blood, White blood, the purity of blood; the purity of White female sexuality, the pollution of African blood and sex." (81)

15. Despite the tribulations encountered by them, the women rejoice the moment of Junebug's graduation. Jessie sings a song of joy:

    Junie graduates tonight,
    Junie makes his speech tonight,
    His gonna tell 'em like it is;
    My chillun starve
    The landlord carves,
    On Judgment Day
    There'll be a mighty price to pay. [. . . .]
    Will the Devil tempt my lamb? (King and Milner 38)

    Yet, at another place she dreams of her son's achievement:

    Could I steal a brighter sun?
    No more than two worlds can equal
    Junie turns hollow days to mellow,
    My Junebug, my son
    It is a valedictorian. (King and Milner 35)

16. When the bill providing support for schools was put before the English parliament in 1807, Mr. Giddy (afterwards, president of the Royal Society) raised objections with the thought that

    it would be prejudicial to their morals and happiness, it would teach them to despise their lot in life instead of making them good servants [. . .] instead of teaching them subordination, it would render them fractious [. . .] it would enable them to read [. . .] vicious books and publications against Christianity, it would render them insolent to their superiors and in a few years the legislature would find it necessary to direct the strong arm of power against them. (Niebhur118)

    To quote from Niebhur:

> Now sir, the old-time Negro is assassinated by this suffrage plan. This new issue, your reader, your writer, your loafer, your voter, your ginger-cake school graduate with a diploma of side whiskers, and beaver-hat, pocket pistols, brass knucks and bicycle, he, sir, is the distinguished citizen whom our statesmen would crown at once with the highest dignities of an ancient and respectable commonwealth. (Niebhur 119)

17. The term 'High Street" conjures notions of segregation based on class. While the Whites are permitted to walk on "High Street," the Blacks are prohibited from doing so, thereby relegating them to a "low" status.
18. The control of the mobility of the African Americans based on class and their quest for physical space has been the intrinsic theme of slave songs too. Blauner quotes a Jamaican slave song which poignantly highlights this particular predicament of the African Americans.

> If me want for go in a Ebo, me
> can't go there
> Since them tief me from a guinea, me
> can't to there
> If me want to go to Congo, me can't
> go there.
> Since them tief me from my tatta,
> me can't go there.
> If me want for go in a Kingston, me can't
> go there.
> Since Massa go in a England, me can't
> go there. (Blauner 36)

The very essence of slavery is its absolute control over the human impulse to move about, since it would simultaneously curb their inner spaces too. The curbing was reinforced through their economic dependence which was inevitable as they were denied proper opportunities in education and jobs which would cripple them forever.

19. Godiva is the wife of Leofric, one of Edward the Confessor's great earls. According to legend, her husband imposed tax on the inhabitants of Coventry. She begged him to remit it, which he jestingly promised to do if she would ride naked through the streets at noon-

day. She took him at his word, directed the people to stay indoors and shut their windows, and complied with his conditions. Peeping Tom who looked out was struck blind. The story is told by Drayton in "Poly Oblion," by Leigh Hunt and Tennyson in "Godiva." Lady Godiva figures as the mother of Hereward in Charles Kingsley's "Hereward the Wake" and in one of Landor's "Imaginary Conversations" (Source: *Oxford Companion to Literature*). Lady Godiva is an important figure since she is one of the early undaunted feminists whose courage remains breathtaking even to this day. At yet another level, she is a woman of the aristocratic class who remains a stark contrast to the African American women.

20. Shange is wounded over the fact that the African American women are not given the roles of Lady Macbeth or Mother Courage on "ethical" grounds. She adapts and demystifies Brecht's *Mother Courage and Her Children* wherein she transforms Brecht's thirty year German war to the post civil war era of the fight between the American cavalry and the American Indians for the south west territory. The mother in the play is an emancipated slave. She elaborates on the efflorescence of the play in her "How I Moved Anna Fierling to the South West Territories" (1984):

> Oz & i decided on mother courage. This waz based on Brecht's [. . .] aristocratic position [. . .] [it] has most to do [. . .] with the actual responsibilities all of us must accept for the machinations of the capitalist state. The history of Afro-Americans is so mired in the sluggish imaginations of racism that our true experiences in the development of this country are looked upon as quirks. how in the hell cd the 14 million blacks freed after the civil war have an insignificant relationship to Manifest Destiny, to miscegenation [. . .] i lived in Brecht's conscious mind for six months [it] gave me the opportunity to ground myself in the history of my people in this land [. . .], i waz raised on but excluded from [. . .] i have resolved the classics for myself. (Shange, *See No Evil* 34-38)

21. A major myth which is unduly attached to the African American race is their sexuality. While the African American women are projected as "Jezebels," and whores, the men's sexual prowess is also highly exaggerated. This idea is suggested in Ralph Ellison's *Invisible Man*, where the black phallus symbolises great force that

White men envy. Towards the end of the novel, he sees his own testes bleeding, suggesting waste of his creative power. Shange bemoans the fact that even talented young men like Sean unfortunately internalise the inflated notions of Black male sexuality as projected by the dominant White culture. Thereby, they remain content with merely establishing their sexual identities. Their creative powers thus go unrecognised and eclipsed for ever. Such men cannot ascend the socio-cultural ladder of the American class systems.

22. Comparing class with the Hindu caste systems, Allison Davis goes on to mention how: "The negro or white person is born into a social class just as he is born into a color caste [. . .] caste [. . .] categorically prevents marriage or intimate social participation outside one's color group [. . .] class restricts marriage and participation to those individuals identified by symbols and behaviour as of an inferior kind and rank." (Davis, *Caste, Economy and Violence* 320)
23. Shange's attitude towards Black men is much-debated when analysing *for colored girls*. Many critics hold the view that Shange as a feminist hates Black men. Erskine Peters in "Some Tragic Propensities of Ourselves: The Occasion of Ntozake Shange's *for colored girls*" contends that "Shange conversely portrays Black men basically as pasteboards or beasts" (81).

    Robert Staples in "The Myth of Black Male: A Response to Angry Black Feminists" insists that "watching a performance [of *for colored girls*], one sees a collective appetite for black male blood" (26).

    On the contrary, Sandra Hollin Flowers in "*colored girls*: Text Book for the Eighties" insists that "Shange demonstrates a compassionate vision of black man—compassionate because though the work is not without anger, it has a certain integrity which would not exist if the author lacked a perspective understanding of the crisis between black men and women" (56).

    Lester A. Neal examines this view in "Shange's Men: *for colored girls* Revisited, and Movement Beyond'. He argues how Shange does not hold men solely responsible for women's oppression (319-20).
24. bell hooks in *Feminist Theory: From Margin to Center* (1984) includes an essay on "Feminist Movement to End Violence" wherein she lashes out against women who equate violence and love. She

contends that it is difficult to motivate such women. The two qualities have been mistakenly intertwined. There are women who fear that "eliminating violence will lead to the loss of love" (124). She argues that the solution for this will not come: "until men and women cease equating violence with love, understand that the conflicts can be resolved without violence and reject the idea that men should dominate women, [until then] male violence against women will continue" (125).

25. One of the most debated works on the African American families is Daniel Moynihan's *The Negro Family: The Case for National Action* (1965) where he discusses marital dissolution, illegitimacy rates and female-headed families. Franklin Frazier's *The Negro Family in the United States* (1966) provides a historical and sociological analysis of Black family life in a period when psychological and biological theories of racial inferiority abounded. The ultimate image of a Black woman that emerges from his work is that of a strong and independent person who placed little value on marriage, engaged in free sexual activity and had no notions of male supremacy. Herbert Gutman's *The Black Family in Slavery and Freedom* (1976) depicts a far more accurate understanding of the Black family predicament. He contends that the female-headed household was atypical before 1925 and generally exaggerated in studies of Black family life. He indicates that there is little evidence of the matriarchal form of household.
26. The term "castration complex" when used in African American Studies is different from what it means in the general use of the term in feminist studies. Feminist studies, responds to Freud's idea. Freud contends that like boys, the first object of love for girls is also their mother; later she moves on to father or men who take the place of her father. The transition from the female to a male love object begins when the girl realises that she does not have a penis, that she is castrated. She "notice[s] the penis of a brother or playmate, strikingly visible and of large proportions, at once recognise[s] it as the superior counterpart of [her] own small and inconspicuous organ (the clitoris) and from that time [. . .] [she] [is] a victim to envy for the penis" (Tong 141). But in African American Studies, the term refers to the metaphoric act of castrating adopted by the dominant White culture to curb the creativity of the African

Americans. In African American Women's Studies, the term refers to a particular myth created by the dominant White patriarchal capitalist culture that the advent of the African American women's movement tended to nullify the existence of the African American men, rendering them powerless. The unwanted internalisation of this myth by the African American men often led to conflicts between the sexes.

27. Jean Carey Bond and Patricia Perry in their "Is the Black Male Castrated ?" argue how the emasculation theory is actually a two-pronged attack:
    (a) The theory alleges that the African American men are weak as they are unable to protect their women and children from the bane of racist, capitalistic poverty. Therefore, they are supposed to be easily "pushed aside by their women in their quest for freedom and by playing their economic ace in the hole."
    (b) Another important aspect of the theory is the fact that the African American women used their bodies by complying with rapists to rise on the socio-economic ladder. (Cade 114-16)
28. Nikki Giovanni's "Woman Poem" sums up the predicament of the African American women and female castration:

    you see, my whole life
    is tied up
    to unhappiness
    it's father cooking breakfast
    and me getting fat as a hog
    or having no food
    at all and father proving
    his incompetence
    again [. . . .]
    it's having a job
    they won't let you work
    or no work at all
    castrating me
    (*yes it happens to women too*) (Cade 13; my italics)

29. Owl is associated with blindness. We speak of blind owl. While she longs for light, she is turned blind. Staring is blinking with the eyes having no sensation at all. To stare into space is empty gaze. Owl is a nocturnal bird while dove is diurnal.
30. Nikki Giovanni's poem "Ego Tripping (There May be a Reason

Why)" (1970) expresses the same idea of inner spirituality and celebration of positive Black womanhood:

I turned into myself as was jesus. [. . .]
All praises all praises
I and the one who would save (Ellman and O Claire 1385)

Chapter 5

Conclusion

Celia: Why do Negroes love the colour red?
Julie: It's for the blood that flows in torrents inside us, beneath your dress, everywhere. (King and Milner 36)

The conversation in Archie Shepp's *Junesbug Graduates Tonight* metaphorically sums up not only the vigour and vitality which surround African American life but also the violence which forms the essence of their existence. Any study of African American life cannot ignore the presence of violence since the race has been subject to it in multiple forms. Both the physical and psychological violence have far reaching consequences, often distorting their being and mutilating their psyche. The violence may appear appalling to a lay person whose knowledge of the history of the race and its tumult in a White man's land may be minimal. But a historical study of African American life proves the fact that "force" and "violence" had been the ruling factors of African American life, since they are the only race brought to the land of god's plenty by force. Their travails did not end there. African American men and women have been lynched and tortured to such an extent that their inner selves are torn asunder. The violence has been so deeply ingrained in their psyche that the creativity of the African Americans has been smothered by liberal doses of violence. Violence therefore produces counter-violence. The aftermaths of revenge and violence are narrated by the chorus in the beginning of Kennedy's *Orestes*. Orestes is in a ravaged mental state, "seized by a raging fever." The greater agony lies in his soul since he is debilitated both by his mother's ghost and Eumenides. His bouts of starvation and sorrowful wails aptly delineate the contours of his anguished psyche.

Apart from the general commentary that the chorus makes in traditional Greek drama with regard to the events past and present, Kennedy actually makes a deeper use of this dramatic technique to rise from the particular to the universal, since revenge and hatred can shatter both the slayer and the slain. In fact, while the slain has only a single death, the slayer's psyche faces death every second as it undergoes the excruciating feelings of guilt. All the waters of the oceans can never wash away the guilt-stained psyche of the revenger. Struck by insomnia, fever, loss of appetite, hallucination and depression, Orestes cries out frequently in a neurotic condition. All that he now asks for is mere sleep:

> Orestes: Sweet wizard sleep. How I needed you. (Kennedy, *In One Act* 144)

His agitated mind yearns for a dawn in darkness. Like Lady Macbeth who suffers from deliriums after the murder of Duncan, Orestes is also a similar prey of hallucinations:

> Orestes: Take the snakes away. Take the snakes with gorgon eyes away. (Kennedy, *In One Act* 142)

Predated with horror-filled images of death, Orestes' greatest revelation lies in the fact that counter-violence would only lead to perdition:

> Orestes: What had we to gain by murdering her? Her death would never bring him back to life. [. . .] It is hopeless. (Kennedy *In One Act* 146)

Drained of humane qualities like love, compassion, mercy, forgiveness and possessed by revenge, his visage appears corpse-like to Menelaus. This is not very different from the Newtonian idea that every action has an equal and opposite reaction. But a negative reaction would only pave way for a pyrrhic victory.

The multiple burdens of race, gender and class form the cumulative effect of a number of hostile forces which jeopardise their existence. Lynching, slavery and all forms of physical and psychological turbulence from every corner lead to a sort of emotional blitzkrieg amongst them. The plays produced by Sanchez, Kennedy and Shange depict the nuances of violence in their works. The multiple burdens, instead of weakening their fountains of creativity have in fact made them strike back with what Eric Fromm would label as "benign aggression" (Fromm, *The Anatomy* 4).[1] In *The Anatomy of Human Destructiveness* (1961) he mentions how "the degree of destructiveness increases with the increased development of civilisation; rather than the opposite. Indeed the picture of innate destructiveness fits history much better than pre-history." (4)

Fromm segregates aggression into "Malignant aggression" and "Benign aggression."[2] The dominant White culture has acted upon the African American race with a sort of malignant aggression since the vicious pleasure it derives at the cost of the African American race is beyond any doubt. But the African American patriarchal culture also cannot be totally free from this form of aggression since, while they react to the hegemony imposed by the White culture in a creative manner through their art forms, they also never hesitate to impose the same forms of violence on their women who are at the rock-bottom of the American socio-cultural ladder. The African American male literature is therefore also guilty of the vindictive power exercised over them by the White race. Therefore, the writing of the African American women is one of "benign aggression" since the women are creatively yet forcibly voicing out their protest against the dominant patriarchal values, both Black and White. In the course of their seemingly aggressive behaviour, the African American women are actually creating and ordering their visionary terrains when their physical existence and their modes of succour are threatened. These subaltern women not only speak, but also carve a niche for themselves in the realm of arts by creating their inner spaces.

The violence may be blatantly shown on the stage as in the plays of Sanchez, or it may be brought out through a series of images as in the plays of Kennedy or still it may be reported as in the plays of Shange, but its presence can never be ruled out. It is little wonder, then that Alice Walker pays rich tributes to the creativity of the African American women who have the alchemical power to transform their sorrows into works of art throughout her *In Search of Our Mothers' Gardens*.

Wherein lies the secret of their resilience and strength? It cannot be just will power or physical prowess alone. The reasons are to be found deeper; it is their deep sense of spirituality, which being their racial inheritance (as the Africans are known for their faith in God), that helps them to remain steadfast despite the multiple assaults. Sonia Sanchez brings to bear this aspect in an interview with Zala Chandler:

> we must be spiritual. We must love spiritual sources that we must rely upon. We must call upon our residual memories. . . . Our spirituality will keep us from becoming cynical, from becoming bitter from becoming harsh. (Braxton and Mc Laughlin 362)

Their deep faith instills in them a sense of inner confidence and resilience which keeps their inner selves alive despite all their vicissitudes. The faith also prevents these women dramatists from wallowing in states of existential angst. The Nietzschean view that "God is dead" holds little for these women dramatists since God is the lynchpin of their lives. Their racio-cultural spirituality makes them accept Christianity, but they do not attempt to go back to their original faiths. Despite the multiple perils they face, faith does not perish. Sanchez in her plays does wage an open verbal war with the White Christian God. Kennedy may look at the White patriarchal faith with an element of doubt, but still she does not renounce it. Although Shange starts her *for colored girls* in a general spiritual tone with the final pyramid scene, she pronounces religion in terms of Christianity for the first time in *boogie woogie* where Layla discovers her true self through the discourse of an evangelist. The rainbow is by itself an immense symbol of hope since Shange could have borrowed the idea from Milton's *Paradise Lost XI.*[3] The deep faith helps the African American women to promote a holistic vision of total emancipation for not only the women of their race but to all other oppressed and coloured women. This vision is the most pronounced in Shange. While Sanchez, writing in the early Sixties voices the turbulence in the lives of African American women, Kennedy also, writing nearly in the mid-Sixties and Seventies, probes into the psychological contours of African American women who are shred to pieces on account of the various jeopardies they face. Shange's sympathies are wider since her first play is significantly named *for colored girls who have considered suicide when the rainbow is enuf*, suggestive of the broader vision of the African American women who are able to empathise with other coloured and oppressed women. The wider perspective is a consequence of her holistic vision of life, stemming from her spirituality. It adds a unique dimension to the African American women's movement. This is one of the major reasons why Alice Walker has called the African American women's movement "womanism" since the term implies maturity and "being grown up." It also necessitates love for "other women" and shows a preference for "women's strength." Above all, not only does it concern itself with the survival of women alone, but the "survival and wholeness of entire people male and female" (Walker xi). It is the African American women's deep love for humanity that broadens their mental horizons and adds vigour to their springs of creativity. As Walker continues to mention, the "womanist" is in love with the finest things of life like "music," "dance," "moon," "spirit," "food," "roundness," "folk," "herself" and above all she loves "struggle." She loves all these things "regardless" of how the dominant culture may perceive them. These qualities are as "inseparable as purple to lavender" (Walker xii).

Apart from their deep spirituality Walker attributes their artistry also to the ancestrally bequeathed springs of creativity which the African American women discover when they go in search of their mothers' gardens. Despite the multiple mutilations, the "vibrant, creative spirit that the black woman has inherited [. . .] pops out in wild and unlikely places to this day" (Walker 239). The ancestral presence and the resilient spirit inherited by them subdues the inherent violence in their times. Walker recollects her mother's skills: "Because of her creativity with her flowers, even my memories of poverty are seen through a screen of blooms" (241).

Their suffering has a subduing effect on the harshness of their progeny's lives. It also makes them find their own creative spaces. They may either find fulfillment through a discovery of the proficiencies of their ancestral women or they may make attempts at re-creating the past. One of the ways through which these women writers evoke the past is through their use of mythology. Adrienne Kennedy has for instance re-created the myths of *Electra* and *Orestes* to prove how certain experiences of humanity remain recurrent in one form or another. Therefore, myths are conveniently adapted by writers from Sophocles to Kennedy to suit their own needs. It also gives a sense of identity since the myth-maker forges individual ideas through recurrently archetypal characters. As Jerome S. Bruner mentions in his "Myth and Identity," "It is at once an external reality and the resonance of the internal vicissitudes of man" (349). Myths impart writers with a universal vision which helps them perceive life in a larger perspective and also to give an eternal quality to their works.[5] The emergence of a post modern era has still not eradicated the use of mythology, not only on account of its archetypal quality, but also because it imposes a form and order into an otherwise chaotic experience. Mark Schorer mention in his "The Necessity of Myths" considers it "a large controlling image" that adds philosophical depth to the ordinary facts of life. Most importantly, (it) possesses an "organizing value for experience." Mythology being an "articulated body of such images" acts as a cohesive factor without which the experience remains "chaotic, fragmentary and merely phenomenal." (360). Therefore myths are deployed continually by writers to project their own penetrating insights and turmoil through a meaningful medium.

Kennedy's *Electra* signifies women's force, persuasiveness and the ability to move into action. The name itself is highly significant as it connotes power and woman as a principle of energy. It is Electra who pushes the slightly hesitant Orestes to action. Electra also signifies the conflict between matriarchal and patriarchal values, since Clytemnestra rules for a brief period. By eliminating her through Orestes, she has paved way for the elimination of pro-White America. Kennedy also has a profound humanistic motive in presenting the myths. She understands that "the rarer action is in virtue rather than in vengeance." Shakespeare,). The myth also serves as a symbolic enactment of the mutual hatred between the American Blacks and Whites. After generations of mutual hate, violence and bloodshed, it is high time that there is a greater amity between the Black and White races and between their men and women. The mere elimination of the White favouring America (Clytemnestra) is not enough, since it does not give any solution to the Black versus White issue. It only further compounds the agony. The fact that Blacks and Whites have to live together necessitates a certain amount of sobriety. The elements of reactivity and sobriety are seen in the character of Helen and Menelaus. Orestes, representing the younger generation of Blacks in America realises that the pursuit of a cycle of revenge would take him nowhere. Tyndareus, of the older generation represents wisdom and sanity as a contrast to the insanity of Orestes. He advises him to move towards a state of resolution instead of engaging in acts of bloodshed:

> Tyndareus: These fits of madness are what you pay for your acts of murder. (Kennedy, *In One Act* 151)

He is further supported by members who also call forth for weapons of diplomacy. All this advice falls on deaf ears, as the siblings also kill Hermione, further aggravating their agony and for which they are persisted until Apollo intervenes. The symbolic intervention of Gods is also an affirmation of the sense of hope that all will be well with them despite centuries of protest and violence. All the playwrights seem to be concerned with the idea of ameliorating and synthesizing all differences. While Sanchez pleads for a universe of faith, Kennedy asks for mutual love and understanding, and Shange moves in the direction of universal bonding through sisterhood.

The fact remains that an easy solution cannot be arrived at with regard to the African American predicament. Even the highest office of America is named "White House," as if to affirm the fact that it is a nation of Whites and Whites alone. The success of Obama is only the beginning of America's "White House" being transformed into a multi-coloured house. The stark reality remains that nature will never exist in a vacuum. Uneasy differences are bound to persist between the different races, and sexes. But like differences, even the struggle against these anomalies would also continue forever, since it is an innate human trait to oppose oppression. The fact has to be conceded that the entire spectrum of African American women's plays could move to greater universal missions.[4] Such a broader concern for life alone would make their art enduring, thereby investing it with a sense of permanence. The first step in that direction has been taken by Sanchez, Kennedy and Shange who advocate peace and more holistic approaches towards the predicament of all the oppressed groups. Their re-births with regard to the triple burdens borne by them is indeed fruitful since their visionary maturity is a product of their resilience, faith and optimism which aids them to embark on the up-hill journey of life in an affirmative manner. These women have seen the medusa's head, but they are never stupefied. They are:

> determined women [who]
> go on plodding
> seeing the rainbow of liberty
> smelling the flowers of freedom
>   riding the clouds of justice
>   sailing the waves toward home
>   wild women

> in the whirlwind
> determined women [who]
> go on. (Braxton and Mc Laughlin xvii)

The area of African American women's theatre indeed does offer a fertile ground for research. While most scholars do prefer to work on contemporary writers alone, not much work has been carried out in the area of the early African American women dramatists like Angelina Grimke, Georgia Douglas Johnson, Mary Burril, May Miller, Eulalie Spence, Zora Neale Hurston and the like. The constraints of working in this area are also many, since the procurement of the texts are indeed problematic. A trip to the relevant American universities may solve the problem. These writers may not have the technical sophistication of the current dramatists, but the plays are important for the fact that they got written. Given the little avenues for the African American women in the latter part of the nineteenth and the early twentieth centuries, these women still dared to protest and transcend their constricted spaces. Even among the modern dramatists, the plays of Shirley Graham, Elaine Jackson, Martie Charles, Pearl Cleage, Aishah Rahman, Glenda Dickerson, Anna Deavere Smith and Susan Lori-Parks, to name a few could be explored. But the same hurdles prevail here too, since there are no precise anthologies of plays by these dramatists. One needs to pore through numerous journals, anthologies etc. to basically discover the texts and then start working on theatre.

Notes

1. Such a re-interpretation of the works of African American women writers is necessary since a thorough study of their works throws light on the fact that their survival is rather creative. They unhesitatingly strike back at the dominant White patriarchal culture with the might of their pens, since this is the best way of presenting their struggle in an enduring manner. Undoubtedly their works may be laden with violence which is an innate part of their lives but their art presents not only their trauma but also their struggle to

overcome the ingrained chaos. The conflict between the pain and the struggle is the fulcrum of their creativity.

1. Aggression is specifically human and not derived from animal instinct. It does not serve the physiological survival of man, yet it is an important part of his mental functioning. It is one of the passions that are dominant and powerful in some individuals and cultures [. . .] destructiveness is one of the possible answers to psychic needs that are rooted in the existence of man [. . .] and [. . .] from the interaction of various social conditions with man's existential needs. (Fromm, *The Anatomy* 208)

   Fromm contends how destroying for the sake of destruction (malignant aggression) is different from the biologically adaptive life-serving benign aggression. He defines the latter thus: "Defensive aggression is biologically adaptive [. . .] the brain of animals is phylogenetically programmed to mobilize attack when vital interests of the animal are threatened. [. . .] Basically the aim is to remove the danger; this can be done [. . .] by flight [. . .] if flight is not possible by fighting. The aim of defensive aggression is not lust for destruction, but the preservation of life." (*The Anatomy* 96) Fromm includes man also in this species.

2. The rainbow as a symbol of hope emerges in Milton's *Paradise Lost* XI. Similarly in *for colored girls* too, Shange uses the rainbow as a spiritual symbol of hope which offers a haven of peace for all the agonized women. It is significant that coloured women represent the different shades of the spiritual colour schema since these women are generally considered unfit for such planes of thought. At yet another level, the rainbow could also be viewed as an optimistic symbol that bonds all these women towards sisterhood. Erich Fromm in *And Ye Shall Be Gods* mentions that the "Rainbow is the covenant between god and man" (182).

3. It is significant to note that the African American women dramatists while being universal are also being particular and the vice-versa. Margaret Wilkerson quotes the words of Lorraine Hansberry in this connection:

   > One of the soundest ideas in dramatic writing is that in order to create the universal, you must pay very great attention to the specific. Universality emerges from truthful identity of what is [specific]. (Wilkerson 9)

Bibliography

Primary Sources

Kennedy, Adrienne. "*A Beast Story*." *Kuntu Drama: Plays of the African Continuum*, ed. Paul Carter Harrison. New York: Grove, 1972.

_____. *People Who Led to My Plays*. New York: Alfred Knopf, 1987.

_____. *Adrienne Kennedy In One Act*. Minneapolis: U of Minnesota, 1988.

_____. *The Alexander Plays*. Minneapolis: U of Minnesota, 1992.

Sanchez, Sonia. "*The Bronx is Next*." *The Drama Review* 12.4 (1968): 78-83.

_____. "Sister Son/ji." *New Plays from the Black Theater*, ed. King Milner. New York: Drummond, 1969. 152-57.

_____. "*Uh! Uh! but How Do it Free Us?*" *The New Lafeyette Theatre Presents: Plays with Aesthetic Content*, ed. Bullins. New York: Anchor, 1974. 165-215.

Shange, Ntozake, *for colored girls who have considered suicide when the rainbow is enuf.* New York: Bantam, 1981.

_____. *three pieces*. New York: St. Martin's, 1981

_____. *See No Evil: Prefaces and Essays*. San Francisco. Momo's, 1984.

_____. *From Okra to Greens/ A Different Kinda Love Story: A Play / With Music & Dance*. New York: Samuel French, 1985.

Secondary Sources

Abramson, Doris E. *Negro Playwrights in the American Theatre. 1925-59*. New York: Columbia UP, 1969.

_____. "Angelina Weld Grimke, Mary T. Burrill, Georgia Douglas Johnson, and Marita Bonner: An Analysis of Their Plays." *Sage* 2.1 (1985): 55-65.

Adams, Karen and Norma Ware. *Woman: A Feminist Perspective*. New York: Mayfield, 1987.

Adams, Michael Vannoy. *The Multi-Cultural Imagination*. London: Routledge, 1996.

Allport, W. Gordon. "Prejudice and the Young Child." *Racism: A Case Book*, ed. Fredrick. R. Lapider and J. David. New York: Burroughs, 1972. 68-76

Althusser, Louis. *Lenin and Philosophy and Other Essays*, trans. B. Brewster. New York: Monthly Review, 1971.

Andrews, William, ed. *Black Female Slave Narratives*. New York: Schomburg, 1982.

Angelou, Maya. *I Know Why the Caged Bird Sings*. New York: Bantam, 1989.

_____. *Wouldn't Take Nothing for My Journey Now*. New York: Bantam, 1994.

Artaud, Antonin. "The Theatre of Cruelty." *The Theory of Modern Stage*, ed. Eric Bentley. London: Penguin, 1980. 51-59.

Ashcroft, Bill et al, ed. *The Post Colonial Studies Reader*. London: Routledge, 1995.

_____, ed. *Key Concepts in Post Colonial Studies*. London: Routledge, 1998.

Bahr, M. Howard et al, ed. *American Ethnicity*. Toronto: Heath, 1979.

Bakhtin, Mikhail. *The Dialogic Imagination*, ed. Holmquist. Austin: University of Texas, 1981.

Baldwin, James. *Blues for Mister Charlie*. New York: Dell, 1964.

Baraka, Imamu Amiri. *Revolutionary Theatre: Selected Plays and Prose*, ed. John Benjamin. New York: William Morrow, 1979.

Barnett, Claudia. "A Prison of Object Relations: Adrienne Kennedy's *Funny House of a Negro*." *Modern Drama* 40 (1997): 372-79.

Bart. B. Pauline and Eilen Geil Moran. *Violence against Women*. London: Sage, 1993.

Barthes, Ronald. *Elements of Semiology*, trans. A. Levers and C. Smith. London and New York: Viking, 1968.

Beauvoir, Simone de. *The Second Sex*. U.K. Vintage, 1997.

Benston, Kimberley. "'Cities in Bezique.' Adrienne Kennedy's Expressionistic Vision." *College Language Association Journal* 20 (1976): 221-48.

Berger, Asa Arthur. *Cultural Criticism*. New Delhi: Sage, 1995.

Berghahn, Marion. *Images of Africa in Black American Literature*. New Jersey: Roman, 1977.

Berlin, Ira, ed. *Power and Culture: Essays on the American Working Class*. New York: Pantheon, 1987.

Betsko, Kathleen and Rachel Koenig, ed. *Interviews with Contemporary Women Playwrights*. New York: Morrow, 1987.

Bhabha, K. Homi. "Of Mimicry and Man: The Ambivalence of Colonial Discourse." *Twentieth Century Literature* 28.3 (1984): 121-27.

_____. "Signs Taken for Wonder." *The Post Colonial Studies Reader*, ed. Ashcroft et al. London: Routledge, 1995.

Blackwell, Henry. "An Interview with Ntozake Shange." *Black American Literature Forum*. 13 (1979): 134-38.

Blau, Herbert. "The American Dream in the American Gothic: The Plays of Sam Shepard and Adrienne Kennedy." *Modern Drama* 27 (1984): 520-39.

Blauner, Robert. *Racial Oppression in America*. New York: Harper, 1972.

Bond, Jean Patricia Perry Carey. *The Black Woman: An Anthology*. New York: Mentor, 1970.

Bloom, Harold, ed. *Ralph Ellison*. New York: Chelsea House, 1986.

Bonner, Marita. *Frye Street and Environs: The Collected Works of Marita Bonner*, ed. Joyce Flynn and Joyce Occomystricklin. Boston: Beacon, 1987.

Booth, A.J. *Saint-Simon and Saint Simonism*. London: Longmans, 1971

Brawley, Benjamin. *The Negro in Literature and Art*. New York: AMS, 1930.

Braxton, Joanne and Andree Mc Laughlin, ed. *Wild Women in the Whirlwind*. New Jersey: Rutgers U P, 1990.

Brown-Guillory, Elizabeth, ed. *Wines in the Wilderness: Plays by African American Women from the Harlem Renaissance to the Present*. Westport: Greenwood, 1990.

Bruner, S. Jerome. "Myth and Identity." *Daedalus* 1 (1959): 349-

58.

Bryant-Jackson, K. Paul "Kennedy's Travellers in the American and African Continuum." *Intersecting Boundaries: The Theatre of Adrienne Kennedy*, ed. Paul K. Bryant-Jackson and Lois More Overbeck. Minneapolis: U of Minnesota, 1992. 45-57.

Cade, Toni. *Black Woman: An Anthology*. New York: Mentor, 1970.

Carlton W. and Barbara J. Molette. *Black Theatre: Premise and Presentation*. Wyndham Hall: Bristol, 1992.

Case, Sue-Ellen. *Feminism and Theatre*. New York: Methuen, 1988.

Cesaire, Aime. *Discourse on Colonialism*. New York: Monthly Review, 1972.

Cleaver, Eldridge. *Soul on Ice*. New York: Delta, 1968.

Cohn, Ruby. *New American Dramatists. 1960-1980*. New York: Grove, 1982.

Collins, Patricia Hill. "The Sexual Politics of Black Womanhood," *Violence against Women*, ed. Pauline B. Bart and Elileen Geil Moran. Newbury: Sage, 1993.

_____. *Black Feminist Thought: Knowledge, Consciousness and the Politics of Empowerment*. Boston: Unwin Hymann, 1996.

Cone, James. *The Spirituals and the Blues*. New York: Seabury, 1972.

Cooper, Anna Julia. *Selected Works* Ed. Elizabeth Chelsea. Westport: Greenwood, 1978.

Cox, Sue. *Female Psychology: The Emerging Self*. New York: St. Martins, 1981.

Crawford,W.H. *Girolamo Savanarola*. New York: Eaton, 1907

Cronacher, Karen. "Unmasking the Minstrel Mask's Black Magic in Ntozake Shange's *Spell #7*." *Theatre Journal* 44 (1992): 177-93.

Curb, Rosemary. "Hetero sexual terrors in Kennedy's Plays." *Intersecting Boundaries: The Theatre of Adrienne Kennedy*, ed. Paul K. Bryant-Jackson and Lois More Overbeck. Minneapolis: U of Minnesota P, 1992. 142-56.

_____. "Fragmented Selves in Adrienne Kennedy's *Funnyhouse of a Negro* and *The Owl Answers*." *Theatre Journal* 32 (1980): 180-95.

Dance, C. Daryl. "Black Eve or Madonna?: A Study of the Antithetical Views of the Mother in Black American Literature." *Sturdy Black Bridges: Vision of Black Women in Literature*. ed. Roseann P. Bell et al. New York: Anchor, 1979. 123-32.

Darwin, Charles. *The Descent of Man*. London: Routledge, 1990.

Davis, Allison. *Caste, Economy and Violence*. New York: Rutgers, 1992.

Davis, Y. Angela. "Rape, Racism and the Capitalist Setting." *Black Scholar* 9 (1978): 24-30.

_____. *Women, Race and Class*. New York: Random, 1981.

_____. *Pornography: Men Possessing Women*. New York: Pedigree, 1982.

_____. *Women, Culture and Politics*. New York: Random House, 1989.

Diamond, Elin. "Mimesis, Mimicry and the Real." *Modern Drama* 32 (1989): 58-72.

Douglas, Mary. *Purity and Danger: An Analysis of the Concepts of Pollution and Taboo*. London: Ark, 1990.

Drabble, Margaret, ed. *Oxford Companion to Literature*. London: OUP 2002.

DuBois. W.E.B. *The Negro America Family*. New York: Doubleday, 1908.

____. "Krigwa Players Little Negro Theater." *Crisis* 32 (1926): 446-52.

_____. *The Souls of Black Folk*. New York: Fawcett, 1961.

Durrant, Will. *The Story of Philosophy*. New York: Washington Square, 1961

Ehrenrich, Barbara and Kartin Stalards. "The Nouveau Poor." *The Racio-Eonomic Policies of the U.S.*, ed. Benetha Wild. California: Plumsfield, 1979. 92-101.

Elam, Keir. *The Semiotics of Theatre and Drama*. Routledge: 2009.

Eliot, T.S. *Selected Essays*. London: Faber and Faber, 1976.

Ellison, Ralph. "King of the Bingo Game." *Dark Symphony: Negro Literature in America*, ed. James A. Emanuel and Theodore L. Gross. New York: Free, 1968. 271-79.

Ellison, Ralph. *Invisible Man*. New York: Chelsea, 1972.

Ellmann, Richard and Rober O'Clair, ed. *Norton Anthology of Modern Poetry*. New York: Norton, 1995.

Fanon, Frantz. *The Wretched of the Earth*, trans. C. Farrington, New York: Penguin 1963.

_____. *Black Skin, White Masks*. Trans. C.L. Markmann. New York: Grove, 1967.

Firestone, Shulamith. *The Dialectic of Sex: The Case for Feminist Revolution*. New York: Bantam, 1970.

Flowers, Sandra Hollins "*Colored girls*: Textbook for the Eighties." *Black American Literature Forum* 15.51 (1981): 51-54.

Foreman, Ann. *Femininity as Alienation: Women and the Family in Marxism and Psychoanalysis*. London: Pluto, 1977.

Forrester, John. *The Seductions of Psycho Analysis: Freud, Lacan and Derrida*. CUP: 1992.

Forte, Jeanie. "Realism, Narrative and the Feminine Playwright: A Problem of Perception." *Modern Drama* 32 (1989): 115-27.

Fortune, M. Marie. *Sexual Violence: The Unmentionable Sin*. New York: Pilgrim, 1983.

Foucault, M. *The History of Sexuality*, trans. R. Hurley. New York: Vintage, 1982. 2 Vols.

_____, *Essays on Knowledge, Power and Sex*, ed. Stephen George. New York: Light, 1985.

Fout, C. John and Maura Shaw Tantillo. *American Sexual Politics: Sex, Gender and Race since the Civil War*. Chicago: U of Chicago P, 1993.

Frazier, Franklin. *The Negro Family in the United States*. Chicago: U of Chicago P, 1966.

Freeman, Jo, ed. *Women: A. Feminist Perspective*. New York: Mayfield, 1987.

Freud, Sigmund. *The Basic Writings of Sigmund Freud*, trans. Proctor, ed.,A.A. Brell. New York: Modern Library, 1938.

_____. *The Question of Lay Analysis*. Trans. Proctor N. Gugg. London: Methuen, 1947.

_____. *The Interpretation of Dreams*. Trans. A.A. Brell. New York: Random House, 1950.

Friedan, Betty. *The Feminist Mystique*. New York: Random House, 1963.

Fromm, Erich. *The Anatomy of Human Destructiveness*. New York: Holt, 1961.

_____. *And Ye shall be Gods*. New York: Fawcett, 1986.

Garrett, Jimmy. "We Own the Night." *Black Fire: An Anthology of Afro-American Writing*, ed. Le Roi Jones and Larry Neal. New York: William Morrow, 1970.

Gatlin, Rochelle. *American Women since 1945*. Jackson and Jackson, Mississippi: U of Mississippi P, 1987.

Gayle, Jr. Addison. *The Black Aesthetic*. New York: Anchor, 1971.

Geis, R. Deborah. "A Spectator Watching My Life: Adrienne Kennedy's *A Movie Star Has to Star in Black and White*." *Intersecting Boundaries: The Theatre of Adrienne Kennedy*, ed. Paul K. Bryant-Jackson and Lois More Overbeck. Minneapolis: U of Minnesota P, 1992.

Giddings, Paula. *When and Where I Enter: The Impact of Black Women on Race and Sex in America*. New York: Bantam, 1984.

Gilbert, Sandra M. *Feminist Criticism in the University*, ed. Gerald Graff and Reginald Gibbons. Evanston: North Eastern UP, 1985.

_____. and Susan Gubar, ed. *Norton Anthology of Literature by Women*. New York: Norton, 1996.

Gilman, S.L. "Black Bodies, White Bodies: Toward an Iconography of Female Sexuality in Late Nineteenth Century Art, Medicine and Literature." *Critical Enquiry* 12.1 (1985): 205-43.

Gitlin. *The Whole World is Watching*. Berkley: California UP, 1980.

Gobineau, J.A. comte de. *Essai sur l' inegalite des Races Humianes*. Trans. Robert Young. Paris: Firmin Didot.

Glass, M. James. *Shattered Selves: Multiple Personality in a Post Modern World*. Ithaca: Cornell UP, 1993.

Gordon, Milton. *Human Nature, Class and Ethnicity*. New York: OUP, 1978.

Graham, Shirley. *It's Morning. Black Female Playwrights: An Anthology of Plays before 1950*, ed. Kathya Perkins. Bloomington: Indiana UP, 1990.

Gramsci, Antonio. *Selections from the Prison Notebooks*, ed. Q. Hoare and G.N. Smith. London: Lawrence, 1971.

Gray, Christine. "Discovering and Recovering African American Women Playwrights before 1930." *The Cambridge Companion to American Women Dramatists*. CUP, 2001. 244-53.

Griffin, Susan. "Rape: The All-American Crime." *Ramparts* 10 Sep. 1971: 26-35.

Gutman, Herbert: "Persistent Myths about the Afro-American Family." *Journal of Interdisciplinary History* 6.2 (1975): 356-79.

_____. *The Black Family in Slavery and Freedom. 1750-1925*. New York: Pantheon, 1985.

Hansberry, Lorraine. *To be Young, Gifted and Black*. New York: Signet, 1969.

Hansberry, Lorraine. *A Raisin in the Sun and the Sign in Sidney Brustein's Window*. New York: New American Library, 1987.

Harris, Will. "Early Black Women Playwrights and the Dual Liberation Motif." *African American Review* 28.2 (1994): 202-12.

Harrison, Paul Carter, ed. *Kuntu Drama: Plays of the African Continuum*. New York: Grove, 1974.

Hatch, V. James. *Black Theatre: USA: 45 Plays by Black Americans, 1847-1974*. New York: Macmillan, 1974.

Hawkes, David. *Ideology*. London: Routledge, 1996.

Henderson, George. *Ethnicity and Race: Critical Perspectives*. New York: Brownwell, 1967.

Hernton, Calvin. "The Sexual Mountain," *Wild Women in the Whirlwind*, ed. Joanne Braxton and Andree Mc Laughlin. New Jersey: Rutgers, 1990. 195-222.

Hoagland, Sarah. *Lesbian Ethics: Towards New Values*. California: Institute of Lesbian Studies, 1988.

Hodges, M. Harold. Jr. *Social Stratification: Class in America*. New York: Plumsfield, 1964.

Hofstadter, Richard. *Social Darwinism in American Thought*. Boston: Beacon, 1944.

hooks, bell. *Ain't I a woman? Black women and Feminism*. London: Pluto, 1983.

_____. *Feminist Theory: From Margin to Centre*. New York: South End, 1984.

_____. *Killing Rage: Ending Racism*. New York: Henry Holt, 1989.

_____. "Straightening Our Hair." *Reading Culture: Contexts for Critical Reading and Writing*," ed. Diana George and John Trimbur. New York: Harper-Collins, 1992. 290-99.

Hull, T. Gloria, Patricia Bell Scott and Barbara Smith. *All the Blacks Are Men. But Some of Us are Brave*. New York: Feminist, 1982.

Hull, T. Gloria. *Color, Sex and Poetry: Three Women Writers of the Harlem Renaissance*. Bloomington: Indiana UP, 1987.

Hulme, Peter. "Polytropic Man: Tropes of Sexuality and Mobility in Early Colonial Discourse." *Europe and its Others*, ed. F. Barker et al. Vol. 2. Colchester: U of Essex P, 1985. 17-32.

Ingersoll, Robert. *Lectures and Essays*. London: Watts, 1921.

Issacs, J.R. Edith. *The Negro in the American Theatre*. New York: Theatre Arts, 1947.

Jackson, Elaine. "Toe Jam." *Black Theatre*, ed. Woodie King and Ron Milner. New York: Meridian, 1971.

Jacobs, Harriet. *Incidents in the Life of the Slave Girl*, ed. Sue Miller. New York: The Feminist, 1982.

Jewel, Sue. *From Mammy to Miss America and Beyond*. New York: Routledge, 1993.

Jones, Lisa. "Beyond the *Funny House*: A Conversation with Playwright Adrienne Kennedy." *Village Voice*. 16 Apr. 1996: 46-48

Jordan, W.D. *White over Black: American Attitude towards the Negro*. Chapel Hill: North Carolina, 1968.

Jowett, Benjamin, trans. *Politics* by Aristotle. New York: Modern Library, 1962.

Jung, G. Carl, *Collected Works*. Trans. William Strachey London: Kegan Paul, 1962.

Kafka, Frantz. *The Complete Works*. New York: Penguin, 1982.

Kahl, A. Joseph. *The American Class Structure*. New York: Rhinehart 1992.

Kanneh, Kadiatu. "Feminism and the Colonial Body." *The Postcolonial Studies Reader*, ed. Ashcroft et al. London: Routledge, 1995. 346-48.

Kaplan. J.D. *The Complete Works of Plato*. New York: Pocket, 1951.

Kathleen Betsko and Rachel Koenig, ed. *Interviews with Contemporary Women Playwrights*. New York: Morrow, 1987.

Katz, Maude White. "End Racism in Education: A Concerned Parent Speaks." *The Black Woman: An Anthology*, ed. Toni Cade. New York: Mentor, 1990. 124-29.

Kennedy, Adrienne. "The Growth of Images." *The Drama Review*, 21.4 (1977): 41-48.

Keyssar, Helene. *Feminist Theatre: An Introduction to Plays of Contemporary British and American Women*. London: Macmillan, 1984.

Killinger, John. *Worlds in Collapse: The Vision of Absurd Drama*. New York: Delta, 1971.

King, Woodie and Ron Milner, ed. *Black Drama Anthology*. New York: Meridian, 1986.

Kolin, Philip. "Orpheus Ascending: Music Race and Gender in Kennedy's *She Talks to Beethoven*." *African American Review* 28.2 (1994): 293-304.

Laidler, W. Harr. *Socio Economic Movements*. New York: Thomas Crowell, 1945.

Lakoff, Robin. *Language and the Women's Place*. New York: Harper Row, 1975.

Lerner, Gerda ed. *Black Women in White America: A Documentary History*. New York: Pantheon, 1972.

_____. *The Grimke Sisters—A Biography*. New York: Schocken, 1971.

Levine, Ann. "Bein' a woman, Bein' Colored: Interview with Ntozake Shange." *Science Christian Monitor* 9 (1978): 20-24.

Leviticus 25:46. *The Holy Bible*. King James Version.

Lind, J.E. "The Color Complex in the Negro." *Psychoanalytic Review*, 1.4 (1914): 404-14.

Locke, Alain. *The New Negro: Voices of the Harlem Renaissance*. 1925. New York: Atheneum, 1992.

Loomba, Ania. *Colonialism/Post Colonialism*. London: Routledge, 1998.

Lowenberg, James and Ruth Bogin, ed. *Black Women in Nineteenth Century American Life*. Pennsylvania UP, 1976.

Mac Arthur, Louis. *Race, Power and Privilege*. Toronto: Schilling, 1999.

Macaulay, Thomas Babbington. "Minutes on Indian Education." Ed. J. Clive. *Macaulay: Selected Writings*. Chicago: U of Chicago P, 1972. 123-47.

Maeterlinck, Maurice. "The Tragical in Daily life." *The Treasure of the Humble*. Trans. Alfred Sutro. London: George Allen, 1908.

Malcolm X. *The Autobiography of Malcolm X*. New York: Grove, 1965. (Told to A. Haley)

Malson, R. Micheline, et al, ed. *Black Women in America*. Chicago: U of Chicago, 1988.

Manning, Susan. "Literature and Society in Colonial America," *The New Pelican Guide to English Literature*, ed. Boris Ford. Vol. 8. New York: Penguin, 1989. 19-27.

Marx, Karl and Fredrich Engels. *Selected Works*, trans. Edward Untermann. Moscow: FLP, 1949.

McDonnough, J. Clara. "Gods and the Owls: The Sacred and the Profane in Adrienne Kennedy's *The Owl Answers*." *Modern Drama* 40 (1997): 391-96.

McKay, Nellie. "Black Theater and Drama in the 1920s. Years of Growing Pains." *Massachusetts Review*, 28.4 (1987): 615-26.

Meigs. E. Susan. "No Place but the Funnyhouse: The Struggle for Identity in Three Adrienne Kennedy's Plays." *Modern American Drama*, ed. Susan Meigs. Canada: Associated UP, 1990. 172-78.

Memmi, Albert. *The Coloniser and the Colonized*. Boston: Beacon, 1967.

Miller, Susan Brown. *Against Our Will: Men, Women and Rape*. New York: Simon and Schuster, 1975.

_____. *Femininity*. New York: Linden, 1984.

Milton, John. *Paradise Lost*, ed. Gordon Campbell. New York, London: J.M. Dent, 1981.

Missner, H. Hannah, ed. *Poverty in the Affluent Society*. New York: Harper and Row, 1966.

Mohammed, Abdul Jan. "The Economy of Manichean Allegory." *The Post Colonial Studies Reader*, ed. B. Ashcroft et al. London: Routledge, 1995. 18-25.

Monroe, Sylvester. "Brothers" *Newsweek* 23 Mar. 1987: 54-86.

Morrison, Toni. *Beloved*. New York: Washington Square, 1987.

_____. *Playing in the Dark: Whiteness and the Literary Imagina-*

tion. London: Picador, 1992.

Moynihan, Daniel. "The Negro Family: The Case for National Action." U.S. Department of Labour, 1965.

Mumford, Lewis. *The Story of Utopias*. New York: Boni and Liveright, 1922

Murphy, Brenda, ed. *The Cambridge Companion to American Women Dramatists*. Cambridge: CUP, 2001.

Nathan, Hans. *Dan Emmett and the Rise of Early Negro Minstrelsy*. Oklahoma: U of Oklahoma, 1962.

Naylor, Gloria. *Women of the Brewster Place*. New York.

Nayar, Pramod. *Literary Theory Today*. New Delhi: Prestige, 2002.

Neal, A. Lester. *Ntozake Shange: A Critical Study of Her Plays*. New York: Garland, 1995.

Neal, Larry. "The Black Arts Movement" *The Drama Review* 12.4 (1968): 29-39.

Niebhur, James. *Moral Man and Immoral Society*. New York: Scrivner, 1960.

Odinga. *Not yet Uhuru*. London: Heinemann, 1967.

Ogunbiyi, Yemi. *New Black Playwrights in America*. New York: Grove, 1978.

Oliver, Edith. "The Theater off Broadway." *New Yorker*. 3 Jan. 1978: 76-78.

Ortiz, Victoria. *Sojourner Truth: A Self-Made Woman*. New York: Lippincott, 1974.

Perkins, Kathya, ed. *Black Female Playwrights: An Anthology of Plays before 1950*. Bloomington: Indiana UP, 1990.

Perry, B., ed. *Malcolm X: The Last Speeches*. New York: London, Pathfinder, 1989.

Peters, Erskine. "Some Tragic Prospensities of Ourselves: The Occasion of Ntozake Shange," *Journal of Ethnic Studies* 6 (1978): 79-85.

Pettigrew, F. Thomas. *A Profile of the American Negro*. Princeton and New Jersey: Van Nostrand, 1964.

Pratt, Mary Lousie. *Imperial Eyes: Travel Writing and Transculturation*. London: Routledge, 1992.

Rangan, V. *Critical Spectrum*. India: Manmohan, 1997

Ranveer, Kashinath. *Black Feminist Consciousness*. Jaipur, India:

Printwell, 1995.

Reinfro, G. Herbert, ed. *The Select Poems of Phillis Wheatley*. New York: Books for Libraries, 1987.

Ribowsky, Mark. "A Poetess Scores a Hit with Play on What's Wrong with Black Men." *Sepia* 25 (1976): 41-49.

Rich, Adrienne. *Of Woman Born: Motherhood as Experience and Institution*. New York: Norton, 1976.

Rodgers, La Frances and Rose. *The Black Woman: A Historical Overview*. New York: Garland, 1987.

Rogers, J.A. *Nature Knows No Color Line*. New York: Dalton, 1952.

Rushdie, Salman. *Imaginary Homelands: Essays and Criticism: 1981-1991*. London: Penguin, 1991.

Schneir, Miriam, ed. *The Vintage Book of Feminism*. New York: Vintage, 1995.

Schorer, Mark. "The Necessity of Myths." *Daedalus* 1 (1959): 359-63.

Scott, John. *Minority Women*. New York: Bell, 1994.

Scott, Patricia Bell. *Double Stitch*. New York: Beacon, 1991.

Sernett, C. Milton, ed. *Afro-American Religious History: A Documentary Witness*. Durham: Duke UP, 1985.

Sertima, Van Ivan, ed. *Black Women in Antiquity*. New York: Scrivener: 1992.

Shakespeare, William. *Othello*. London: Macmillan, 1942

_____. *The Tempest, ed.* A.W. Verity. New Delhi: Surjeet, 1988.

_____. *Julius Caesar*. Cambridge: CUP, 1989.

Shange, Ntozake. *A Daughter's Geography*. New York: St. Martin's 1983.

_____. *Nappy Edges*. London: Methuen, 1987.

_____. "Daddy says." *New Plays for the Black Theatre*, ed. Woodie King Jr. Chicago: Third World, 1989.

Showalter, Elaine. "Autonomy and Assimilation in Afro-American and Feminist Literary Theory." Ms. IACIS, Hyderabad, 1985.

Sloane, Patricia. *Visual Nature of Color*. New York: Design, 1989

Southern, Eileen. *The Music of Black Americans: A History*. New York: Norton, 1971.

Sowell, Thomas. *Ethnic America—A History*. New York: Basic, 1981

Soyinka, Wole. *Myth and the African World View*. Cambridge: CUP, 1990.

Spillers, Hortense. "Mama's Baby, Papa's May Be: An American Grammar Book." *Diacritics* 17.2 (1987): 78-89.

Spivak, Gayatri Chakravarty. "Three Women's Texts and a Critique of Imperialism." *Critical Inquiry* 12.1 (1985): 43-61

Stanley, Julia Penelope and Susan. J. Wolfe "Towards a Feminist Aesthetic." *Chrysalis* 6 (1978): 59-67.

Stanton, Elizabeth Cady et al, ed. *History of Woman Suffrage*. Vol. I. New York: Arnold, 1969.

Staples, Robert. "The Myth of Black Male: A Response to Angry Black Feminists." *Black Scholar* 10 (1979): 24-33.

Stephan, N.L. and Gilman. S.L. "Appropriating the Idiom of Science." *The Bounds of Race: Perspectives on Hegemony and Resistance*, ed. D. La Capra, New York: Cornell UP. 72-103.

Stoker, Bram. "Dracula." *The Book of Gothic and Horror Stories*, ed. Cathleen Jackson. New York: Free, 1992.

Strindberg, August. *Select Plays*. New York: Penguin, 1974.

Tannahill, Reay. *Sex in History*. London: Abacus, 1981.

Tate, Claudia. "Ntozake Shange." *Black Women Writers at Work*. New York: Continuum, 1983. 149-74.

Tener, Robert. "Theatre of Identity: Adrienne Kennedy's Portrait of the Black Woman." *Studies in Black Literature* 6.2 (1975) 1-12.

The Holy Bible. King James Version.

Thiong'o, Ngugi wa. *Decolonising the Mind: The Politics of Language in African Literature*. London: James Currey, 1986.

_____. *Homecoming: Essays*. London: Heinemann, 1972.

Tillyard, E.M.W. *The Elizabethan World Picture*. New York: Penguin, 1990.

Timpane, John. "The Poetry of a Moment: Politics and the Open Form in the Drama of Ntozake Shange." *Modern American Literature* 4 (1989): 91-101.

Todorov, Tzvetan. *On Human Diversity: Nationalism, Racism, and Exoticism in French Thought*, trans. C. Porter. London: Harvard UP, 1993.

Tolls, Robert. *Blacking Up: the Minstrel Show in Nineteenth Century America*. New York: OUP, 1974.

Tong, Rosemarie. *Feminist Thought: A Comprehensive Introduction.* London: Unwin Hyman, 1989.

Vaughan, M. *Curing Their Ills: Colonial Power and African Illness.* Stanford: Stanford UP, 1991.

Viswanathan, Gauri. *Masks of Conquest: Literary Study and British Rule in India.* London: Faber, 1990.

Walker, Alice. *In Search of Our Mother's Gardens.* New York: Harcourt, 1983.

_____. "The Diary of an African Nun." *The Black Woman: An Anthology.* New York: Mentor, 1970. 38-41.

_____. *Coming Apart: Youcan't Keep a Good Woman Down.* New York: Harcourt, 1981.

_____. *Color Purple.* New York: Washington, 1982.

_____. "The Abortion." *Breaking Ice: An Anthology of Contemporary African American Fiction,* ed. Terry Macmillan. New York: Penguin, 1990. 630-38.

Wall, Cheryl. *Women of the Harlem Renaissance.* Bloomington: Indiana UP, 1995.

Washington. T. Booker. *The Story of the Negro.* New York: Doubleday, 1929.

"Was Jesus Black-Skinned?" *Hindu* 29 Mar. 2001: 16.

Weber, Max. *Class, Status, Party.* New York: OUP, 1948.

Wellek, Rene and Austin Warren. *Theory of Literature.* New York: Harcourt Brace, 1956.

Wilkerson, Margaret. "The Sighted Eyes and Feeling of Lorraine Hansberry." *African American Review* 17.2 (1983): 3-12.

_____, ed. *9 Plays by Black women.* New York: Mentor, 1986.

_____. "Diverse Angles of Vision: Two Black Women Playwrights." *Intersecting Boundaries,* ed. Paul K. Bryant-Jackson and Lois More Overbeck. Minneapolis: U of Minnesota P, 1992. 58-75

Wood, Allen. *Karl Marx.* London: Routledge, 1981.

Woodie, James. *Race, Class and Power—The Black Situation.* Chicago: Hammond, 1986.

Woodson, Carter G. *The Miseducation of the Negro.* Washington: Associated, 1933.

Young, Jr. Whitney. *Beyond Racism.* New York: McGraw Hill: 1969.